SURVIVING PRETRIAL

The Ultimate Survival Guide to Being Busted & Prosecuted by the Feds

BILAL KHAN

Bilalywood Publications, 2023

Copyright © 2023 by **Bilal Khan**

All rights reserved. No part of this publication may be reproduced, distributed or transmitted in any form or by any means, without prior written permission.

The author does not claim any copyright in case opinions, quotations, or laws referenced throughout this book and are provided under the doctrine of public domain. The graphic of the United States on page 30 is a public domain graphic provided by the United States government.

Book Layout © 2017 BookDesignTemplates.com
Cover Photo © 2021 iStockphoto.com | Goroden Koff | 1346156687
Cover Design © 2023 Hunter Grey using Coverjig.com

Surviving Pretrial: The Ultimate Survival Guide to Being Busted & Prosecuted by the Feds/ Bilal Khan -- 1st ed.

ISBN **979-83729670-0-7** (KDP Hardcover)
ISBN **979-83720325-6-9** (KDP Paperback)

Legal Notice

The information provided in this book is for informational purposes only and is not intended to be a source of advice with respect to the material presented. The information and/or documents contained in this book do not constitute legal advice and **should never be used without first consulting with a licensed attorney to determine what may be best for your individual needs.**

The publisher and the author do not make any guarantee or other promise as to any results that may be obtained from using the content of this book. You should never make any investment decision without first consulting with your own financial advisor and conducting your own research and due diligence. To the maximum extent permitted by law, the publisher and the author disclaim any and all liability in the event any information, commentary, analysis, opinions, advice and/or recommendations contained in this book prove to be inaccurate, incomplete or unreliable, or result in any legal losses or errors.

Content contained or made available through this book is not intended to and **does not constitute legal advice** and no attorney-client relationship is formed. The publisher and the author are providing this book and its contents on an "as is" basis. **Your use of the information in this book is at your own risk.**

While there are some references to actual cases, names have been changed to protect privacy. Hypothetical cases mentioned are not in reference to any person, case, or event. Any names that may seem identifiable are merely coincidental and do not reflect any specific names of defendants who are known to the author.

To Mom, Dad, Casey, Dan, Sarah & Zech– without you, I would never have survived pretrial or anything else before or since.

If the facts are against you, argue the law. If the law is against you, argue the facts. If the law and the facts are against you, pound the table and yell like hell.

- Carl Sandberg

The more corrupt the state, the more numerous the laws.

- Tacitus, 55-120 AD, Roman historian

Contents

Part One	Introduction	13
	Rule #1 (Slow Down!)	16
	Rule #2 (Shut the Hell Up!)	17
	Recommended Readings & Resources	18
	What is Pretrial?	24
	Detainee, Prisoner, or Inmate?	26
Part Two	Criminal Law Concepts	30
	Structure for the Federal Judicial System (graphic)	33
	Circuit Court Map (graphic)	34
	Arrest	35
	Charging Documents	42
	Reading & Understanding	53

	Charges Reading & Deciphering a Case Opinion	80
	Judges	91
	Prosecutors	96
	Attorney-Client Privilege	98
	Fundamental Rights of the Defendant	113
	Strategic Decisions & Your Lawyer	121
Part Three	Crash Course in Criminal Procedure	124
	Initial Appearance	129
	Preliminary Hearing	135
	Detention Hearing	140
	Arraignment	146
	Guilty Plea Hearing	151
	Status Conference	161
	Frye Hearing	164
	Suppression Hearing	168
	Franks Hearing	178

	Curcio Hearing	183
	Faretta Hearing	186
	Competency Hearing	191
Part Four	Lawyers	196
	Getting a Lawyer	200
	Hiring a Private Lawyer	208
	The Lawyer Interview	214
	Vetting a Lawyer	244
	Lawyer's Fees	249
	Contract	256
	Inspecting a Lawyer's Work	265
Part Five	Defense Tactics	274
	Trial Strategies	275
	How to Write a Motion & Brief	302
	Motion to Proceed Pro Se	313
	Speedy Trial Demand	322
	Fighting for Bail	331
	Correcting the Record	341
	Plea Bargaining	358

Part Six	Sentencing	392
	Presentence Report	393
	Sentencing Mitigation Videos	455
	Sentencing Memorandum	461
	Sentencing Proceedings	467
Appendices		
	Guidelines Sentencing Table	480
	Guideline 2D1.1 (Drug Guidelines)	482
	Drug Quantity Table	490
	Guideline 2G2.2 (child pornography guideline)	492
	Guideline 2L1.2 (immigration guideline)	501
	Guidelines Used for Calculating Criminal History	510
Acknowledgements		532

Part One

Introduction

When you are sitting in jail and all of a sudden you get called to go to court, your heart rate is going to skyrocket. You are going to get super sweaty and feel extremely anxious. That only gets worse through each step of the process of going to court. As each handcuff is clicked into place, the belly chain secured and the leg irons locked, you will wonder if there will be news cameras there. You will wonder if your family will be there. You will worry about what everyone will think of you. Then, as you sit in the dog kennel to be transported to the courthouse, you have those same thoughts while you are greeted with the stench of the hundreds or thousands before you who took that same ride. What's going to happen? Will I get out of jail today? Am I going to prison now? These, and other, questions keep mounting in your head as you pull into the courthouse.

The officers lead you into the courthouse where you are placed in a cell. Perhaps that cell is filled with hundreds of people. Or maybe it is completely empty and you are by yourself. In either case, as you stand there with your hands cuffed and legs shackled, the pressure mounts even more. Where is my lawyer? Am I going to see him before court starts? Does he know that I am even at court? In about twenty minutes, you are going to find out that all of this anxiety, pressure, and nervousness was for naught because the hearing was a "status conference" where your lawyer simply says he needs more time!

The only reason that you are nervous at that stage is that you don't know what's going on. It's sad really because your lawyer knows but he didn't explain it to you. Hell, even the officers at the jail know what the hearing is all about. But, nobody is telling you. That's what Surviving Pretrial is here to cure.

Surviving Pretrial is broken in six parts. Part One is "Introductory Matter" and that is where we are going to cover some information that you will need to employ from beginning to end. Part Two will teach you how to break down and read a statute. We will also learn where to find various law and even how to decipher a case opinion. In Part Three, we are going to have a crash course in criminal procedure by discussing every kind of hearing you may be required to attend. Part Four is where we will cover everything about Lawyers. In Part Six, we will open the Armory and give some tips and tricks that may come in handy for you. Last but not least we will examine Sentencing in Part Six.

Rule Number 1:

Slow Down!

My brother once told me "the gears of justice grind slowly." He couldn't have been more right. They grind so slowly that you can take your time with everything. In fact, take up knitting. You now have the time to do it!

The prosecutor's biggest weapon is **knowledge**. You can dull that weapon by taking your time, learning all the material, and making good decisions. This is the long game. A criminal prosecution can take many months to finish. Don't start throwing money at lawyers until you decide that is what is right for you.

Rule Number 2:

Shut the Hell Up!

People are out to get you. And no, I'm not being paranoid. Do not talk to anyone about your case. If you are in jail and asked, just say, "I'm fighting it and that's all I can say about my case." Only a snitch would be upset that you don't talk about your case. Don't talk with anyone. Not friends, not family and definitely not other inmates. Your life literally depends on it. Only speak with your lawyer in a private area where nobody else can hear you. In fact, act like an NFL coach who hides his mouth when talking. Don't fall victim to the many opportunists out there who don't care if you go away forever. And protect your family and actual friends by not telling them anything either.

Recommended Resources and Readings

This is a section that is usually tucked at the end of nonfiction books. I decided to put it in the front to make it as obvious as possible. These are resources that I used and believe should be considered by every criminal defendant. Hopefully they provide you with the same knowledge and support I got out of them.

Suggested Resources

Douglas Passon, Esq.
10565 N. 114th St., Suite 101
Scottsdale, AZ 85259
1-480-448-0086 or 1-800-846-3909
info@dougpassonlaw.com
DougPassonLaw.com

If you are facing an uncertain sentencing hearing or there is a concern that the judge has it out for you, then **you need to have your lawyer call Doug.** His profession is sentencing mitigation. And you should contact him as early in the process as you can. The second you realize there is a strong likelihood you will face sentencing is the time you should call him. But, if you are later in the game, you should still call him. He offers a number of services including the creation of sentencing mitigation videos, plea negotiations, sentencing strategy, and much more. But he is also incredible at drafting letters to probation officers, prosecutors, and judges to ensure you are humanized throughout the process. Any money spent with Doug will be the best money ever spent. Even if you are using public defense, if your family wants to donate money to your cause, then I would send it to Doug and continue with the public defender. You will not be disappointed.

>**Vincent J. Ward, Esq.,**
>**The Ward Law Firm**
>**PO Box 7940**
>**Albuquerque, NM 87194-7940**
>**(505) 944-9454**

Vince is a superb federal trial lawyer. I owe him my life. If you need a lawyer who will work hard for you and you intend on hiring one, I personally recommend him if you can afford him. He is someone who won't waste your money and will maximize your investment as far as it can go. He is extraordinarily honest and is someone you can talk to. I just wish I met him before we hired the lawyers who couldn't have cared less. I can easily attest that

Vince is a lawyer who will care for you as a person. He will not judge you. He will fight for you every step of the way. He won't lie to you.

> Walt Pavlo
> Prisonology, LLC
> 11231 US Highway 1 #310,
> North Palm Beach, FL 33408
> (617) 858-5008
> prisonology.com
> info@prisonology.com

I have never used Prisonology, but Walt is well known and has a great team to help with prison issues. He is also a good contact for mitigation issues.

> Alan Ellis
> The Law Offices of Alan Ellis
> 2023 Revival Lane
> Rio Vista, CA 94571
> Phone: 415-235-9058
> alanellis.com
> aelaw1@alanellis.com

Alan is the most experienced federal sentencing specialist in the country. He has been recognized by judges, defense lawyers, and others as being the absolute best. Alan was counsel of record on my case and I have referred friends to him. I will continue to do so because he fights tooth and nail for his clients. He will use any tool available to fight for you including getting Doug Passion, Walt Pablo, and others involved in your case of it will help. Alan specializes in sentencing, appeals and post conviction relief. There is a caveat. When we discuss getting a lawyer in this book. I make clear that you don't want prosecutors to recommend an attorney. Alan is recommended by prosecutors. Oddly, one of my prosecutors recommends him. What I can say is this, as unfortunate as it is that Alan is recommended by DOJ prosecutors, he really is a great criminal defense lawyer. His knowledge and experience is second to nobody.

Books to Read

- <u>The Criminal Law Handbook: Know Your Rights, Survive the System, Sixteenth Edition, by Paul Bergman J.D., Sara J. Berman J.D., Published by Nolo. Available on Amazon</u>

This book is a must own for anyone in jail on criminal charges. It will help you understand the nuances of criminal law well beyond the federal specifics we discuss here. I can't stress just how much this book taught me.

- <u>The Prisoner's Self Help Litigation Manual by John Boston and Daniel Manville, 2010, available on Amazon</u>

While you are in jail, you need to learn your rights as a prisoner. That is the only way to make sure they don't screw with you too badly. This book taught me about my rights and I used it to successfully sue a jail or two.

- <u>Black's Law Dictionary, Pocket Edition, 6th, available on Amazon</u>

Having a law dictionary will save you a ton of time when trying to figure out what everyone around you is saying. Black's is awesome. And it's pocket edition is perfect for the jailed defendant.

- <u>Federal Prison Handbook: The Definitive Guide to Surviving the Federal Bureau of Prisons, by Christopher Zoukis, available on Amazon</u>

Chris Zoukis knows how to do time. He's done it and brings a great book with tons of advice for new inmates. He has a consulting service to help navigate prison specific issues for you. While I have never used his services, I have read his books. And if more inmates followed his advice, they would have way fewer problems in prison.

- <u>Directory of Federal Prisons: The Unofficial Guide to Bureau of Prisons Institutions, by Christopher Zoukis, available on Amazon</u>

This book details every federal prison. It also provides insight from inmates in those prisons as to the political landscape, violence and special issues. While I can attest that it was accurate when it was originally published, it doesn't appear to have been updated in several years. Hopefully, Chris is able to bring us an updated version in the near future.

What is Pretrial?

It is important to understand what "pretrial" means for our purposes since there are different definitions out there. Sometimes it means all the events that lead up to a trial. While that is technically true, your pretrial experience will not end until the case is either dismissed or your are sentenced to go to prison.

In **<u>Surviving Pretrial</u>**, we define "pretrial" to mean the time from when the arrest occurs up to and including the day the judgment is entered in the case. Pretrial does *not* include the appeal, post conviction proceedings, or other events that occur following the entry of the original judgment.

When talking about "pretrial" in the physical sense, we are talking about the time you are either in custody at a jail, in a halfway house or out on bail. The physical aspect of pretrial is one of purgatory. Most pretrial defendants feel as if there is no light at the end of the tunnel and live in a state of despair. If you or a loved one is sitting in pretrial, rest assured that the feelings of despair can and will end.

In order to reduce the amount of anxiety you will undoubtedly experience, Surviving Pretrial will help shed some light on the events that any pretrial defendant or their family and friends are facing. The only reason pretrial feels like purgatory is because it is never truly understood. Those that "help" the pretrial defendant also have little understanding as to what it means to be sitting, waiting and wishing for the case to be over. At the end of the day, their lives continue on.

In order to shed light on both the temporal and physical aspects of pretrial, we will take you on a guided tour of each and every aspect that a pretrial defendant must face. At the end of this tour, you should be able to understand critical legal jargon, self-advocate and enforce your rights without fear.

Detainee, Prisoner, or Inmate?

If you are ordered incarcerated during the pendency of the case you will feel like a prisoner. That's because you are a prisoner. In most systems, the ability to bail out is not a right. There are innumerable reasons, which we will discuss at length later in this book, why a judge can order you to stay in jail pending the outcome of the case itself. No matter where you are held, you will hear people claim that you are a "pretrial detainee" or an "inmate" or use some other adjective to describe your status. In the Maricopa County jail system, for instance, you will be referred to as "UNSENTENCED." In most jails around New Mexico, you will be referred to as a "detainee." Others will simply call you a "prisoner." What's the difference? Nothing.

In the law, someone who has yet to be convicted of a crime is not a traditional prisoner, but they are still held against their will and subjected to onerous conditions. Unless you are one of those insane contestants on 30-Days In, you are not in jail by any specific choice you made on any given day. You will hear people say, "You put yourself here." Don't listen to them. Until you walk into court and say you are guilty or a jury renders a verdict saying you are guilty, you are considered innocent under the law. But, while you are considered innocent under the law, the fact remains that jail is far worse than most prisons in America. Jails, which hold the innocent and guilty together, generally are underfunded and presume that their prisoners are only going to be in that jail for a short period of time.

It is ridiculous that the system believes jail is a short term issue. In the federal system, the average defendant will remain on pretrial for well over a year before they are sentenced and sent to a prison. Sadly, the judicial system views the government's power to incarcerate presumptively innocent citizens as virtually limitless. So long as they bring you into court for some sort of hearing, and a judge orders you detained, they can treat you just like, and often times much worse than, the convicted prisoners in a formal prison.

The biggest difference between someone who has yet to be "convicted" of a crime and someone in pretrial has to do with punishment. Our system of criminal justice punishes most criminals to a term of isolation from society. While some people believe that you go to prison in order to receive a punishment, the prevailing correctional theory is that being in prison is the punishment. While you are in some form of pretrial detention, you will also be isolated from society in all the ways convicted prisoners are. You will probably become very vocal about your presumption of innocence and later realize that your assertions of innocence mean nothing.

We will explore your rights regarding the detention environment in detail later in this book, but it is important that you understand, right now, that the only thing that separates you from a convicted prisoner is that the jail system cannot make you work, except for requiring you to keep you and your living area clean. The jail can, and will, utilize corrective methods such as solitary confinement if you violate their rules. No amount of yelling, screaming or tantrum throwing will change any of this. While you are in jail, you are a prisoner just like the rest.

Hopefully, the United States Supreme Court will one day create a dividing line between convicted and un-convicted prisoners. But as it stands now, there really is no line. As I said above, jail conditions are often times worse than prison conditions. For instance, in many jails, you will not even see an ice cube. But, in most prisons (at least in the federal system), you will see ice machines in every housing unit. In some state prison systems, you can have your own television set. Many jails only allow you to have video visitation or visitation through glass with a phone while most lower security prisons allow you to have in person contact visits.

As a matter of legal theory, there is a major difference between someone who has not been convicted and someone who has been convicted. In practice, however, it means very little and you would do yourself a favor to remember that you are being held against your will by the strongest force our country has to offer: the government.

☐

PART TWO

Criminal Law Concepts

This book has been in my thoughts for the last decade. Ever since I faced the federal gauntlet, I have wanted to get information to everyone so we can level the playing field a little. Prosecutors use knowledge as their weapon of choice. The know the facts of the case. They know the law. They know the rules of procedure and evidence like the back of their hand. They know every loophole and trick to take advantage of. You know nothing. And if you **THINK** you know criminal procedure, you probably don't have the knowledge necessary to stand toe-to-toe with a federal prosecutor. The only way to level the playing field is to learn your rights and enough criminal procedure to not be lost. In much the same way a mechanic looks to the customer who has never turned a wrench, the prosecutor looks at you like a moron. They are super cocky. They don't believe that you will learn any of the stuff in this book. There is nothing cooler than watching a prosecutor find out they are arguing a case against a defendant who knows his rights.

Unfortunately, a large number of criminal defense lawyers also presume that their client has no idea what's going on and leave them in the dark. They may throw phrases at you that you don't understand in order to confuse you so you just "trust" them. Your life is on the line here and "trust" is something that must be earned, not implied.

Law is something that can be learned by literally anyone. In fact, the Supreme Court has said time and again that the general public is presumed to know the criminal law. In law school, lawyers get to go on a nice tour of law as if their are touring America for vacation. Well, maybe not like vacation. They have to learn a lot in three years including: civil law, criminal law, constitutional law, real property, probate, and the list goes on. So we can give them a little break. You need to learn criminal law in rapid fashion. You don't have a semester to take a criminal law course and you certainly haven't had any instruction into the fundamentals of law. Like how to read and decipher case opinions or statutes. Or even where to find the law. Or the types of law that even exist in our complex society called the United States of America. We have to cover all of these for your journey through pretrial to move from the turbulent dirt road to smooth pavement.

Structure for the Federal Judicial System

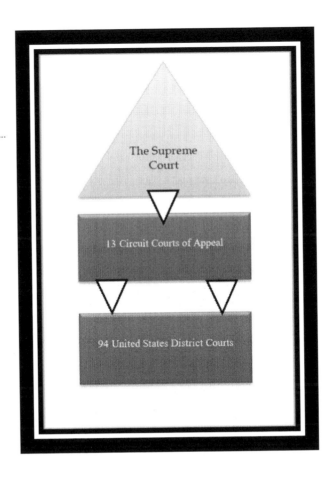

Circuit Court Map

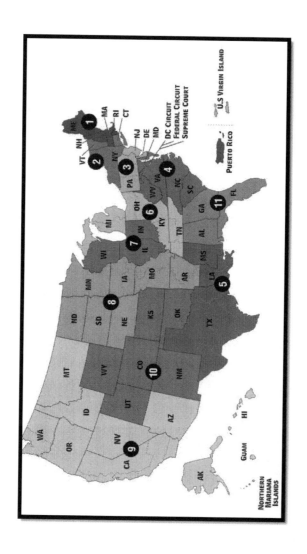

Arrest

When you are "under arrest" you are in the government's physical custody. Whether it is the local police, the sheriff, the state police, or one of the many federal agencies, if you are being questioned or had handcuffs placed on you, it is safe to presume that you have been arrested. The police officers or agents that are speaking to you may say that you are "free to leave" or that you are only being handcuffed for your protection. That is a load of bullshit and you shouldn't listen to them. Once you are behind the police station doors, leaving is far from easy. Some defendants are not in such an obvious arrest situation. Instead, they are on the side of the road during a traffic stop or they are in their own house during the execution of a search warrant.

IF THE POLICE HAVE SPOKEN TO YOU ABOUT SOMETHING THAT YOU COULD BE IMPLICATED IN PRESUME YOU HAVE BEEN ARRESTED.

It is true that the law defines the arrest as being the point at which your freedom of movement is fully restricted. In layman's terms, you can't leave by your own free will. Under the law, the placing of handcuffs on someone is usually considered an arrest. There are times where you are considered under arrest when the handcuffs are not taken out. For the purposes of this section, we are concerned with your first contact with someone from the prosecution team. It could be a police officer, federal agent, prosecutor, or any number of government personnel. Even the post office has people who investigate crimes.

No matter if you are under arrest in the formal sense, or in the broader sense that we are using here, you absolutely must know that you have the right to never say a word to anyone in the government about the alleged crime or anything else that could help them convict you. There are a number of legal theories where this derives from. For instance, the Fifth Amendment to the United States Constitution prohibits the government from forcing you to be a witness against yourself. You will hear of people "take the 5th" and then stop answering questions. The First Amendment to the United States Constitution also prohibits the government from making you say anything at any time as well. Just like you have the right to speak, you have the right to not speak too.

Let's use a hypothetical. Sammy is asleep and the local police bangs on the door saying, "Search Warrant!" Sammy wakes up and finds his way to the door and is met by an army of police with automatic weapons. They take him, handcuff him for his "own safety" and then "clear" the house (which means searching for other people and weapons). After clearing the house, the police officers take the handcuffs off Sammy and tell him to sit on the sofa. One of the officers says, "Hey Sammy. I know this is a little weird. But I have a warrant to search the house for evidence of drug dealing. Do you know anything about that?"

What should Sammy do? Should he say he knows something about drug dealing? Should he deny everything at all costs?

Sammy has the "right to remain silent." Surely, you have heard of that right somewhere! Sammy also must know that anything he says "can and will be used against" him in court proceedings. In this situation, the police don't have to warn Sammy of his rights, but Sammy has every right to invoke them at any time. Sadly, Sammy is like most others and couldn't read Surviving Pretrial until he was sitting in jail. No matter the scenario, it is likely that Sammy would land in jail no matter what he does, so he should "remain silent."

Scenario number one is that Sammy knows something about the drug dealing going on. Sammy knows that his roommate, whom was conveniently not home or on the lease for the apartment at the time of the search, has been dealing pills for extra cash. Sammy never thought anything of it, but now that the police are there, he decides to cooperate and tell the police about the roommate.

> *Sammy says, "My roommate Brian has been selling pills. But I don't know much about it."*
>
> *"How long has this been going on?" the officer asks.*
>
> *Sammy responds, "about six months."*

Sammy is now in hot water. His knowledge makes it look like he is part of a drug conspiracy. In the apartment, they find some pills and plastic baggies. Because Sammy said he was involved, the police arrest him. **WAIT!!! WHAT???**

Sammy never said he did anything, you say? You're right. But **everything** that Sammy says **will** be "used against" him. The police are allowed to fill in the blanks where it suits them. They will twist statements to meet their needs. I know, it's really messed up and America has a lot of work to do to fix these problems in criminal law. But, we aren't going to fix those in your case, and you need to understand that literally anything you say can be used against you.

Scenario two is that Sammy, knowing that his roommate is involved with drugs, doesn't want to get in trouble. Thinking he is smarter than the system, Sammy decides that he will deny deny deny. "I don't know anything officer." The officers still find pills and baggies. Will the police officer believe Sammy? Probably not. Cops are there to make a case; not set anyone free. It is likely the police officer will conclude that Sammy is lying.

Lying is far worse than explaining what is going on because it generally shows that you have a guilty conscience under the eyes of the law. The sad reality is that Sammy could have been telling the truth that he knew nothing and the same result would occur.

Scenario three is that Sammy says absolutely nothing other than his name to the police officer. He politely tells the officer that he does not want to talk without a lawyer present no matter what. All the officer has in his hands are the pills and baggies. That's it. There are no statements to present to the judge. So, when we fast forward to a court hearing a decent lawyer will be able to show the judge that (i) Sammy never lied, (ii) Sammy had no knowledge of the activities of his roommate, (iii) the evidence was located only in the roommate's bedroom, and (iv) Sammy is not involved. While Sammy was still arrested, it is far more likely for the case to resolve in Sammy's favor if he stays quiet. Why is that? That's because your silence cannot be used against you. Even when the police read your rights out loud, they conveniently leave out the right that your silence cannot be used against you in any way. The prosecutor cannot go in and tell the judge, "Sammy never told us anything and he should have if he wasn't guilty." That's not how our system works. The prosecutor must prove their case without your help. *If you help them, that's on you.*

Anyone that has had experience with the criminal justice system knows that speaking to the police regardless of innocence is a bad idea. However, the vast majority of people questioned by police do not have prior experience with the criminal justice system. They only know what they were taught in school many years prior: The police are your friend and are there to help. Sometimes cops are helpful, but most often they are there to make a case against someone.

That doesn't mean if you spoke to the police that all is gone. Just like your statements can be used against you, so can theirs. It's just harder. We will talk more about this later especially when looking at how lawyers tend to respond to confessions. If you spoke to the police, all I can say is: "what is done, is done." If you didn't speak to the police, I congratulate you. If you didn't speak to the police and feel like you offended them in some way (the cops are very good at making you feel that way), don't sweat it. They are not your friend. Their primary job is to build a provable case that you, or someone you are connected with, was involved with the commission of a criminal act.

Charging Documents

In America, we have an **accusatorial** system of justice. The government accuses you and must present competent evidence to prove the accusation. In order to make the process fair, you have to be given notice of the charges against you. This is done in one of several ways. One way is to file a criminal complaint. Another is to get an indictment. And a final way is to file an "information." Each system varies in what is required in order to properly charge someone with a crime. For instance, in some states, a regular citizen can walk into the courthouse and file a criminal complaint against someone. In most other states, a criminal charge must be presented by the government. Most jurisdictions have different rules for different levels of charges. While each jurisdiction has its own methods for presenting the charge, all of them absolutely must provide you adequate notice of the charges so you can defend yourself.

A charge represents an allegation of illegal conduct. It can be as minor as a traffic infraction or as major as a homicide. One way we are all given notice is when the legislative branch of government makes something a crime. They present and vote on bills and once passed, the legislature must provide a list of "elements" that would cause a violation of the law.

For instance, homicide has several basic elements. First, homicide can only be committed against another human being. Put another way, you cannot commit a homicide against your pet. Second, homicide requires that you intended to kill the other human being. So, if you go outside and shoot your dog in the head, you can rest assured that you will not be charged with homicide. You were given notice, in the form of statutes, that tell you homicide requires a human being be intentionally killed. That doesn't mean you couldn't be charged with animal cruelty or animal abuse; those charges have far different elements than homicide. The legislature also must give notice of the potential penalties allowed. For instance, some jurisdictions allow the death penalty. Others permit life in prison. Just because you never read the law does not mean that you haven't been given "notice" that the criminal law exists. The United States Supreme Court has held that all regular citizens are presumed to know the criminal law.

The second type of notice is the actual charge. Once you have been accused of committing a crime, the government must attach a charge to the accusation. The charge uses one of the statutes to inform you what the government intends to prove in the case. That can be done with a citation, complaint, indictment or information.

A "**citation**," "**notice to appear**," or "**summons**," are synonymous. That is they are a piece paper that a police officer gives to a target informing them they must show up to court or pay a fine. These are most commonly issued for traffic violations or other minor infractions. For instance, most police officers will not usually effectuate a formal arrest for jay walking. Instead, they would give a citation stating that the offender must either pay a fine or go to court. Just like the more major charges that we are dealing with here, you have a right to contest the citation in a court of law. The principles behind a citation are the same. The citation will usually tell you whatever statute or ordinance you violated, the facts relied on to support the charge, and what you must do to respond to the citation. If you were cited for speeding, for instance, the officer would fill out a form citation outlining all the relevant facts such as how fast you were going, how he determined your speed (LASER, pacing, etc.), time of day, road conditions, etc. He will likely fill out a section that tells him to name the ordinance or statute you violated and he will write a date that your appearance is mandated by. Just like any other situation involving the police, you are under no obligation to speak with the officer. A police officer that goes beyond "good day" is trying to get more out of you. He may say, "do you know how fast you were going?" Your response may tell the officer that you had been drinking alcohol and now you are facing DWI charges. (This happens literally every day on the streets of the United States).

You probably have very little concern for citations if you are reading this book, so we will move on to the next type of charging document. But, if you are felony defendant, then you should know that citations will become part of your life since everything from probation officers to local police issue them to people with "records" constantly. In any event, the next kind of charging document is called a "**complaint**." There are two major types of complaints in law.

The first is the **civil complaint** which allows regular people to complain about some wrong that another person committed against them. If you were in a car accident, and you wanted to sue the other driver, a civil complaint would start the process. In the criminal world, it is called a "**criminal complaint**" and achieves the same exact result: opens a court case.

The criminal complaint does two things. First, it tells the court that it has a new case to hear. Second, it tells you the charges you are facing **AT THAT TIME**. In a nutshell, the criminal complaint keeps the prosecution honest. It shows they are not just making up some case out of the clear blue sky but are instead proceeding based on their understanding of the gathered facts. Once a judge is informed that a complaint is filed, the judge will make sure to schedule hearings that are necessary to deal with the case. Judges know that criminal complaints involve the jail system and do not want anyone to sit around for no reason. If the prosecutor or police officer didn't file a complaint, they could do what they please without any oversight from the judicial branch. Thankfully, the Revolutionary War put a stop to that!

In order to understand the complaint let's go back to Sammy. Now that he has been arrested, and the police told him, "we believe that you knew what your roommate was doing and you were part of it," they are ready to file a formal charge. The police decide to charge a conspiracy in a criminal complaint. In making the charge, the police officer uses a criminal complaint to tell a judge and Sammy that:

> On or between January 1, 2018 and September 5, 2019, Sammy did knowingly enter into a criminal conspiracy with others known and unknown, including but not limited to Brian Abner, to distribute controlled substances in and around the District of Wyoming, in violation of 21 U.S.C. § 841, to wit: oxycodone.

The government has now placed Sammy on notice of what they believe they can prove at trial. The words used in the charge have specific legal meanings. For instance, "conspiracy" is a fancy term for a criminal contract between two or more people. "Controlled substances" are defined by statutes. Finally, the charge tells you exactly where to find all the elements of the crime: 21 U.S.C. § 841. Don't worry, we will get into how to read the law a little later.

The criminal complaint will also set forth some set of facts that build up to the charge. In Sammy's case, the police may say that they had been watching

Brian for some time, that they took custody of Sammy's cell phone and found numerous phone calls to Brian, and that they interviewed Sammy who said he knew about Brian's activities.

So long as the criminal complaint sets forth "probable cause" to believe that the target committed the charged crime, the criminal complaint will stand. Probable cause is about the lowest proof standard that exists in the law. It is very low. Basically, as long as a police officer or agent swears under the penalty of perjury that the facts are true, that is enough. And unless the police officer brazenly lies, the officer will probably be believed by the first judge to review the complaint.

In the federal system, the criminal complaint is a common mechanism for federal agents to secure an arrest warrant. More than anything, the federal agents usually believe they have enough information to bring the target in for questioning and want to use the charge to scare the target into talking. It is a very effective tactic. Most people honestly believe that they can mitigate the problem by talking to the police. But, once the complaint is in, the process will continue forward no matter what you say.

It is by no means a requirement that a criminal complaint be filed to bring a case against someone. Instead, the federal prosecutor can choose to skip the complaint and go straight to a grand jury and seek an indictment. Under federal law, you have a right to be charged by an indictment issued by a grand jury. The indictment is a document that lays out the specific charges and is approved by a grand jury. Not every state uses indictments issued by grand juries, but it is the most common way of securing a formal felony charge against someone. A "grand jury" is a jury that simply votes to approve or deny a prosecutor's charging decision. In some systems, you are given notice so you can testify if you want before the grand jury. In the federal system, it is pretty rare to be informed of the grand jury's schedule.

Regardless of the system, most attorneys and legal scholars agree that testifying before a grand jury is ill-advised. That's because the grand jury proceeding does not allow your own lawyer to go in with you. The prosecutor asks all the questions. Because of that, and because the grand jury only requires a majority vote, it is extremely difficult to convince a grand jury to not issue the indictment. If you are thinking of testifying before a grand jury, you are going to definitely want to consult with a lawyer.

The final type of charging document is called an "**information**." Some systems are permitted to rely on an information to make a formal charge and proceed to trial. Most systems, however, only use an information to make enhanced charges that require notice. For instance, if a prosecutor is planning on seeking the death penalty, in many jurisdictions the prosecutor will file an information which informs the defendant that the death penalty is on the table and what charges are being relied on for the death penalty. It is common to see an information filed in federal court in drug cases where the defendant has prior drug felony convictions. Called an "851 Information," that information will state that the government is seeking an enhanced penalty (double the minimum and maximum) and spell out the prior convictions it will rely on. The government has the burden of proving the existence of the prior felonies and you have a right to contest that. Thus, the information puts you on notice. If an information is being filed in your case, you need to make sure and ask your attorney what the meaning of it is specifically. Do not let your attorney leave until you understand what the information says.

Many attorneys scare the hell out of their clients with threats of indictments and other charging documents. It is sad they do this since the right to receive notice of the charge is protected by the United States Constitution and every single state's constitutions. All of them require that you be given notice of the charges so you can prepare a defense. The indictment process may seem easy, but for prosecutors is time consuming. Because of the time required to present a case, it does stop prosecutors from routinely changing the charges and allegations. Think of the charging document as a flashlight that lets you see your enemy for the first time. Now, instead of a dark blob at the end of a dark room, you can see that the monster has definition. You can develop some strategy to survive because you can see it.

While a charging document helps shed a lot of light on the charges that you must face, the fact remains that a prosecutor can change the charges. The longer the case is in the court system, the harder it is to change. But, it is possible. For instance, there are times that a charging document isn't written properly and you ask for it to be dismissed. If it is dismissed "with prejudice" that means the charge can never come up again. But, if the charge is dismissed "without prejudice" the prosecutor can walk right back in to the grand jury room and secure a new indictment. Many defendants wonder why a lot of lawyers do not seek dismissal of the charging document as a matter of course, and this is the precise reason why. If you do that, all you have done is delay the inevitable for a little more time. Most savvy lawyers will use the error to help negotiate a plea agreement that is favorable for you if you believe that a guilty or no contest plea is the way to go. If you are intent on challenging the case fully, then demanding your lawyer to seek dismissal of the charges regardless of the outcome may be perfectly reasonable. No matter the course of action, remember the charging document removes the wiggle room from the prosecutor's case.

Reading & Understanding Charges

Legal reading is very different from reading a novel. That doesn't mean you can't do it. It just means you need a little practice so you can understand how to read and understand charges. In order to accomplish our task, we are going to present you with several example charges and then provide specific instructions in how to break them down to understand them. Because the criminal law is very large, we will only be able to cover a couple of common charges that are seen. But, no matter what the charge is, the principles are the same.

Charge # 1

> *On or about January 23, 2019, in the Northern District of Illinois, Tim Jansen did knowingly possess with intent to distribute 100 grams or more of a detectable amount of heroin, a Schedule I narcotic controlled substance, in violation of 21 U.S.C. § 841(a).*

Step One: Break down the charge

The charge must inform you as to the who, what, where, when and how. Looking at the charge we know:

- ➢ **Who: Tim Jansen**
- ➢ **What: 100 grams or more of a detectable amount of heroin.**
- ➢ **Where: Northern District of Illinois**
- ➢ **When: January 23, 2019**
- ➢ **How: Possession with Intent to Distribute**

These four pieces of information are vital. Usually, the "who" is an easy one. But that isn't always the case. What if your name is Tim Jansen, but you weren't in the "Northern District of Illinois" on "January 23, 2019?" That would mean the what doesn't matter at all. If you could prove that you were not anywhere in the Northern District of

Illinois on January 23, 2019, then it should be clear they got the wrong guy.

Taking the opposite, what if you were in the Northern District of Illinois on January 23, 2019 but you didn't have "heroin" on you at all? Then you are likely going to challenge the allegation that you had heroin. Your intent would not matter at all. Now, if you did have heroin, but its purity was only 20%, then you may challenge that you had 100 grams or more of heroin. Breaking the charge down into understandable parts will allow you to isolate what is and is not challengeable.

What if all of it is true? Well, that doesn't mean all hope is lost. The government is telling you what they are planning on proving. For instance, if the prosecutor messed up and left in "January" from another case, and meant to put in "February" instead, that could cost them the case. Well only if the prosecutor fails to catch the mistake and the case makes it all the way to trial, it will be very difficult to convince a judge that the date should simply be changed because that would violate your rights to notice. (This is where moving for dismissal of charges is a highly strategic decision that must be weighed with an attorney).

Step Two: Find out the law

Now, let's look at "how" the crime allegedly occurred. You may be thinking that this would mean the actual events and you would be partially right. But, the "how" also concerns the definitions of the words. Words have meaning. In law, the rule is that if a word is used, it has a meaning of some sort and courts are supposed to apply that meaning when interpreting the law. For instance, what does "possession" mean? Is "possession with intent to distribute" the same as "possession"? Does 500 grams mean the weight of the actual heroin or all the additives too? The law has to define all of these things so you have an idea of what the charge actually means. And, indeed, the law defines all of these words.

For you to better understand this, we must first understand where "law" comes from. Law, at its core, is an understanding between a government (in the olden days, the King; today, the federal or state government) and a group of people (the citizens) as to what is permissible and what is not. In America, law is developed through various processes outlined in each state's constitution or, for federal law, the United States Constitution.

The United States Constitution has placed the power to pass laws in the hands of the legislative branch which is called "Congress." Congress will present a bill and then argue about it for a while. After that, they will vote whether they want the bill to be considered a law or not. If the vote carries through the entire Congressional process, then it is sent to the President to be signed. If the President doesn't want it to become law, then the President can refuse to sign it, and then Congress will have a chance to override the President. Unfortunately, it is beyond the scope of this book to discuss the intricacies of Congressional processes. What you need to know is that after a bill is turned into law, it is codified as a "statute" in a big collection of books. Every state and the federal government has a set of statutes which have all of their laws placed into them. The federal set of statutes consists of 36 "Titles" and contain thousands upon thousands of statutes within them. The Title of a set of statutes can guide you to what you are looking for.

In the federal system, Title 8 is for "Immigration and Naturalization," Title 18 is for "Crimes and Criminal Procedure" and Title 21 is for "Food and Drugs." These three Titles are the most commonly referenced when you are involved in a federal *criminal* case.

Turning back to Tim Jansen, in order to find out where the actual statute is, the indictment tells us to go to: 21 U.S.C. § 841(a). This is an abbreviated way of saying "Title 21" of the "United States Code" statute or section "841" and paragraph "a." With that information, if you have access to the United States Code, you would find:

> § 841. Prohibited acts.
>
> *(a) Unlawful acts. Except as authorized by this title, it shall be unlawful for any person knowingly or intentionally --*
>
> *(1) to manufacture, distribute, or dispense, or possess with intent to manufacture, distribute, or dispense, a controlled substance; or*
>
> *(2) to create, distribute, or dispense, or possess with intent to distribute, or dispense, a counterfeit substance.*

In much the same way we took the charge in Step One and broke it down, we can understand the statute by breaking it down into readable parts. While we will still look at the who, what, where, when, and how with the statute, the difference will be that we are *not* concerned with the facts of any specific case. Our goal in this step is simply to understand what the "elements" of the crime are. An "element" is a condition to gain a conviction. The government is required to prove each individual element beyond a reasonable doubt. So, with 21 U.S.C. § 841(a), we have the following breakdown:

> - Who: Any Person
> - Where: In a specific district of the United States
> - What: controlled substances
> - When: Any day after the statute became law
> - How: manufacture, distribute, dispense or possess with intent to distribute or dispense

While the "when" can be a vital issue and should always be evaluated, in most cases it is not an issue. But, it is still important to understand what we are looking at. The United States Constitution prohibits any state and the federal government from prosecuting anyone for a crime before the law that made the act criminal became a law. That is why we must always know the day the statute became a law. For instance, if a defendant sold a drug on January 5, 2019 by that drug was not defined as a drug for purposes of the statute until January 6, 2019, then the defendant could not be convicted of the crime. The law that prohibits such a conviction is called the "ex post facto clause" of the United States

Constitution. For Tim Jansen's purposes, though, heroin has been a controlled substance for many years and the law prohibiting its distribution and private possession has been around for decades. So, Tim will probably not be contesting the when as far as the law is concerned.

Next, the government will have to prove that the event occurred in or is somehow connected to the United States (federal) or the state where the charge lies. You will notice that the statute does not make any mention of this. For the most part, criminal statutes regulate the conduct of people within the borders of the United States or within the prosecuting state. For instance, if you commit a crime in Indiana, it is unlikely that Texas would be able to prosecute you for it. Why do I say "unlikely?" That's because there are times where conduct of a person can be regulated outside of the country. For instance, there are federal laws that prohibit people from not reporting their income and paying their taxes while they live in a foreign country. Typically, if a statute applies outside of the jurisdiction, it will be spelled out. But, it is vital you verify your understanding of this with a knowledgeable lawyer.

There is a second part to the "where" that is extremely vital and can become a significant issue in any case called "venue." The United States and most state's Constitutions mandate that a criminal trial occur in the "state and district" where the crime was allegedly committed. Under federal law, "districts" are defined by Congress. For the most part, each state can be considered its own district under federal law. However, many of those states are divided into multiple districts. For instance, if you are charged with committing a crime within the Western District of New York, the government will have to tie you to the Western District of New York. As a matter of example, the Bronx is **not** part of the Western District of New York. So, if you know that you committed the crime in the Bronx and there is absolutely nothing tying you and the criminal activity to the Western District of New York, then you may want to proceed to trial. Remember, however, that this is very complicated and it is absolutely vital that you speak with a knowledgeable lawyer about whether you have such an argument. Do not just run to the courthouse and start screaming that the venue is wrong because all that will happen is a transfer of the venue. Strategy is key in preserving a venue issue.

The "what" gets a little more complicated. You will notice that the statute doesn't list out the "controlled substances" that fall under the purview of the law. For instance, is "cinnamon" a controlled substance that could land you in jail? It is a "substance" and, in many ways, it is "controlled" (such as by the Food and Drug Administration certification process). Thankfully, cinnamon is NOT a "controlled substance" for purposes of the drug laws despite the use of the phrase. That's because in Title 21, where we found our statute, there are definitions for many of the terms.

> *(6) The term "controlled substance" means a drug or other substance, or immediate precursor, included in schedule I, II, III, IV, or V of part B of this title [21 U.S.C. § 812]. The term does not include distilled spirits, wine, malt beverages, or tobacco, as those terms are defined or used in subtitle E of the Internal Revenue Code [26 U.S.C. § 5001, et seq.].*

The definition tells us where to find what is prohibited. When we turn to 21 U.S.C. § 812, we find the list of schedules which has a list of all controlled substances. We find that opiates (the class of drugs heroin belongs) are considered Schedule I narcotics. Accordingly, it is regulated and prosecutable.

Step Three: Straighten out the facts.

"What" is a very important consideration and should never be disregarded. Was the heroin 100%

pure? For the garden variety drug cases, not likely. That means the weight may not be 100 grams of heroin, but is 100 grams of heroin *and* non-drug fillers. If that is the case, the government may not be able to prove that Tim Jansen possessed 100 grams.

Whether the government can prove that Tim Jansen had 100 grams or more doesn't mean that he can't still be convicted. But, it does mean that the penalties could be lower. For instance, having 100 grams or more of heroin is subject to a 5-year mandatory minimum term of imprisonment while less than that - even one gram less - has no mandatory minimum attached to it.

"How" is just as critical as "what" when evaluating the facts of the case. We already know that Tim is charged with possession with intent to distribute heroin. Tim contends that he never intended to distribute it at all and the reason he had such a large amount of heroin was because he lived far away and didn't want to have to go back and forth. Tim's contention is definitely plausible and a savvy lawyer could use that to convince the prosecutor that Tim had no intention to distribute (i.e. to get a good plea bargain) or even convince a jury that Tim is only guilty of simple possession. That could result in a sentence of decades less in prison.

Tim would do himself a lot of favors by writing down his own version of events. Not only will it help ground him, but it will be something to show and discuss with his attorney when the time is right. Most people operate in a narrative world and there is no reason to depart from that in Step Three. Because Tim already knows that he needs to be prepared to discuss the facts of the case with his lawyer, he writes the following:

> *It is true that I had heroin on me. I was driving from Indiana to Illinois because it is very difficult to find heroin in Indiana. It is a long drive to get to Illinois though so I only go once every three months and buy enough for the three months. I got into heroin because of pain pills after a car accident. I broke my back and the doctors gave me morphine pills for months. Before I knew it, I couldn't get through a day without it, but the doctors stopped prescribing them to me. I tried finding pills and eventually I found heroin. I know I shouldn't be buying or using heroin and I need help. I never meant to be a dealer, I have never sold or given heroin to anyone.*

This short explanation of what happened will help Tim's lawyer determine what the case is all about. First, the lawyer will now know that the critical element in question is whether or not Tim intended to distribute the heroin or if he was really trying to stock up. Now that the lawyer knows this to be the critical element to attack, the lawyer can develop an investigation plan. That plan may include finding the medical records that may support Tim's assertion that he is addicted because of a broken back. The lawyer may also determine that he wants to speak with the local police in Indiana to determine if Tim had ever had any trouble with the law there involving distribution or even possession of drugs. If Tim's story is to add up, there shouldn't be any hint of distribution activity in the local area.

Using this three step process will allow you to understand the charges before you and what the issues are. This three step process can be used for any charge. Let's try another one.

Charge # 2

On November 10, 2018, in the District of Wyoming, Dwayne Wallings committed murder within the definition of 18 U.S.C. § 1111 in that, with malice aforethought and by means of shooting, Dwyane Wallings unlawfully killed Special Agent Robert Joseph, who was then an officer of the

Federal Bureau of Investigation of the United States Department of Justice engaged in the performance of his official duties in violation of 18 U.S.C. § 1114.

Step One: Break down the charge

- Who: Dwayne Wallings
- What: Murder
- Where: District of Wyoming
- When: November 10, 2018
- How: Shooting

Step Two: Find out the Law

When a charge is structured as it has been here, there are several provisions of the law named. One of them is for definitional purposes while the other is the actual allegation.

Notice how the charge says "committed murder within the definition of 18 U.S.C. § 1111..." When you see something like that, you know that the charge is not for a violation of 18 U.S.C. § 1111 but is cited to allow everyone to know what definitions are being used. The definitions are vital and need to be look at as well. Thus, we open the United States Code to Title 18 and find Section 1111 and find:

(a) Murder is the unlawful killing of a human being with malice aforethought....

So, 18 U.S.C. § 1111 defines "murder" as "unlawful killing" of a "human being" with "malice aforethought." Two of these definitional phrases have common meanings and should be easy to figure out. First, the killing must be "unlawful" which means not supported by law in any way. Second, it must have been of a "human being" which means it must have been someone of the human race. Finally, the murder must have been committed "with malice aforethought."

There are many types of lawful killing. You may recall the trial out of Florida where a security guard was tried for murder when he shot a young man during a scuffle. The security guard maintained that he was defending himself and was authorized by law to shoot and kill the young man that died. In Florida, the law is called the "stand your ground" defense. Every jurisdiction has definitions of what is lawful and unlawful. In Dwayne's case, what if the FBI Agent attacked him without provocation or lawful objective and Dwayne thought his life was in danger? Would he be legally permitted to defend his life? That is for a jury to decide, but it has long been held that self-defense is usually a lawful purpose when a killing is involved (this is very complicated and, if you are facing a murder case and you claim self defense, then you absolutely need to consult with a lawyer).

Is a baby in utero a "human being" within the definition of the law? What about a person in a persistent vegetative state? You would think that this is an easy point of contention, but when you look at all the possibilities, there are defenses that have been and continue to be mounted under this element. Obviously, if Dwayne killed a dog that was the property of the FBI, no matter how much that dog was loved by its handler, it would not be murder within the definition provided at 18 U.S.C. § 1111. Things get a little more complicated when we start look at all the possibilities for homo-sapiens (human beings) that exist in our society. For the most part, despite common religious belief to the contrary, a human being cannot be a baby in utero since that baby is not breathing on its own. As a result of this legal definition, if a baby is terminated before it takes a breath on its own it is not likely a murder. In the cases where things are not so obvious, strategy will be key in mounting a defense to this element.

The final element is "with malice aforethought." When you see the word "with" next to an element it usually is an element of intent. That means it is something that the defendant wanted to do; it wasn't an accident. Malice aforethought is a legal term that has a definition in law that is well accepted. When there are legal terms that you need to know better, you should consult a legal dictionary such as Black's Law.

Suffice it to say, in order to prove malice aforethought, the prosecutor must bring evidence to show that the killing was intentional (i.e. not an accident) and premeditated (i.e. planned). That means Dwayne may have a legal defense available to him. Being woken up unexpectedly and feeling the need to protect yourself doesn't seem like someone who had an intention to kill someone or even that they planned to kill anyone. Because Dwayne can now pinpoint a potential legal issue, he should write that down so he can discuss it with his lawyer.

Because Dwayne is now informed about the law as it relates to his own case, he can have a meaningful conversation with his lawyer. Put another way, Dwayne will be able to determine if his attorney is not properly representing his interests.

Step Three: Straighten out the facts.

Remember, this is the section where the defendant writes his own version of what happened. The police have already generated a ton of reports which outline their "findings." It should not come as a surprise, but the police are not very diligent in making sure the facts are objectively true. They will usually only look for the facts that support their own theory of the case and then write a report to support that theory. In other words, the police follow the process for writing a novel as opposed to learning the truth. If nothing else, Dwayne is able to communicate his version of events so his attorney can get his head around what really happened.

> *So, I went to bed on November 9, 2018 at about 11:30pm. Nothing was going on. Early in the morning, I heard something crash like someone was breaking into my house. I grabbed my gun, ran into my closet and yelled for the person to get out of the house. They didn't respond to me. Right after I yelled for the person to get out, my closet door was opened and I saw a gun pointed at me. I was scared and I shot the person to protect myself.*

Notice how there is no talk about the law in Dwayne's narrative. There is no need to talk about the law. This section gives the defendant the opportunity to talk about the facts. And, in Dwayne's case, the facts are very interesting. First of all, it is clear that he didn't "intend" to kill anyone. He only intended to protect himself. Second, he claims that he was in the closet hiding because he was afraid. Finally, without any warning or announcement, the closet door was opened and a gun was pointed at Dwayne's face. Dwayne's version of events will allow a legal investigator and his attorney to compare the police's claims and develop a case for self defense.

True Story Example

Let's look at a case that really happened. I was involved with helping a defendant (we'll call him Fred) in county jail that was charged with a sex offense and kidnapping. The state of New Mexico charged Fred with criminal sexual penetration in the fourth degree and kidnapping in the first degree. In New Mexico, a fourth degree offense comes with a penalty of 18-months in prison that can be suspended and probation granted. A first degree offense has a minimum of 18-years and probation cannot be granted. Fred was very scared that he was going to spend a lot of time in prison.

The three steps we outline above are important, but if there is a step that you cannot complete because of your personal situation, make sure to at least get the third step done. There should be no excuse for not ensuring your version of events is fully understood by everyone supposed to help defend you. In Fred's case, because we weren't able to access a law library, and his lawyer was not communicating with him (more on that later), we were stuck with only working out his version of events.

Fred came to me in a frantic state exclaiming that court did not go well. He informed me that his lawyer, whom he never met before, came to him with a plea "bargain." According to the lawyer, in return for a guilty plea to both counts, the state would agree to "only" 18 years in prison. Fred was shocked. But, up until the time the offer was made, Fred didn't really do anything to make sure his case moved in a direction to end as favorably as possible. By waiting so long to worry about his case, Fred made it substantially more difficult to fix the problems in the case. But that didn't mean we weren't going to try. There were other problems in Fred's way. The jail we were held at didn't have a law library, getting books mailed in was virtually impossible and we didn't have any dictionaries to use. That means we could not complete steps one and two. All we had in our arsenal was step three, so that is what we concentrated on. After a lot of prying, Fred told me the following story:

> On a Friday night, me and my girlfriend (the victim in the case) went out to dinner. At that dinner, my girlfriend told me that she was pregnant with our baby. I was excited, but I knew that my girlfriend was using meth. So I told her that she needed to stop using drugs and if she needed to get into treatment, then we would figure it out together. That sparked an argument between us. Later, my girlfriend arranged for a taxi to pick us up and take us to a hotel where we were staying together. At the hotel, we got into another argument about the methamphetamine use. I guess people were concerned about our arguing and called the cops. When the cops showed up, my girlfriend disclosed her age, her pregnancy and her relationship with me. The police arrested me.

Fred also told me that his girlfriend was 15 years old, that she was planning on keeping the baby, and that they were planning on marriage. Fred's case clearly warranted an arrest. After sitting in jail for several weeks, Fred was told that he was indicted by a grand jury for two counts.

First, and not surprisingly, Fred was charged with Criminal Sexual Penetration in the Fourth Degree (New Mexico's statutory rape law). Second, he was charged with Kidnapping in the First Degree. All Fred had in his possession was the indictment. While he had a phone call with his lawyer who told him not to worry, he hadn't met the lawyer until he went to Court and was given the offer. Because he had the indictment, I looked at it and found out why they were charging him with kidnapping. The prosecutor was operating under a theory that when they got into the taxi together, that was kidnapping.

As I said, we didn't have a law library, so I was stuck with only looking at the charging document and using common sense. Common sense can get you in trouble when evaluating law and you should avoid it if at all possible. However, if you have no choice, it can at least help you communicate with your lawyer. In the case of a kidnapping, common sense dictates that there must be some sort of force involved. Fred's story had no indication of force. That means the "offer" given by the state was baseless and he was right to be concerned that his lawyer wasn't doing anything. What was Fred to do?

Fred had waited a very long time to get concerned about his case, and it would have saved him a lot of stress to take the bull by the horns and be involved from the start. But, we aren't here to judge Fred's procrastination; it is indeed very common among defendants. Fred wasn't too late, there was still time, and that is what he needed to understand. Unfortunately, we only had like two days before he was due back in court to either accept or reject the offer.

In order to stop the madness, the first thing we did was draft a letter to his lawyer. That letter put forward Fred's version of events and put emphasis on the fact that at no time was the "victim" compelled to do anything. She is the one that called the taxi, she got in, she directed the taxi and she paid for the taxi. Fred also made very clear that his girlfriend was still his girlfriend and did NOT support the state's case. Fred understood that her lack of cooperation only could go so far because she could be compelled to testify. Given her age, it was clear that Fred would be found guilty of statutory rape unless the heavens opened up and a Christmas miracle occurred during trial. The letter thus made clear that Fred would be fine with pleading to the fourth degree charge and face the judge for punishment.

We put something else in the letter to hopefully wake the lawyer up. We used the phrase **"ineffective assistance of counsel"** to explain that her lack of investigation and diligence on the case was unacceptable. We didn't need to give her legal citations to demonstrate that she wasn't being a good advocate for Fred, we just laid out the facts. We concluded our paragraph about ineffective assistance of counsel with a caveat. If the lawyer didn't start doing the job she was supposed to do, Fred would be immediately informing the judge of the problems and ask for a new lawyer. (We will get into how to do all this in a later chapter.)

Since Fred was going to be in court again in two days, we didn't mail the letter. I instructed him to bring the letter to court, hand it to his lawyer, and demand that she read it right in front of him. So, two days later, Fred went to court and told his lawyer to read the letter. She became alarmed, which was precisely the effect we were looking for. She went over to the prosecutor and even showed the prosecutor the letter (this is a very odd step for any lawyer to take, but so is getting a letter accusing ineffective assistance at a hearing). The lawyer and prosecutor asked the judge if he could reschedule the hearing for another week so they could meet up with each other and discuss the case further. The judge agreed and reset the hearing. Fred didn't have to say a word.

A week later, Fred went back to court and the lawyer sat with him and explained that the prosecutor was not willing to drop the kidnapping charge but would consider reducing the sentence considerably. This was the right direction but not enough. Before he went to court, I explained to Fred that it would always be his choice and nobody can force anything. Believing that he had a decent case to present that he never kidnapped anyone, when the lawyer told him the better, but still bad, news, he vehemently declined the offer. The lawyer told him that he will have to tell the judge that he declined and then the lawyer advised him to not make any extra comments to the judge. The lawyer was sadly mistaken that Fred would remain quiet. He fully intended to tell the judge what was going on.

In New Mexico, and many other states, (but not the feds) it is common for a judge to make sure that the defendant knows that an offer was made and that there is no right to get another one, or even the first one. The judge will make sure that the defendant actually wants to take the offer or reject it. If the defendant wants to reject it, then the judge may ask them why. Most defendants just say that they don't want to take it. Fred used that opportunity to explain to the judge exactly why. He said:

> *Your Honor, the reason I am not accepting the offer is because I cannot plead guilty to something I didn't do. The state is saying that I kidnapped my girlfriend. I didn't. In fact, she is sitting behind me in support of my defense. I have no problem accepting responsibility for the criminal sexual penetration charge because it has now been explained to me that being four years older than her makes me guilty. I did not kidnap her ever.*

We prepared that statement before court and Fred understood that it should only be read if they didn't give him a deal worthy of consideration. After reading it, the Judge looked at the lawyers and said that the lawyers should go into the other room and have a conversation about next steps. The prosecutor agreed to drop the kidnapping charge, a sentence of probation and even agreed to having the record expunged if he completed his probation with success. The offer meant he wouldn't even have to register as a sex offender.

This is an extreme case of using the three steps, as best as possible, to secure a great result. More often than not, though, using these three steps will not be so dramatic. You should not presume that you will have any specific result just because you went through the three steps. The steps, more than anything, will give you an opportunity to understand everything that is happening. They also will allow you to communicate with your lawyer and determine whether your lawyer is actually doing their job.

No matter if you are charged with DWI or terrorism, using the three steps outlined above will allow you to understand what the prosecutors are planning to attempt to prove in court. It is their case to prove. You may not agree with their version or even their charges. What you want the case to be and what it is are two totally different things and what you want is not going to happen just by sitting there. In order to defend yourself, you must understand what is coming. Once you know what is coming, you can determine what is contestable and what isn't. You can develop a strategy to poke holes in the prosecution's case. Use these three steps to gain an understanding of the charges so you can defend yourself.

☐

Reading & Deciphering a Case Opinion

Before we get into reading and deciphering a case opinion, I want to make one thing clear. Reading case opinions is very hard because it is dense. Legal writing uses a flow that can be confusing and quite boring. You must always hone your reading skills by reading, reading, and reading more. And I don't mean case opinions either. The more you read (whether for work or leisure) the better you will become at understanding the context of an entire document and the faster you will become in reading generally. Reading for leisure will expose you to new words and phrases that can help you get better at understanding what judges are saying. Don't just read cases in your life. Read other entertaining stuff to ensure that you are always improving your reading skills. It doesn't matter if you have a Ph.D. or are a high school drop out. **EVERYONE CAN IMPROVE THEIR READING THROUGH MORE**

PRACTICE. Oh. And don't be afraid to open a dictionary to learn a word if you don't know it.

Case opinions are the pastor's lessons if you will. Just like a pastor will try and give you his interpretation of what the Bible may mean in some context, judges provide interpretations of the law as applied to facts. Opinions are written by judges to explain their reasons for applying the law the way they did. Case opinions have been written for hundreds of years. Those old opinions are part of history and are even referenced today in our own legal world. For instance, the Magna Carta is commonly spoken of even in American law because it was so important for the development of a free democracy hundreds of years before America was even a thought. All of the decisions of the United States Supreme Court and every inferior court are available to read today. Thankfully, the majority of them have been made electronically available which makes it significantly easier.

So, what makes a case opinion "law" that must be followed by your judge? Location is the answer. Your case is being heard in a "district court." That "district court" is in a "district" of the United States. All the districts have been decided by Congress long ago and it is pretty rare for them to add, delete, or change them but they certainly have the power to do it. A "circuit" has a group of "districts" in it. There are 13 circuits in the federal system. Districts within a circuit must follow "published" opinions from their Court of Appeals and do not have to listen to other circuits' decisions. And the Supreme Court is the final authority. When they speak on issues concerning federal law, then ALL lower courts must follow it. Only Congress and the Supreme Court can overturn an opinion of the Supreme Court. And Congress can't really figure out how to order dinner, so you shouldn't hold your breath waiting for them. It is rare for the Supreme Court to overrule itself, but it does happen. One of the most famous decisions (Roe v. Wade) was recently overturned and has opened a whole new can of worms regarding abortions.

It happens a lot that defendants will read district court opinions and point to them as if they should be applied exactly the same with them. But, district court opinions have zero authority in other cases. Sure, you can always show a judge what another judge did previously to try and convince them to do the same, but they do not have to. After being told that the district court opinions aren't really powerful, you'll probably turn to appellate decisions (decisions for the Courts of Appeal) in order to try and convince your lawyer is right. But then your lawyer will point out that the opinion you are looking at is "unpublished." And you will look at the lawyer like he has fifty heads because you were just told that appellate decisions are what matter. And they do. But only if they are "published." It is very confusing because you are looking at the cases in written form so that means they are all "published" right? No. Publication in the appellate world speaks to whether the opinion is selected for a specific set of books called the Federal Reporter. There is no such distinction with district court and Supreme Court opinions. How do you tell the difference? Generally speaking, at the beginning of the case there will be a note that says if it is unpublished or published. If it is a brand new opinion, it may use the word "**PRECEDENTIAL**."

What does all this mean. It means that if you want to present a legal claim to a court, your strongest legal basis will come from the Supreme Court. If the Supreme Court hasn't answered your question directly, then you will want to point to a published appellate opinions from the circuit your district is in. If you can't find any support there, then you will look for unpublished opinions (which are opinions not published in the Federal Reporter, but instead in some other book like the Federal Appendix or LEXIS Reporter) from your circuit. If you can't find anything there, then you look for published opinions from OTHER CIRCUIT

COURTS. When that yields no results, then you look for unpublished opinions from other circuits. And, if all that doesn't help, then you look to other district courts all over the country to see if anyone has applied the law in a way that helps you to similar facts as yours.

Whew. Now you know the strength of each level of case opinion. But, you also have to separate the meat from the cow. In case opinions there are two parts. **Holding** refers to the specific answer to a question. **Dicta** (singular is dictum) refers to all the fluff that judges use to justify their position. Holding is what matters. Dictum doesn't really matter but can be persuasive if used correctly. Determining which is which is very hard and lawyers screw it up constantly. So, don't beat yourself up if you incorrectly refer to something as holding when it's not. That's the whole point of debating the issues and it is ok to debate a point with your lawyer (but within reason).

The way I do all of this is I write a question at the top of my piece of paper that I want to research. And then I go down the list to find cases in each category and list each case's holding so I can have a discussion about it later. Let me show you how I do it.

Surviving Pretrial · 85

First I generate a "problem" to research.

Problem: Can the police enter a house without a search warrant if they believe that evidence could be destroyed?

Then I start researching words from the problem in the case digests.

We are going to look for cases in the following order (I live in the Tenth Circuit, so I will use that for the primary Court of Appeals):

- Supreme Court
- 10th Circuit Court of Appeals (published)
- 10th Circuit Court of Appeals (unpublished)
- Other Circuit's Court of Appeals (published)
- Other Circuit's Court of Appeals (unpublished)

The trick to finding cases that matter is to search district court opinions first. District court's answer specific questions and provide citations to all kinds of cases. That is where you can find the cases you need. So I am going to run a search in all the district court's within the Tenth Circuit for:

> *"warrantless entry"* and *"destruction of evidence"*

I am going to put in the quotes along with the word "and." This is called Boolean searching and helps confine your search. For more information on how to use Boolean search principles, check out Wikipedia: Boolean Searching (https://en.m.wikipedia.org/wiki/Boolean_expression).

Google Scholar and most other (free and paid) electronic law libraries allow Boolean search principles to be utilized.

After running the search, I am looking for any cases that have both of those phrases in them. I would prefer to find cases of a criminal variety, so I am looking for cases that have "United States" in the plaintiff spot (i.e. United States v. xxxxxx). I see a fair amount of results on my screen. I decide to click on the first one that involves the United States as the plaintiff which is *United States v. Cannon, 2021 U.S. Dist. LEXIS 11270 (D.N.M. 2021)*. In reading the opinion of Magistrate Judge Yarborough, I see a discussion about a "four-part test" to "determine whether the likelihood of destruction of evidence justifies a police officer's warrantless entry." In discussing the test, Judge Yarborough points us to *United States v. Aquino, 836 F.2d 1268, 1272 (10th Cir. 1988)*. I immediately know this is a published opinion because it's citation is to the Federal Reporter. (The Federal Reporter abbreviations are "F.," "F.2d," "F.3d," and "F.4th." When F.4th gets full then it will add F.5th (but that will be a long time from now).) So, I go to *United States v. Aquino* and read it. Trying to decipher the holding in a case like this is difficult because Circuit Judge Seymour didn't specify it in exact words. There are two ways to figure out the holding when it isn't clearly spelled out in the case. One way is to read other cases that discuss the case you need to find a holding on. If a judge states that a case made a certain holding, it is fair to use that one as your understanding. Otherwise, you can read the case and try and develop what the holding is yourself. I have been doing this a long time and know that Aquino held that where there is sufficient reason to believe a person is engaged in dealing drugs, even when there are no controlled buys, the police can enter the home in search for drugs. But, Circuit Judge Seymour has a warning built into the opinion about the police not really taking any steps to try and secure a warrant suggesting that the case was a close call. (Close calls are great because they can point you in a direction that could help you). For now though, I am concerned with learning more about warrantless entries and destruction of evidence.

To that end, I see a discussion of the same four elements that Judge Yarborough discussed and I also see that the Tenth Circuit is relying heavily on "Payton." I look through the opinion and find that "Payton" is for *Payton v. New York, 445 U.S. 573 (1984).* I immediately know this is a Supreme Court case because of the citation to the United States Reports. (The Supreme Court opinion citation abbreviations and names are: S. Ct. (Supreme Court Reporter), U.S. (United States Reports), L. Ed. (Lawyer's edition), and L. Ed. 2d (Lawyer's edition second). There are others that are really old, but this should get you started pretty well.)

I go find *Payton v. New York* and read that case. There is a trick to determining the holding of the Supreme Court. It's called the "Syllabus." The syllabus doesn't form any part of the opinion so you don't want to quote it directly in an argument. But it will summarize the case and provide you with a paraphrased holding. Not all cases provide a syllabus, but they are more common in present day Supreme Court practice so you might as well benefit from it. Lawyers use Supreme Court syllabi to determine if the case has any bearing on what they are researching. It really speeds up the process. According to the syllabus, the Supreme Court held that "The Fourth Amendment ... prohibits the police from making a warrantless and nonconsensual entry into a suspect's home in order to make a routine felony arrest."

My list now looks like:

- Supreme Court: *Payton v. New York*, 445 U.S. 573 (1984)
- Tenth Circuit (published): *United States v. Aquino*, 836 F.2d 1268
- District Court: *United States v. Cannon*, 2021 U.S. Dist. LEXIS 112705 (D.N.M.)

Now I am going to scour more current cases in the Tenth Circuit that cite and reference *United States v. Aquino* and/or *Payton v. New York*. I am going to try and find any cases that more closely fit my own fact pattern and then add them to my list in their proper places. Make sure to take notes about what each case discusses and whether the defendant won or lost because it is a real pain to try and remember all the cases that you will read through.

Case research is an art form. The more you do it the easier it will get. But you have to remember not to take cases out of context or forget their place in law. Case opinions are not the end all for your case. They are really only helpful in trying to convince the judge that your application of the law is the correct application. No two cases have the same fact pattern. You may believe that your reading of a case's facts require a judge to make a decision one way or the other. **THAT ISN'T HOW IT WORKS.** The judge **CAN** disagree with you. The judge **CAN** rule against you. Nothing is guaranteed. Understanding the holding of an opinion will, however, help you communicate your position to your lawyer. Absolutely provide your notes to your lawyer to help him out. The more researchers, the better. Don't get case crazy. And, for the love of God, do **NOT** start quoting cases like Bible-thumpers quote Bible verses by taking them totally out of context. Make sure any discussion you have about a case gives effect to the entire context of the case you are reading.

Judges

Canon 1: A Judge Should Uphold the Integrity and Independence of the Judiciary

An independent and honorable judiciary is indispensable to justice in our society. A judge should maintain and enforce high standards of conduct and should personally observe those standards, so that the integrity and independence of the judiciary may be preserved. The provisions of this Code should be construed and applied to further that objective.

Code of Conduct for United States Judges, 2019

Defendants erroneously believe that the judge is some protector for them. And while the judge is there to ensure that your rights are not trampled on, it would be wrong to assume the judge is there to protect you from everything. If you or a loved one is facing a criminal case, you need to understand who a judge is and what she does. First, a judge is an umpire. She is there to call balls and strikes for and against both parties. Second, she is there to resolve disputes between the parties. Finally, she is there to enter a judgment in favor of someone. Whether it is a civil case, criminal case or a traffic ticket, these three jobs do not change. The judge is not your friend, enemy or opponent.

Each state and the federal government have different qualifications for judges and even have different levels of judges. They even give the judges different titles like: Magistrate, District Judge, Supreme Court Judge, Justice, Appellate Court Judge, etc. Some are voted in. Others are appointed. Unfortunately, because each jurisdiction is different, this book cannot go into the details of each jurisdiction. No matter what their title is, whether they are voted in, or appointed to be a judge, their job remains the same. Their job is to make sure that the law is followed and the proceedings are fairly conducted.

As you can imagine, criminal cases are not the most civil of proceedings that can occur. The defendant surely doesn't want to be there and the lawyer wants to help their client. The prosecutor's job is to get a conviction and put that person in jail (not seek the truth). While everyone will usually refer to each other with terms of respect, the proceedings themselves will be filled with numerous contentious issues (unless your lawyer sucks).

Imagine you are at trial and the prosecutor makes some disparaging comment about you that is clearly not true. Most lawyers would ask the Judge to intervene; some Judges would intervene without being asked if the error is egregious. As you have seen on Law & Order, your lawyer will say "Objection" and then offer some basis for why there should be a call in your favor. If the Judge agrees, she may do anything from declaring a mistrial to instructing the jury to disregard the statement or even ordering the lawyer to go to jail for contempt. In this way a Judge is just like an umpire in a baseball game. The Judge is there to witness every moment of the trial and determine if a rule is violated by either side. Remember that the Judge's job is not necessarily to protect you, but the proceedings themselves. You benefit from this and it is indeed a constitutional right. Imagine the prosecutor set all the rules. You would have no chance.

The reason we are even discussing this is that there are too many moments where a defendant starts sending letters to judges asking them to dismiss the case, fire prosecutors for being biased and get a new lawyer. While you are permitted to file motions and other documents, you must follow the rules in order to do so. Each jurisdiction has its own rules. For instance, if you aren't happy with your lawyer, there is very little a judge can do. You can ask the judge to have a new lawyer assigned (a topic we cover in full later), but the judge is by no means obligated to grant your request and they routinely deny such requests. You can ask the judge to allow you to represent yourself. But, you need to understand that the judge didn't decide the charges to bring against you. The prosecutor decides that, and there is very little a judge can do about it. Even if the judge believes you are innocent, if the prosecution has presented probable cause to a grand jury, the charges will remain and the case will have to proceed to trial to give the prosecution an opportunity to prove the charges.

Don't get me wrong, sometimes you need to go to the judge to get things worked out and to protect yourself. Fred's story is a great, albeit rare, example of that. However, if you don't understand the judge's job, you will drive yourself nuts trying to get things done. The judge is there for both sides, not just yours. When asked to decide something, the judge will weigh a bunch of factors and may not rule in your favor. You may feel like the judge is "biased" against you even though the judge is actually doing his job well.

Prosecutors

> The United States Attorney is the representative not of an ordinary party to a controversy, but of a sovereignty whose obligation to govern impartially is as compelling as its obligation to govern at all, and whose interest, therefore, in a criminal prosecution is not that it shall win a case, but that justice shall be done. As such, he is in a peculiar and very definite sense the servant of the law, the two-fold aim of which is that guilt shall not escape or innocence suffer. He may prosecute with earnestness and vigor -- indeed, he should do so. But, while he may strike hard blows, he is not at liberty to strike foul ones. It is as much his duty to refrain from improper methods calculated to produce a wrongful conviction as it is to use every legitimate means to bring about a just one.
>
> Justice Alexander Sutherland
> United States Supreme Court
> *Berger v. United States*, 295 U.S. 78
> April 15, 1935

There is no nice way to put this, and many prosecutors will likely be offended for my saying so, but prosecutors are biased and they do not like you. Their job is simple: **WIN**. You will read books and cases that talk about the ethical obligations a prosecutor has to "serve justice" and be "fair." On paper, that all sounds great. But, in practice, the fact remains that prosecutors are people who, like most, want to win. While I agree that prosecutors shouldn't use a lot of the tactics that they do employ, it just can't be denied that they do employ unethical tactics to win their cases. Just because the prosecutor doesn't like you is not a reason to have the prosecutor removed from your case. In fact, it is nearly impossible to convince a judge to force a prosecutor off the case. It is likewise nearly impossible for the prosecution to force your lawyer off the case. You will save yourself a lot of heartache if you realize the prosecutor is there to win their case. They are not there for you. They are concerned with getting their case done and going home. That's it. Most of them will forget about you the moment the gavel falls and the case is over.

Attorney-Client Privilege

As a general rule, attorneys are not permitted to disclose information provided about a client or their case to anyone without first getting the client's express permission. This is called the "attorney-client privilege" and is very powerful. But, the privilege has its limits and you need to understand these limits to properly benefit from it. First, if you decide to talk to others about your case, then you have nullified the attorney-client privilege insofar as the information you disclosed. Second, if the lawyer was or is part of the criminal enterprise, in any way shape or form, then there is no attorney-client privilege. Third, if you disclose an intent to commit a crime in the future, the privilege does not apply. Finally, the attorney-client privilege does not protect physical evidence of a crime.

Keep it quiet!

The attorney-client privilege instructs attorneys to never disclose confidential information about a client, their case, or their disclosures without first getting the express permission of the client. The privilege belongs to the client, not the attorney. All too often, though, clients decide to speak with others about conversations they had with their attorney including specifics about trial strategy and other case specifics. In that situation, the attorney-client privilege is nullified because the client did not keep the information confidential. That is the precise reason why most attorneys do not like speaking with family, friends or significant others about a client's case even when its authorized. If the government can find a way to pierce the attorney-client privilege, it will. Let's consider several hypotheticals to better understand this:

Hypothetical #1

Donna was arrested and is sitting in the jury box awaiting her court hearing. Just before the court is called into session, Donna's attorney comes to the jury box to introduce himself and tell her that she is in good hands and he will speak with her more after the hearing. Even though she is trying to be quiet, Donna tells the lawyer in front of the other defendants that she committed the crime. Is the information protected?

Donna's lawyer certainly wouldn't go off and tell the prosecution, or anyone else for that matter, that she just confessed to the crime. And no amount of pressure should push her lawyer to tell anyone that fact. What Donna didn't know though is that the defendant sitting to her left wants to get a deal with prosecutors and heard Donna say that she was guilty. That defendant tells his lawyer who he heard Donna say she was guilty and wants to try and get a deal from the prosecutor to turn over the information. The prosecutor bites, gives the defendant a better deal because of the information, and now the prosecutor bases her own strategy on the fact that Donna is guilty. There is nothing the lawyer and Donna can do because Donna disclosed the information in front of other people.

Hypothetical #2

Jimmy hired a lawyer to represent him in a case where he is charged with failing to register as a sex offender. The gist of the case is that Jimmy decided to get his own apartment and didn't report his change of address to the Sheriff. Jimmy's defense is that he never moved out of his parent's house and still lives there. Jimmy's parents are paying for the defense and Jimmy wants his parents to know what is going on. So Jimmy tells his lawyer to tell his parents "everything" that is happening in the case and that there are no secrets between them. Should the lawyer tell the parents "everything?"

It is always difficult being in the middle of two parties that have a vested interest in the outcome of the case. Surely, Jimmy's parents want the best for him and are indeed paying large sums of money to the lawyer in an effort to get the best result possible. Jimmy doesn't want his parents to think that he is shutting them out of his life or case. The lawyer knows all of this. While experienced lawyers may know how to tactfully approach this situation, it is common for lawyers to simply state that they will not discuss case specifics with anyone but the client. If Jimmy's parents are made privy to all of the confidential information, then the information is not protected by the privilege. Why on Earth would Jimmy's parents turn around and tell anyone what they heard? Jimmy's parents probably wouldn't do this intentionally, but what if they are called as witnesses in the case? If the prosecutor asks the parents questions as witnesses, there is very little that can be done if any of those questions will result in the disclosure of damaging information.

Hypothetical #3

John is sitting in jail pending charges for drug distribution. His attorney arranges to speak with him on an unrecorded line in order to maintain the attorney-client privilege. John is called to the case-manager's office and handed the telephone receiver. On the other end, John's attorney is already waiting. But, the case-manager is still in the room. What is John to do?

The problem here is very common when pretrial prisoners are trying to speak with attorneys about a case (in fact, it happened to me). Hopefully John understands that the jail is a government place and all the people inside it are the government's people - no matter who runs it. Even if it is privately run, the fact remains that all the money for the jail comes from the government. Thus, it is a government place with an interest in making the government, not the defendants, happy. As a matter of law, a criminal defendant has a right to speak with his attorney privately. That means the defendant's conversation cannot be listened to in any way (the jail can observe the attorney and client together to make sure no contraband is passed between the two). The case-manager is in violation of the attorney-client privilege. Even so, John must assert the privilege and ensure it remains protected. Put another way, you can't un-ring a bell.

If John doesn't say anything and has the conversation with the lawyer and the case-manager hears everything, the case-manager could tell the prosecutor everything that he says regardless of the context. Sure, the case-manager will say they would never do any such thing, but suffice it to say that the case-manager's salary depends on the happiness of those that pay it. What should John do in this situation? Because the lawyer could not possibly know who is present in the room, John should immediately tell his lawyer who the call is not private. If John's lawyer is worth his salt, John will be in for a treat because the lawyer will probably be upset and make their disdain known to the case-manager (it was a lot of fun to watch a jail's case-manager be yelled at by a legal team threatening to sue). In many facilities, the case-manager will not leave the room no matter what a lawyer says and if that is the case, the lawyer should probably file a motion of some sort with the court explaining the violation of John's rights and seek some sort of relief. Even so, John and his lawyer would probably be best suited to not speak about anything in particular if the call is not truly private.

Probably the most effective way to be private with an attorney is through the mail. However, no matter where you send any mail from, the outside of the envelope should say "**CONFIDENTIAL: ATTORNEY-CLIENT PRIVILEGE**" or something to that effect. That way nobody could claim to not know they were invading the attorney-client relationship "by accident." In jails and prisons, letters between lawyers and their incarcerated clients should be opened in front of the client and only briefly inspected for contraband. Please know that the jail or prison will have specific rules to ensure that your mail is properly treated as privileged. If you and/or your lawyer do not follow the exact rules, then the jail or prison would be justified in breaching the privilege.

Lawyers Who Are Criminals

> ### Warning
> *If your lawyer was involved in the alleged crime in any way then it's safe to assume he has no care for you and you should not trust him as a lawyer for you.*

Because there are numerous legal considerations that go into virtually every business deal, even criminal enterprises use lawyers. In many of these cases, the lawyer is complicit in the crime and are probably profiting off it. When that happens, the government has a right to also go after the lawyer for committing crimes and the lawyer will not be able to keep secrets under a doctrine called the "crime-fraud exception." The crime-fraud exception allows the government to pierce the attorney-client privilege when the attorney and the client are engaged in a mutual criminal enterprise. Put differently, if your lawyer is later indicted for something that doesn't involve you, then your files are probably safe from use in a court of law. If you and the lawyer were in cahoots, then there is no privilege and all files, records and memories in the lawyer's head are potentially admissible in the case.

If you have a lawyer who **could be** implicated in any way in the case, then it is highly advisable to steer clear of that lawyer for your defense and seek a lawyer you have never met. Honestly, you'd be in better hands with a high-school debate club student, a jailhouse lawyer, or even yourself than with a lawyer who is also trying to save his own skin. It happens where lawyers involved in crimes with non-attorney defendants are quick to convince those defendants to keep a unified front and let the lawyer-defendant "take care of everything." Anything and everything you say to that lawyer can be used against you and, if that lawyer is really conniving, he will use that information to strike a deal for himself while hanging you out to dry.

I am already charged with a crime, so who cares?

The privilege only protects you from the lawyer spilling the beans about past conduct. They are not allowed to protect information about a crime that may be committed in the future. Further, if the lawyer is told about a crime and offers some level of "advice" to help make the crime less detectable, they would be part of a criminal conspiracy. Even if they are not said to have engaged in a conspiracy, they are officers of the court and have a duty to uphold the law. Just because you are charged with a crime and you have a lawyer doesn't mean you can get away with everything in the future. So, be careful not to disclose any intention to commit a crime in the future.

There is a fine line between asking a hypothetical question regarding the application of law and seeking advice on actually committing a crime. For instance, it is permissible to ask a lawyer what the elements of terrorism are for educational purposes. However, if you go to a lawyer and ask how to avoid detection for an element, you may not be protected by the attorney-client privilege. Most attorneys view the attorney-client privilege in a very broad way. Those attorneys will usually maintain the confidences of the client regardless of what the client may say. They may even justify keeping the client's confidence by viewing the question as one of a hypothetical nature rather than as a confirmation of an intent to commit a criminal act. It is extremely rare to hear of an attorney reporting a client for voicing an intent to commit a criminal act, but it does happen. No lawyer wants to wake up one day, turn on the news, and see a validation that someone was hurt because of a criminal act they could have prevented.

This rule is highly applicable while you are in pretrial. It has less to do with the crimes you allegedly already committed and is instead concerned more with the possibility of other crimes being committed. Let's look at a hypothetical example:

George is charged with selling 20 grams of heroin in violation of the law. During discovery, George's lawyer informs him that a person has been acting as an informant against him. The lawyer doesn't tell George the name, but George is fairly confident as to whom the snitch is. George looks at his lawyer and says, "I am positive that Johnny told on me." George is fuming. He and Johnny grew up together. How could Johnny tell? In his state of anger, George says to his lawyer, "well Johnny is in my housing pod, and I am going to walk out of here and kill him." In this example, George's lawyer will probably report the threat to authorities and that information will probably get back to the prosecutor thus weakening George's case in many ways.

Taking the same example, if George's lawyer has no basis to believe that George can even get to Johnny, then the threat may seem idle. In such situations, a lawyer may tell George that he is "not going to do anything to Johnny because it will hurt your case." Assuming that nobody is spying on them, the conversation is private. Nobody would have a clue if nobody said anything. The lawyer, though, will have to live with the prospect that he could have protected a witness' life. Thus, do not ever assume that your lawyer will sacrifice his own ethics and morals for your benefit. It is one thing to be honest about what you have done in the past so the lawyer can strategize for you and quite another to ask a lawyer to simply allow someone to get hurt. If you make a hyperbolic statement to your lawyer and you, in fact, do not intend to do anything, then make sure you immediately explain that to your lawyer. Criminal lawyers do understand that you are under a lot of stress and will be understanding if you say something hurtful to your case because of that stress.

Physical Evidence and the Privilege

The attorney-client privilege only protects statements made between an attorney and client. While the rule has been interpreted to mean written statements made in connection with developing a case, it does not mean physical evidence of the crime itself. How does that work?

Linda shot and killed her husband with a .38 caliber gun that is registered to her. The police never found the gun because Linda has kept it in her car. Linda never gave any statement to the police and the police believe that the crime was committed by a house burglar. Because she is scared, Linda goes and hires a lawyer to help her stay out of jail. During her first appointment, Linda brings the gun and hands it to the lawyer and tells the lawyer who she used that very gun to kill her husband. What is protected?

In Linda's situation, the lawyer is absolutely required to turn the gun into the police. It is **physical** evidence of a crime and the lawyer certainly doesn't want a gun in his office. The lawyer, however, does not have to tell the police how he acquired the gun, who his client is or any of the statements made to him about where the gun was used. He simply will walk into the police station and say, "I believe this may be evidence of a crime that was left at my office." The lawyer should not release any of the information learned as a result of the meeting that produced the gun. An ethical lawyer will **not** clean the gun or remove trace evidence from it such as DNA or fingerprints. If he does that and the police figure that out, he can - and will be - charged with obstruction of justice for tampering with the evidence. And, please do not mistake the hypothetical as advice to obstruct justice, but if the gun was already cleaned before it came to the lawyer, well, that is a problem the police will have to figure out.

If you have already been arrested, this is not likely to be an issue since it is highly likely the police have already seized the evidence sufficient to hold you. There are times, though, where you may need to use this rule to your advantage while in pretrial. Here is a true story.

I was helping an inmate with his case. He was charged with and convicted of possessing child pornography on a computer. The police came to his house, seized the computer, found the evidence and proceeded with the prosecution. The inmate's lawyer secured a plea bargain for the mandatory minimum and everything was working out well for the inmate. Just after sentencing, the FBI went to his wife and gave her back the computer. The wife knew that computer had child pornography on it and didn't want to get in trouble. Under the law, possessing the computer with child pornography on it is illegal - even if she had no desire to ever view it. When he told me this, I immediately was concerned that his wife could be charged with possession. Make no mistake, the federal government has no problem charging people with crimes that they (the FBI) perpetuated. I explained the rule to the inmate about physical evidence and how it could benefit his wife in this situation. Thus, his wife immediately took the computer to the lawyer and explained to him that the FBI brought her the computer and she believes it contains child pornography. The lawyer took possession of the computer and brought it to the prosecutor and made a record of what happened to protect the wife. Had she held on to the computer and it was found later, she could have been in a lot of trouble.

It is ok to bring physical evidence of a crime to your lawyer. It is probably better to give it to your lawyer rather than allowing the police get it first. The police will eventually get it but will be done in a way that is most protective to you. It doesn't matter if the "evidence" is of a crime you had nothing to do with. As a final example, imagine you are walking down the street and stumble upon a bloody knife. If you pick it up and take it to the police, they will likely question you and even believe that you are connected to whatever crime the knife is part of. That is not a good scenario for simply being a good citizen. If a lawyer brings it to the police, the lawyer will have the advantage of knowing all the intricate details of the law in order to keep you protected while also being a good Samaritan.

Fundamental Rights of the Defendant

> *It is ... recognized that the accused has the ultimate authority to make certain fundamental decisions regarding the case, as to whether to plead guilty, waive a jury, testify in his or her own behalf, or take an appeal.*
>
> Chief Justice Warren E. Burger
> *Jones v. Barnes*, 463 U.S. 745
> July 5, 1983

Whether you are represented by an attorney that you hire or one appointed by the court you will ultimately be responsible for any and all errors that occur throughout the proceedings. You are the one that gets to sit in jail for years to come if an error occurs. With that said, attorneys are professionals and are permitted substantial discretion in how to present your case to the court. Regarding what motions to file, objections to lodge, witnesses to call to the stand, and other "strategy" matters, the lawyer makes the call. To be sure, that is why you have a lawyer. They are the ones that know the rules and are the ones with the experience to make those decisions. That discretion is, however, not boundless and there are certain fundamental decisions the defendant must make themselves. Put differently, a criminal defendant facing charges has several important decisional rights. No matter what a lawyer may want to do, these are rights that the lawyer may not intentionally interfere with. First, you have the right to decide how you will plead. Second, you have the right to decide if you will testify in your own defense. Third, you have the right to decide if you want to proceed via a judge trial or a full jury trial. Fourth, you have the right to decide whether to take an appeal. Fifth, but only if you can afford to, you have the right to choose your counsel.

You will be presented with at least one opportunity to enter a plea to the charges against you. Typically, this is done at an arraignment. No matter if the proceeding is a formal arraignment or something else, the fact remains that no one can decide the plea but you. In the federal system, the rules say that a defendant can plead "not guilty," "guilty" or "with the court's permission, no contest."

Thus, if you are going to federal court and you want to plead "not guilty," there is absolutely nothing anyone can do to force you to say anything else. This right is vital because it means that a lawyer cannot decide whether there will be a trial or not. If your lawyer tells you, "we will not go trial," rest assured that your lawyer cannot make that call. If you want to go to trial - even if doing so will result in your demise - the lawyer has no choice and must help you through an entire trial. From this right flows the right to decide if you will accept or reject a plea bargain. The lawyer absolutely must communicate any and all plea offers from the government to the defendant and the defendant has the absolute right to decide if he will take the bargain or not. No matter if your lawyer believes the bargain is terrible or believes you will absolutely win at trial, the lawyer cannot make the decision of whether to accept or reject the offer without your express approval either way. Any time you are asked for a plea, you have the right to decide what that plea will be.

Many defendants who go to trial want to testify. It is often not advisable for a defendant to take the stand because prosecutors can use the opportunity to really paint the defendant poorly and virtually all criminal defense lawyers recommend against it. Be that as it may, the Constitution protects your right to decide whether you will take the stand. If you want to take the stand at your own trial, your lawyer cannot stop you from doing so. In many jurisdictions, the judge will have a small hearing without the jury present to discuss whether the defendant will testify or not. Often, though not required, the judge will ask the defendant personally and if the defendant declines, the judge will make sure the defendant is fully aware that it is his call - not the lawyer's. Because there are many pitfalls to testifying, I personally advocate for having a thorough discussion with your trial lawyer about whether you should or shouldn't take the stand and consider it fully before making a decision. I do not, however, advocate for any attorney or other legal support person to make the decision for the defendant.

If you proceed to trial, meaning you do not plead guilty to the charges, you have a Constitutional right to have a trial by jury. A jury is usually twelve people selected through a process called voir dire (pronounced vore deer). In some state systems the number of jurors is different. For instance, in Florida, a six person jury may decide a criminal case.

The Founding Fathers wanted to ensure that people would be judged by their peers as opposed to just the government. "Peers" does not have the same meaning as when you were in high school. It simply means people who live in the community just like you. The Founding Fathers didn't want the government to decide such serious issues without supervision. Thus, the Founding Fathers ensured that the People would first have to permit the government the power to punish someone in each case. A criminal defendant automatically gets a jury if they want it. There are times where a jury may not be beneficial for the defendant. That's because not all trials turn on the facts (such as whether you did it or not) but instead concentrate on complicated legal arguments (such as whether what you did was actually illegal). In those cases, it could be a good strategy to waive a jury and ask for the judge to be the only one that decides the case. Because you would be losing the benefit of a non-government decision-maker and also losing the benefit of having more than one person unanimously decide if the case was proven by the government, you will have to make the decision as to whether to have a judge or jury trial.

The right to appeal a criminal conviction or sentence imposed is not always guaranteed. In the federal system, Congress has authorized criminal defendants to file at least one appeal to the United States Court of Appeals no matter what. In some state systems, if you plead guilty, then you give up the right to present an appeal altogether. But, if the system you are in promises you the right to an appeal, then you are the one that gets to make the decision. A lawyer has a Constitutional duty to generally ask if you want to appeal and, regardless whether the lawyer supports the decision to appeal or not, they must help you open an appeal if you want one. What happens on the appeal is another game but it is your call if you want to appeal. Your lawyer can tell you that there is no chance for an appeal to be successful or give you some other "advice" trying to get you to avoid an appeal, but if you specifically say you want an appeal and one is available under the law, they must help you with getting it started.

The right to choose your lawyer is not an absolute right because it really depends if you can afford to even hire a lawyer. If you can't afford to hire a lawyer, then one will be appointed. When a lawyer is appointed, you do not have a right to have a lawyer of your choice. Sometimes defendants will see an appointed lawyer they perceive as better than theirs and ask the court to change the lawyer to that one. Sadly, that is not how it works. If you can afford a lawyer, then it is very difficult to keep that person out of the court. For this reason, if you want a lawyer who doesn't even live in the same area, or even practice criminal law regularly (which is probably a bad idea), you can hire them and they will likely be given "permission" to practice in a one-time case capacity. This is called "pro hac vice" practice. So if you have a case in Utah, but you like a lawyer from New York, the New York lawyer will probably be permitted to come in and represent you. This is more common in federal and capital practice rather than in typical state practice. In very rare situations a lawyer of your choice will be disqualified for a conflict of interest, but it is very hard for the government to succeed in these challenges and are indeed extremely rare.

Flowing from the right to choose your lawyer is the right to not have a lawyer at all. If you choose this route, never forget that "a lawyer who represents himself has a fool for a client." That maxim tells lawyers, and self-represented litigants, that it is impossible to maintain an objective mind when you are the one in the hot seat. Thus, it is highly advisable to have a lawyer represent you. But, it is recognized that if you want to defend yourself, the court system cannot interfere with that right so long as you understand the risks of self-representation.

You, and only you, have the right to make these decisions. Nobody can make them for you. If you think about it, it makes sense that someone who is incompetent is never found guilty and often sent home or to a hospital because they cannot make the decision of whether to plead guilty or not. Since they can't make that decision, the system cannot progress past the arraignment because the defendant can't make a proper decision. No matter what any lawyer may say, these decisions are fundamental and only the defendant gets to make the final call. Always remember that. If you feel **<u>ANYONE</u>** is pressuring you to decide one way or the other, that would be the time to tell the judge. The judge will remind everyone that these five decisions are yours to make without fear of any problems from your own lawyer.

☐

Strategic Decisions & Your Lawyer

Lawyers are terrible communicators outside of the courtroom. Very few possess the ability to communicate with criminal *defendants* because they speak an entirely different language. If they could actually explain their job to you, they should say that their job is to ensure that your rights are protected throughout the process, translate the legal jargon into language you can understand, and make decisions about how to present your case. The Supreme Court of the United States has spoken about this on many levels and has explained that a lawyer is entitled to make strategic decisions about how best to proceed towards the client's goal, but the client makes the decision as to the ultimate goal.

No matter if you hire a lawyer with your own money, someone else's money or have one appointed to you, you are in charge the *ultimate* outcome of the case. As we discussed previously, only you can make the decision of whether to plead guilty or proceed to trial. If you choose to proceed to trial, no amount of strategy the lawyer employs can contravene that decision.

While you will make decisions that effect the *ultimate* outcome of the case, your lawyer will make decisions about what *motions to file, when to file motions, what objections to lodge, what questions to ask witnesses, and what witnesses to call.* If you instruct the lawyer who the case is to proceed to trial, they will be in charge of planning the defense's case and will make all other on-the-fly decisions that need to be made. This is precisely why you have a lawyer.

Being involved with your case as a defendant is important. But you need to also realize what a lawyer's job entails. For instance, when you call up a surgeon and say that you want the arteries in your heart to work better, you aren't going to be over his shoulder and tell him everything to do to get your arteries opened up.

You have elected to use a professional to captain your shop so you should let him be the captain. That doesn't mean you shouldn't pay attention and inform the lawyer when they aren't steering the ship properly, but it does mean you have to give them a chance. If you see the boat heading for an ice berg, the by app means tell your lawyer about the problem. If the boat is going to sink, then by all means, get a new lawyer. But, don't be a micromanager and allow your lawyer a sufficient chance to prove whether he is a fit captain or not.

Part Three

Crash Course in Criminal Procedure

Criminal law is vast. It is a specialty in and of itself. It is estimated there are over 5000 criminal offenses under federal law. The problem is your exposure to its procedures and nuances has been too limited for you to understand what is going on. But, if you hope to survive a prosecution, you need to learn it and learn it fast. In this Part, we are going to go through every type of hearing and also explain certain events that occur during a criminal trial. Before we delve into all of those we need to go through some basics.

When you were in Middle and High School, you probably looked at your teacher like they were crazy. Who needs to know about the American Revolution or the Civil War anyway? You are about to find out that criminal defendants need to understand all of these subjects on at least a basic level to effectively mount a defense. There are a ton of books out there that explain all of these subjects. Here, I am going to give you a short explanation of the important parts and why they are important to you as a criminal defendant.

History is everything in law. It's what pushes laws to be made and what forms people's feelings about issues. The American Revolution was the war that the Founding Father's fought in order to break from the English monarchy. There were many things that the American colonists were pissed at such as: taxation without representation, unchecked searches and seizures, religious persecution, private trials, trials without lawyers to help, and restrictions on the right to dissent from the King. The argument regarding taxation resulted in the Boston Tea Party. By destroying the tea, the people said Americans won't be subjected to an arbitrary tax by the King. It is said that one of the reasons why coffee is so popular in America is because of the Boston Tea Party. Make no mistake, the rebels who tossed the tea into the harbor were considered criminals to the King. But, America celebrates their history.

Unchecked searches and seizures were common during colonial times. The King gave his officers the power to enter homes without consent, search for imports, and seize imports or charge duties on those imports. The officers did not need to get any other permission from anyone. The King's "writ of assistance" permitted them to do as they please. That, of course, pissed everyone off.

Religious persecution is something that everyone talks about even today. There is a misconception that America was founded on Christian principles. And while certain Christian principles have shone through the years, the fact remains that the formation of the United States of America did not specifically adopt Christian principles. Instead, the Founding Fathers wanted all people to be able to worship in their way, at their time, and by their own theology. It is true that when the Mayflower sailed, the Pilgrims and Puritans were trying to distance themselves from theological ideals and Ecclesiastical courts with which they disagreed. But there was a 300 year period between the Mayflower and the American Revolution. By that time, the people had found they didn't like it when a King, Emperor, or anyone else for that matter, would tell them what they should believe in.

Since the dawn of man, governments have used their power for tyranny and persecution. One of the ways they succeeded in this was by closing proceedings to determine a citizen's guilt to the public. This practice actually predates the time of Christ. Roman criminal trials were known to be conducted in private. Those in charge didn't need to answer to anyone. Sure, the Kings of past had no problem hanging a condemned prisoner in the public square. But that was after someone already passed judgment that the prisoner was guilty of the crime charged. The Founding Fathers wanted this practice to cease forever.

Another way government persecuted citizens was by trying them for crimes without any help from a lawyer. The law is complicated and always has been. The majority of people brought before trial were uneducated in basic studies and never had any education in complex legal application and theory. The Founding Fathers knew that access to a lawyer is the only way to ensure that a trial is fair by making it a Constitutional right to have a lawyer available to help the defendant.

This history is what formed the laws that America lives by today. Are they perfect. Most certainly not. But they have solved a number of problems that have repeated throughout history. A judge can't just throw everyone out of a public courtroom for no reason. A defendant's guilt must be announced publicly, not as a method of embarrassment or disgrace, but as a way to make sure the government isn't acting arbitrarily. The Church has no power to dictate how you life, feel, think, or act. The Ecclesiastical laws of old have no existence because they only served to persecute other religions. Searches and seizures are not permissible without approval from a neutral arbiter whether through case law or individual analysis. The formation of all the types of hearings you are about to learn about comes out of this history. That's because the formation of the United States Constitution also comes directly out of this history. Now let's look at all the types of hearings you could be required to attend.

Initial Appearance

When I was brought into court for my initial appearance, I was about ready to fall over from a heart attack. I didn't have the foggiest idea of what was about to happen. Nobody told me that I was going in for an "initial appearance" and even if they did, I had no idea what that meant. I was terrified that there would be news cameras everywhere. I felt humiliated that my parents would see me shackled and wearing an ugly green jumpsuit. I was horrified because I thought that my parents would hear about all the awful things the government claimed I did.

The officers led me into the courtroom and it was packed. It wasn't packed with cameras or protestors or anyone screaming at me. Instead, everyone was sitting around like it was a train station waiting for the next train. I learned that the majority of the people sitting there were lawyers waiting to speak for their clients. Next were the cops and agents that needed to testify for one reason or another.

Otherwise, it appeared to be people's families waiting for their loved ones. My family was there and it was then that I realized that I was more than happy to see them. I forgot about my cuffs and waved at them. They waved back. I now knew that no matter what was about to happen, I had my family supporting me. But I still had no idea what was going on.

As it turns out, the initial appearance is about the least climactic event you will experience. All that happens is the judge lets you know, well, that you have a court case and you have been arrested. You already know that. So what is the point of this?

The initial appearance is one of the most important hearings that happens in the court system. You don't even realize it, but several things are happening which are vital to the protection of your rights. First, a judge is forced to look at your file and your face. The judge is forced to acknowledge that a human being's liberty is at stake. Second, a message is given to the police and prosecutors that they cannot speak with you at all without your lawyer present. Finally, it makes sure you understand your rights.

The questions you are asked will be routine and will have little to no bearing on the actual outcome of your case. You will be asked your name, date of birth, and other demographic information that verifies you are the right person in front of the judge. You may also be asked if you are taking medications and if you are in jail if your medical needs are being cared for. Answering these questions does not admit to anything that is being alleged against you. The judge's questions are designed to not ask you anything about the alleged offense. The most important question you will be asked during this hearing is whether you need a lawyer or if you have retained one.

Very few people would have had time to have found a private attorney by the time this hearing is taking place. If you did retain an attorney, and he or she isn't there, simply tell the judge you have a lawyer and would like to wait for them to be present before you answer anything. The judge will respect that demand because it is your right to have a lawyer of your choice present for a hearing. But, if you are like the roughly 95% of defendants who don't know which end is up, never mind having a lawyer retained, then you are going to want to ask the judge to appoint a lawyer.

The United States Constitution demands that all defendants be provided an attorney to represent them at all "critical stages" of a criminal case. It is safe to refer to court hearings as "critical stages" no matter what is supposed to happen at them. It doesn't matter if you have millions of dollars. At this stage, you may not be able to locate a lawyer to help you in the initial stages. Asking for appointed counsel does not mean that you are waiving your right to hire a private lawyer later. You can always go from public to private defense at virtually every point of the case.

Once there is a lawyer on the case, the government is on notice that it cannot speak to you about the case in any way without your lawyer present. The police would love nothing more than to interrogate you until a trial begins. But, the United States Constitution protects your right to remain silent and to have a lawyer during all critical stages of the case. The law behind this is a bit complicated and we will talk about it more later, but suffice it to say that having a lawyer, whether appointed or hired, is vital to protecting your rights.

I already had a lawyer when I was brought in for my initial appearance but he was not aware that I was being brought in for an initial appearance until it was too late for him to get there. When I looked around the courtroom, I couldn't find him and I started getting nervous. Because it was an initial appearance, there was a public defender there for everyone who needed an attorney. I explained to her that I had a lawyer and she understood. When it came time to talk to the judge, she explained that my attorney couldn't make it. We still went forward with the hearing since the judge just wanted to ask me some simple questions. The lawyer standing next to me was prepared to stop me from incriminating myself accidentally.

By the end of the hearing, I left feeling like nothing happened. That is what you should feel. Towards the end of your hearing, the judge will issue some orders. One of those orders will probably be the date and time of the next court hearing. The judge will also likely state what kind of hearing that will be. For instance, the judge could say, "I am setting a detention hearing for May 1 at 830 in the morning." It is important to pay attention to the kind of hearing you are going to attend so you can be ready for that hearing. If you didn't hear it or didn't understand, ask your lawyer. You may not be able to ask your lawyer right after the hearing because the whirlwind is about to begin again. The officers in the court are going to move quickly to get you out of there. It is not uncommon for defendants to be swept out before they can even say goodbye to their lawyer. If you can't speak to your lawyer for whatever reason, you need to remind yourself that the criminal justice train moves like molasses. You will have more than enough time to speak with your lawyer later. So don't stress yourself out because you now survived your first pretrial hearing: the initial appearance.

Preliminary Hearing

Although there are exceptions to this rule, it has become common-place for the government to use "criminal complaints" to open cases against defendants. Because these complaints are not vetted by a grand jury, and they are used to have you arrested, you are entitled to a "preliminary hearing" for a judge to determine if there is actually "probable cause" to believe you are properly charged with the alleged crime. Often times, defendants waive the preliminary hearing. A preliminary hearing is not required to be held if you have been indicted by a grand jury.

I waived my preliminary hearing in federal court and I regretted it. My attorney came to me and said that he "made a deal" with the prosecutor that if I waive the preliminary hearing, he would get access to the discovery faster. It sounded good to me, so I waived the hearing. He also told me that the hearing would be very specific about what was alleged that I did and it would be embarrassing. I can't stress enough how much I regret waiving the hearing.

First, we only got 50 pages of the 4000+ pages that were yet to come. The only "discovery" turned over was the search warrant, which I already had, and an inventory list of items seized. That's it. So, I didn't get anything in return for the waiver. I later learned that a preliminary hearing would have yielded far more "discovery" for us than was provided. Basically, my lawyer lied to me to get out of preparing for a preliminary hearing. In fact, this is one of the primary reasons I even decided to write this book.

Understand, that you are not required to waive the preliminary hearing or anything else for that matter. One of my friends in prison once said, "So you want me to make the government's life easier so they can put me in jail?" Waiving the hearing makes their life easier and yours harder. That's it. The best advice I could give anyone is to not make this decision through emotion. If your lawyer legitimately has a solid offer of something concrete from the prosecution and you want to accept, then go ahead and waive the hearing. But, even if you are guilty as hell, if you are not getting anything in return then force the government to do their job. No matter what, it is your choice.

There is a huge benefit that comes with preliminary hearings. Prepared lawyers use the hearing to lock in testimony from the lead police officer on the case and further get some insight into the government's theory of the case. It is a hearing that your lawyer gets to "cross examine" the witness called. If the prosecutors decide to change their theory of the case later, or the police officer gives conflicting testimony later, the preliminary hearing transcript will become a useful tool in destroying their credibility.

The chances of a preliminary hearing releasing you from jail is slim to none. And, the "evidence" that is introduced will not seem favorable to you. It is virtually guaranteed that the testimony will make you cringe as you hear it. The police officer will not be nice. In fact, the police officer and prosecutor will make you sound as horrible as they can. It's their job to do that and do it they will. But none of that really matters to your criminal case. After they bash your character, your lawyer will be able to question the officer and show that the police officer is probably making conclusions without all the facts which is extremely common. Your lawyer will be able to show that the bashing of your character is based only on conclusions made and not extensive investigation. Moreover, the judge sitting there has heard everything under the sun. They deal with criminal defendants and know that what is being said isn't always provable or even reasonable. Most importantly, your lawyer will be able to find out what the police and prosecutor are thinking about your case.

The preliminary hearing is not meant to end a case against a defendant. It is really just a bump in the road for the prosecutor and ensures that the prosecutor isn't just filing a complaint for no reason. In other words, it is a very rare day where the prosecution loses and the defendant is released. Probable cause is a very easy standard to meet. But there is a lot to be said about holding the government to the fire. Even if you are planning on eventually pleading guilty, ordering the government and your lawyer to conduct the preliminary hearing sends a message that you aren't just going to bend over and take it up the ass. It sends the message that, if necessary, you will fight for your freedom.

It is vital to remember that the preliminary hearing will not likely release you, no matter how prepared your attorney is. On the flip side though, it will not be the final hearing. The government still has the burden to prove each element of the crime beyond a reasonable doubt. It is far harder to prove something beyond a reasonable doubt than to establish probable cause. The prosecutor must show they have a legitimate reason to believe they can win their case and there are numerous rules that they must follow to do it. If you waive the hearing, you are allowing them to bluff if they want to. If you hold them to it, the absolute worst that could happen is that the case moves forward. If you waive the hearing, there is a 100% chance of the same result. Hopefully the decision you make is one made from logic and strategy rather than emotion.

☐

Detention Hearing

I have yet to meet a defendant who isn't concerned about the detention hearing. As the name implies, the detention hearing will decide whether or not you will be held in jail for the duration of the pretrial process.

It is a common misconception but the federal constitution does not guarantee you "bail" during a criminal case. Instead, it just guarantees that if bail is granted, it won't be "excessive." When you are facing a federal case the judge must follow the Bail Reform Act when determining whether to grant you bail. The federal system relies less on money and more on conditions when granting bail. That doesn't mean that money isn't going to be ordered as "security" for your presence in court but it probably won't be some absurd amount of money that you could never access. That's because a judge can simply order you detained without bail if they so desire.

More often than not, the detention hearing will immediately follow the preliminary hearing. While these hearings generally happen on the same day, they are not the same thing. The preliminary hearing looks to whether there is probable cause to believe you committed a crime. The detention hearing looks to whether there is reason to believe that you are a danger to the community or a flight risk while the case is pending. The judge will figure that out through presentations by the prosecutor and your lawyer. Often times, though, the defense lawyer is not prepared to properly argue a detention hearing. It will be up to you to make sure your lawyer is prepared by ensuring they have access to appropriate evidence, witnesses and other information to present to the court. A short-cut for a lot of lawyers is to request a Pretrial Services Report. While a Pretrial Services Report is usually very helpful for a defendant, it should not be the end of the defense lawyer's preparation for the hearing.

It is frequent for the United States Probation Office, Pretrial Services Division, to prepare a report for the judge to review which discusses whether you should be released and what conditions should be given. Part of that report is developed through an interview with you and that generally occurs on the same day as your initial appearance. The probation officer will ask you a number of questions about your home, job, income, and other demographic information. It is probable that the probation officer will also want to interview someone who you propose can be responsible for you while you are out of custody.

The judge can allow you to be released with only a few conditions or could place extreme restraints on your liberty while released. As the law stands now, it is absolutely important to know that if you are granted some level of bail, you will not receive any credit against any sentence imposed later. However, if you sit in jail you will get credit for that period of time. The choice will ultimately be up to you.

Defendants who are released can be placed in a halfway house or put on house arrest. These types of conditions of bail can be pretty extreme and many defendants who have experienced both opine that jail is a better option. There is no right answer though. If you are placed on house arrest, you will be given a GPS monitor that cannot be removed. You will be expected to only go places that are approved by a probation officer before you go. Sometimes, you and the probation officer can work out a little schedule for common occurrences such as grocery shopping. For the most part, you will be sitting at home. Unlike jail, if you are on house arrest, you will have your own bed, kitchen, television and light switch. While you can't leave very often, and you will face other restrictions for sure, the biggest benefit will be the ability to communicate with your attorney without the prying eyes of other defendants trying to curry favor with prosecutors by trying to gather information about you. You will be able to help your lawyer prepare for the case to come and be comfortable while doing it.

In jail, it is a royal pain in the ass to set up private legal calls. I was in county jail for 4 ½ years and after about three years inside, the prosecution turned over some CD's with recorded phone calls on them. Over 100 of those calls were attorney calls and each and every one of them was reviewed by a federal agent. We objected and the judge didn't really care, so nothing happened with that except for the prosecutor being able to listen in as we were arguing about strategy and other issues including my intentions going forward.

If that weren't enough, in jail it is extremely difficult to review the discovery in your case or even write a letter to your lawyer about your case without some other inmate trying to see it. In my case, another inmate who I didn't know from a hole in the wall, called up the prosecution and told them he learned a lot of things about me. It didn't matter that

90% of what he said was completely false, because he had gotten into my attorney letters and was able to come up with some things (that were innocuous) that were true. The prosecutors treated him like platinum and buried me without batting an eye.

Far worse than house arrest is being placed in a halfway house. In a halfway house you will be given rules just like jail but you will probably be permitted to go to a job every day. You will have to be back at the halfway house by a certain time and any movement will have to be requested. Worst of all, you will not get any credit for time served in a halfway house and if you mess up while you are there, even slightly, you could be taken straight to jail and have your bail revoked by the judge.

In any case, the decision on whether to accept the bail conditions or go to jail will be yours. If you don't want to put up with any of it, then just tell your lawyer you want to stay in jail and he will arrange for you to waive the hearing. I am willing to bet that you would like to have a full detention hearing and at least have whatever freedom you are granted at your disposal.

There is something that many lawyers do not tell their clients about the detention hearing; it can be appealed immediately. If you lose the hearing and it was held by a magistrate judge, then you are entitled to a review of the decision by a District Judge. If the District Judge also denies it, you can appeal it to the Court of Appeals. These appeals require a fair amount of work so lawyers tend to not mention it. But if you went forward with the hearing and you are denied bail, you can and should demand that your lawyer appeal the decision immediately.

It is important to know that the detention hearing is something that will be important to you and will decide whether you sit in jail or are released pending trial. Remember that this hearing does not decide whether you are guilty of the crime. It is only meant to allow a judge to decide if allowing you out of jail will result in your flight from the case or further criminal acts.

Arraignment

The federal constitution guarantees that you will be charged by an indictment issued by a grand jury. The right is important in that, in theory, there is a barrier between the defendant and the government consisting of regular people. In practice, the right to a grand jury's issuance of an indictment holds little actual value to the defendant. The indictment itself would have been drafted the by the prosecutor for approval. The indictment, however, is an extremely important document as it tells you what the government intends to prove at a trial. In order to make sure that you received and understand the indictment, the judge will hold an arraignment in order to explain the charges to you and to take your formal plea to those charges.

In the vast majority of arraignments that take place in federal court, the defense waives the "reading" of the indictment. Generally speaking, most defendants have little to no desire to hear the charges read out loud to the whole world. So long as you have read the charges and understand them, then it is perfectly fine to waive the reading. Just know, as with any waiver, if you don't want to give up the right to have it read to you by the judge, then you don't have to. If the judge conducts the reading, then she will read each and every word of the indictment out loud and into the record.

After the reading is completed or waived, the judge is going to ask you questions similar to those asked at your initial appearance. Where the arraignment becomes vital is when your defense is going to be based on something like the defense of "not guilty by reason of insanity." That defense, and several others, are required to be asserted at the arraignment. It is important to speak to your lawyer if you think there is a reason to think that you need to assert a specific defense.

The most important thing that is going to happen at your arraignment is the taking of your plea. over 99% of pleas taken at the arraignment will be "not guilty." Because of this, most attorneys just assume their clients will plead guilty and not speak with them about the types of pleas and the benefits and risks of each.

I was railroaded at my arraignment and I spent years trying to go back to it and correct the error. I had already been in jail for roughly nine months by the time I had an arraignment. The reason was because my lawyers kept telling me that I needed to waive the indictment period because "we don't want to piss of the prosecutor." In hindsight, I now know that the indictment is my right and nothing to be scared of. But I listened to my lawyers. Well, when the arraignment came around, my lawyer just told the judge that my plea was "not guilty." I actually didn't even know I was going to court for an arraignment. I wish, to this day, that I simply pled guilty to the indictment on that day which is what I wanted to do anyway. Since I didn't speak up, I lost the right and all my arguments over the next ten years would fail as a result.

You have a right to plead either guilty or not guilty at the arraignment. Whatever plea you want to enter, make sure you tell your lawyer very clearly by saying, "I want to plead [guilty or not guilty]." If you decide to plead guilty, you are pleading guilty to the charge or charges as listed in the indictment. If you decide to plead not guilty, then the case will be scheduled for further proceedings. The most important thing to know is that this is your decision alone. As we discussed previously, many lawyers just assume that you want to plead not guilty at the arraignment. But if you tell them you want to plead guilty, and they say "not guilty" on your behalf, then you should absolutely speak up. All you have to say is, "Your Honor, that is not the plea that I want to enter." That will stop everything instantly. The judge will undoubtedly ask your lawyer to speak with you about what is wrong. If you clearly tell your lawyer you want to plead guilty though, then he must do everything in his power to help you do it.

If you want to plead guilty, you need to understand the biggest risk you face is that there are no bargains or agreements that restrict the judge from imposing any sentence within the statutory range. For instance, if you are charged with trafficking in more than 100 grams of heroin, then you are looking at a sentence of 10-Life. That means the judge is authorized to impose a sentence from 10-years in prison to Life in prison when you are sentenced. It is absolutely vital that you know the statutory range for each count that you intend to plead guilty to. Another major risk is that it will be virtually impossible to challenge the validity of your plea later. The judge will definitely make sure that you aren't on drugs, drinking, or suffer from some mental disorder before accepting the plea. If the judge has any concerns about your ability to understand the consequences of entering a plea, she will likely order that the hearing be continued until you are tested. However, if you are obviously not insane, the plea will be accepted and backing out of it will be virtually impossible.

It is extremely rare for a defendant to enter a guilty plea at the arraignment. Usually, your lawyer doesn't even have the discovery in the case to even help advise you on what is a good course of action. It is generally more advisable to plead not guilty at the arraignment since that doesn't harm you in the least while a guilty plea ensures you will be sentenced. If you can't decide, then you should enter a not guilty plea.

☐

Guilty Plea Hearing

At some point in the case you may decide to plead guilty. In fact, well over 95% of federal criminal defendants do just that. For instance, if you decide to accept a plea agreement you will have another plea hearing so you can plead in accordance with the agreement. There is a secret a lot of attorneys will keep from you. That secret is that you can literally ask for a guilty plea hearing at any time. You simply need to tell your lawyer to schedule a guilty plea hearing.

These hearings are usually conducted by a United States Magistrate Judge. That is done by consent. If you do not want to consent to a Magistrate Judge taking your plea, then you don't have to. You can demand a United States District Judge take the plea. There, however, does not seem to be any strategic advantage to demanding the United States District Judge conduct the hearing. But since it is your right to do that, do not be afraid to exercise it if you want to.

There are two arguable benefits to entering a plea in front of a United States District Judge. Specifically, it is possible for the judge to actually accept the plea agreement as written at the hearing. Although, that is a rare case. Most judges will defer the decision of whether to accept the plea agreement until after a presentence report is entered. The other arguable benefit stems from whether you have to speak up and assert your rights as we discuss in depth later in the book.

In a nutshell, when you accept a plea bargain, what you understand is written and what is written are two different things. What is written is what will control. So, if your lawyer tells you that the plea will get you a sentence of probation, but that is not clearly written in the plea agreement, you will need to speak up during the hearing. The rule goes that if you remain quiet, you bear the brunt of the error that comes. Virtually every defendant is told by their lawyer to not say anything at these hearings except to answer questions posed by the judge and to just tell the judge that you understand everything. That is a really, really bad idea. I cannot stress this enough. In my world, when I help a prisoner file a § 2255 motion for ineffective assistance of counsel or breach of the plea agreement, the first thing that the judge says in denying the motion is that the defendant didn't say anything during the plea hearing. Don't fall victim to that.

There is another thing that could happen at a guilty plea hearing. You can always assert a not guilty plea. In fact, the judge will tell you just that. If you are confused about the agreement or something you thought was promised was not actually promised, then you may want to say not guilty.

Now, because the court went through the trouble of scheduling the hearing and all the lawyers are present, the judge will probably ask you why you aren't pleading guilty. You should tell her why. If your lawyer never reviewed the agreement with you and you really have no idea what it says, then say so. If your lawyer told you that you were only getting five years in prison but you never saw that written, or heard the judge mention that, then you should say so. "Your honor, my lawyer told me that this plea, if accepted, guarantees a five year prison sentence. Is that true?" The judge will tell you the truth. Moreover, it will be on the record. So if the judge says, "Yes, if I accept this plea, it guarantees a five year prison sentence and not more than that," then it will be very difficult for the government to argue otherwise. But if the judge says, "Well, it appears this is a non-binding plea so even if the court accepts the agreement it can give you any sentence in the statutory range," you may want to plead not guilty since your understanding was completely different. If you do this, rest assured there will be a gasp in the courtroom.

I was never told that I could schedule a plea hearing at anytime and just sat by and awaited a superseding indictment that charged me with more serious crimes. Had I known I could have walked into court and entered a plea to the indictment before the superseding indictment was filed, I would have. I would have likely faced substantially lower penalties in the end. But I didn't know.

One day, my attorneys scheduled a plea hearing for me without my knowledge or consent. It did not go well for them. By that point, I had enough and I was speaking up. I was woken up at like six in the morning, went through the strip search process to go to court, got shackled, transported, and caged. My blood pressure was through the roof. I was nervous. That's because, I had no idea what I was even there for. Putting two and two together, I thought it was a status conference. Just before the hearing was set to begin, my lawyers had a legal visit with me in the courthouse. They said, well we are here for a plea hearing. I lost it. We started yelling at each other and

I told them in no uncertain terms that I was not going to plead guilty and they were insane to just assume that.

Oh, but this story gets crazier. When we got into the courtroom the District Judge was there. My lawyers had to now tell the judge that there would be no plea hearing. The District Judge was less than pleased. The hearing was an absolute waste of time. To try and soften the blow to themselves, but not me, my attorneys outright lied to the judge and said that I changed my mind. I was never asked in the first place, so I couldn't have changed my mind. In any case, for the first time in literally eighteen months, I was informed we were scheduled for trial in less than three weeks time. I was not at all aware of that fact. My lawyers had told me countless times that we would have negotiated a plea bargain or would have filed a ton of motions. None of that or any other trial preparation had occurred. Shocked doesn't even begin to describe what I was feeling at that time. The last time I felt even close to that heated was during a training exercise in the Marine Corps that involved crawling through mud and water while under barbed and razor wire with flares, grenades and machine guns going off.

I semi-corrected the errors when I did plead guilty two weeks later. It was more cathartic than anything but at the plea hearing I was asked if I was satisfied with my attorneys' performance and representation. I did not answer in a way that was expected. I told the judge that I had no idea if I was satisfied. Until the case is done how could anyone know? The judge eventually pressed me so I acquiesced and said that I was satisfied up through that point. Soon after this plea hearing, I fired those guys and hired new lawyers. By the time I entered a plea with the new lawyer, all of my lawyers were terrified of what I could possibly say. They knew that I knew my rights and I was no longer just going to sit by and get raped.

No one case is alike. Always remember that.

When you are at a guilty plea hearing, you can always continue to assert your right to a trial by pleading not guilty. You are under zero obligation to waive a trial. Ever. It is your constitutional right to go to trial. In fact, the entire purpose of the hearing is to make sure that you are making a decision of your own free will and without improper coercion. That is precisely why you need to say something if some promise is missing from the agreement and wasn't said. It has happened that prosecutors will concede the promise and the judge will write it into the agreement to make sure it's on the record. It would also be part of the transcript. It is also possible that the prosecutor will not concede and then you will have to decide if you want to accept the agreement as now understood. Saying nothing will result in you entering a plea bargain that you don't understand and quite possibly under terms that are not favorable to you.

Questions Regarding Counsel's Performance

There is something that routinely occurs at guilty plea hearings and is incredibly unfair. The judge is probably going to ask you if you "are satisfied" with your attorney's performance and advice to you. Nearly every defendant answers "yes." And that is a major problem if you are ever going to try and claim ineffective assistance of counsel later. I personally did not answer by simply saying "yes." I qualified the answer by saying that you could never know if your lawyer's advice and work were satisfactory until all the dust settles and the proceedings are over. Needless to say, the courtroom gasped. The judge really didn't know what to do with it. So, he just pressed on and told me that I had to answer the question. As a result I said, "well, up until right this moment now, I guess so."

I have thought about this in depth since and can't find anything in the law that requires a judge to ask that question in order to accept a guilty plea. The biggest problem with a judge asking this question, in my opinion, is that the judge is seeking to protect the case from constitutional attack without giving you a chance to really seek advice on how to answer the question. Your lawyer cannot provide you conflict-free advice about how to answer that question because he has a vested interest in the answer.

I believe that you should do a couple of things to stave off this question. What I am about to say has not, to my knowledge, ever been done in court. And there aren't any cases that I can find that really discusses the issue. But, if more and more defendants press this issue, I believe judges will cease the practice of asking.

First, before you go to the guilty plea hearing, tell your lawyer to file a document expressly informing the court that you cannot, and will not, answer any questions regarding your attorney's performance or your satisfaction with his work. Your lawyer will probably look alarmed. All you have to tell your lawyer is, "Look, I don't want to waive any of my rights. And I know that judges ask defendants if they are 'satisfied' with their lawyer's work. If I answer 'yes' then it will be used against me if a problem is discovered later. This isn't an attack on you. I just want to protect my rights." Whether your lawyer files anything or not is not really a game-ender but it is nice to warn the lawyer where your thoughts are with it.

Second, when you are the hearing, if the judge asks you if you are satisified with your lawyer (or anything that is similar to that) you may want to respond:

Your honor. I am not a lawyer. I don't have the benefit of asking a conflict-free lawyer about how I should answer that question because it seems like certain answers could waive my rights in some way. As a result, I am going to have to respectfully object to the question because I can't be represented by anyone right now regarding how to answer that question. Furthermore, I have read Rule 11 of the Federal Rules of Criminal Procedure and nothing in it says that the court needs to verify a defendant's satisfaction or lack thereof with his counsel. I want to enter a plea today, but I am not prepared to answer that question and I doubt I could ever be prepared to. If I am forced to, then I would say that "up until right now, I am satisfied but I reserve the right to confer with new counsel later and still make a claim of ineffective assistance of counsel if it is later discovered that my attorney's performance wasn't satisfactory."

You can read that word-for-word to the judge. You can even show it to your lawyer before you ever get to the hearing. Any lawyer who truly believes in the Constitution would agree that you can't reasonably be expected to answer any such question and should help you object.

Status Conference

Judges want cases to end. In fact, it is their job to make sure that all cases are heard and decided in an orderly and fair fashion. In order to do that, judges set small hearings called status conferences to check in with the lawyers. If you are released on bail, it is likely you will have to show up to the hearing just so the judge can make sure you will show up. If you are in custody, it is actually common for status conferences to be held without you present. For the most part, that's ok, but you should still find out what happened at the conference.

If you are taken to the conference, you will realize that very little will happen at it. It will probably only be about ten or fifteen minutes long. These hearings are used by judges to make sure that nobody is just dicking around for no reason. The judge will want to know if there have been any discovery issues, if any motions are anticipated, if the trial date is acceptable, and/or if either side needs anything to make the case move along.

For instance, let's say that you have been sitting in jail for six months under an indictment. You pled not guilty and your lawyer still has not received the discovery in the case. Your lawyer could use that hearing as an opportunity to inform the judge of the problem and the judge can demand the prosecution get its act together.

A status conference is also an opportunity for you to connect with your lawyer and lodge any objections that you may have regarding your lawyer's performance on the case. However, you shouldn't expect to take up too much of the court's time.

Suffice it to say that if you have objections, any time you are standing in front of the judge it is the time to lodge them. You need to make sure that your objection is at least legally arguable and grounded in fact as opposed to speculation. For instance, let's say your lawyer has never been to visit you and you only spoke to him at the arraignment. You have never seen the discovery. You have never been asked for your version of events in the case. You haven't even been able to tell your lawyer what your ultimate goals are. When you are standing in front of the judge, you will want to say something and you would be right to because the law says that you have the right to the *effective assistance* of counsel throughout the case. Simply explaining the facts to the judge and uttering the words "*possible ineffective assistance of counsel*" will usually be enough to light a fire under your lawyer's ass. If your lawyer still doesn't get his act together, you have now made a record about the problems which will protect you if you raise the issue again, on appeal or in a post-conviction motion.

Status conferences are a place of potential opportunity to speak to the judge if you need to. It is also a great opportunity to at least connect with your lawyer about the status of the case. Otherwise, they are meant to help move the case along. The system of justice moves like molasses and if there weren't status conferences your case may not move forward at all.

☐

Frye Hearing

In a landmark case called *Missouri v. Frye*, the United States Supreme Court made clear that a defendant has a right to be informed of the existence and terms of a plea offer. Before this case, it was common for lawyers to not tell their clients about a plea offers and hold out on their behalf for a better offer. Well, if you would have wanted the offer and you weren't told about it, then there is a huge problem. Your only recourse is usually discovering the fact of the offer through public records requests and then pursuing a post-conviction motion. That is very difficult to pull off to say the least.

After the Frye decision many, but not all, district courts recognized that finding out about a plea offer that was never communicated is virtually impossible. In order to protect defendants from that injustice, many district courts conduct something called a Frye Hearing. However, it is not a uniform practice throughout the districts.

The prosecutor is usually the one that requests a Frye hearing because they don't want to deal with a claim in the future. Since the prosecutor has zero control over what your lawyer tells you, it is a good practice to make sure that you were told and in fact want to reject the offer. If you have no idea about the hearing until you arrive, then you probably have no idea about the plea offer. If that is the case, you need to absolutely speak up and inform the judge that you were never told of any plea offer and that you would like to be informed of the specifics so you can make an educated decision. Because of the decision in Frye, it is becoming less of a problem since lawyers are terrified of being found ineffective. A lawyer's failure to communicate a plea offer to the defendant is definitely ineffective.

If you are called to a Frye hearing you will want to pay close attention and you may want to ask the judge questions about the plea agreement's benefits and consequences. So long as you don't waste the judge's time with irrelevant questions, it is likely she will answer your questions. The judge is going to ask you if you were informed of a plea offer made by the prosecution. If you weren't informed, do not lie about it to protect your lawyer. Your life is the line here. Your lawyer will get to go home each and every night and watch the football game with his buddies regardless of what happens in the courtroom. Your lawyer may tell you to just nod and say yes. **Don't do that**. All that will do is protect your lawyer and hurt you. Be forewarned though that what you say in court has long lasting effects. In fact, if you ever try and challenge anything that happened in court, what you say at the previous hearing will be considered virtually absolute. You will not be able to take it back. So, please only say what is absolutely necessary to get your point across and nothing more.

After the judge asks you if you were informed of the offer, the judge will ask you if you understand what the offer gives you. Again, do not worry about making anyone look good and tell the truth. If you don't understand something, then say something. If you can't read or understand the agreement, then you need to speak up and say exactly that.

It is ok, and even advisable, to ask the judge some questions to make sure you understand what it is you would get and not get. For instance, many, if not most, plea agreements in federal court are "non-binding" on the district judge. That means the judge doesn't have to listen to anything in the agreement and can sentence you to any amount of time in the statutory range and there is nothing you can do about it. If you aren't comfortable with that, then you may want to reject the plea. Asking the judge if your plea is "non-binding" is a good question then. So is, "do I have to do prison time with this agreement?" or "How much prison time do I have to do with the agreement?" The point is ask questions that relate to the agreement and your understanding of it.

If you decide that you actually want to take the plea agreement after going over it, a topic we will cover in great detail later, you can tell the judge that you changed your mind and want to take the plea. But if you tell the judge at the Frye hearing that you reject it, then the plea is gone and it is likely another one will not be offered. While it is not impossible to get it back, it is extremely hard. So, make sure you understand everything before making a decision one way or another.

It is entirely possible that you will not be given a Frye hearing if you plan on rejecting a plea offer. But, if one is held, it is highly beneficial to your decision making process. The only significant downside to a Frye hearing is that it will be impossible to claim that you didn't know about the plea agreement or its terms later since there will be a record of you being specifically informed. That's ok because it is far better to know and make the decision up front than try and backpedal anyways.

Suppression Hearing

In our system, a trial is not simply a presentation of witnesses and evidence. It is a presentation of *competent* witnesses and *admissible* evidence. There are numerous rules that govern the admissibility of evidence and it is common for the police and prosecutors to ignore those rules when acquiring evidence to use against you. When the defense wants to call a foul on the prosecution for how it gathered evidence, it moves to suppress, or throw out, that evidence.

Suppression hearings follow the filing of a Motion to Suppress. The Motion to Suppress will seek to throw out confessions or evidence seized in violation of the defendant's rights. It seems simple enough. For instance, if the police violate your Fourth Amendment right to be free from unreasonable searches and seizures, you should expect that the court system would uphold your constitutional rights and punish the police for violating them. As with everything in law though, it sounds far more simple than it really is.

The path to getting a suppression hearing is long and winning is rare. That doesn't mean they shouldn't be pursued. Often times, suppression hearings are used by defense lawyers to at least try and weaken a prosecution's case in order to push for a better deal. They are also a useful tool in convincing the prosecutor that there is a defense that could win. When that is the goal, it doesn't really matter if you win or lose. What matters is whether the prosecution thinks you will win. If they do, they will probably sit down and strike a deal with you. The point is, if they have no reason to believe you will win anything, then they have no incentive to bargain with you.

Suppression hearings vary in degree. Some take only a few minutes while others can take more time than a full on trial. If the issue the defense is complaining about is fact intensive, the suppression hearing will likely have several witnesses brought into court to testify. If the facts are not in dispute, then the suppression hearing could be as simple as pointing out to the judge the legal arguments for both sides so she can make a decision.

As far as a defendant is concerned, the biggest question that should be answered before showing up to the suppression hearing is whether or not you will be expected to testify at that hearing. There are a number of things you need to know before you agree to take the stand. In all events, you absolutely need to have a conversation with your attorney about all of this *before* the hearing takes place.

Simply put, what you say in court can and will have lasting effects over your case. It is common for defendants to testify at suppression hearings, get trapped in a lie and have that very lie used to enhance their sentence in the end. If you are going to testify, you need to make sure that you and your lawyer have a very long conversation as to your version of events and the facts that will come out. A smart lawyer will set up a mock examination where they have another person that you don't know come in and cross-examine you so you can get a flavor for how these things go. Suffice it to say that if you intend on going into a suppression hearing and lying about anything, it is a virtual certainty the lie will be exposed and cause you more harm than good.

You also must consider what winning a suppression issue actually means. For instance, even if you win a suppression hearing there is no guarantee that you will win the whole case or that it will be dismissed. Popular culture has made it appear that a police officer's failure to read a defendant their rights or a violation of a defendant's Fourth Amendment rights will result in an immediate dismissal. In the real world, that is simply not true. More often than not, a win at a suppression hearing only weakens the prosecution's case; it doesn't usually end it.

During the suppression hearing, it will be very tempting to bug your lawyer about everything that is happening. While you should be prepared to help the lawyer pinpoint factual errors in testimony, you should really try and sit back and let your lawyer do his job. I recommend having a list of the facts that must be established in order to win the suppression hearing. Your lawyer should have no problem outlining that for you days, or even weeks, before the hearing takes place. For instance, if you are pushing to suppress a statement you made to the police because they failed to read you the Miranda warning, you and your lawyer will have to prove:

i. **that you were "in custody" as that term is defined by the law;**

ii. that officers engaged in interrogation by asking questions directly relevant to the investigation; and

iii. that nobody informed you of your right to remain silent or to consult with an attorney prior to questioning.

The ultra-majority of claims involving suppression of police interviews centers on the "in custody" requirement. In order to prove that you were "in custody," your lawyer will have to show that you were placed in a situation that would cause a reasonable person to believe they were not free to leave. This is way harder than it sounds to prove. For now, suffice it to say that your lawyer is going to have to bring forward evidence and testimony to establish that you were not free to leave. It doesn't matter what you believed at the time. What matters is what a "reasonable person" would have believed and that "reasonable person" does not exist. Basically, if you are handcuffed and brought into a police station and put in an interrogation room you are entitled to be informed of your rights. But, if you were brought into your bathroom at home and the officers stood in the doorway to prevent you from leaving, a court may find that you were still free to leave and not "in custody." Such a finding would cause you to lose the suppression motion.

Because it's is a critical fact that needs to be proven, it would be ok, expected even, for you to politely inform your lawyer if you don't believe he established that fact before it is too late. When the witnesses are gone, it is too late. That is why you have the list of facts that must be established.

Continuing with our example for suppression of a police interview, let's say the police officer that questioned you is on the stand. The prosecution asks the officer a bunch of questions to make the officer look like the most perfect officer in the world. Your lawyer, in turn, (at least in theory) destroys the officer's credibility. But, if your lawyer failed to ask the questions that really matter, no amount of credibility destruction will help. Lawyer's are people too and they make mistakes. In the heat of battle it is easy to forget what lines of questioning need to be conducted. Until you are put in that situation you have no idea how hard it really is.

The first time I presented a case to a judge was my own post-conviction case in a state court. I had been through countless hours of classes and have drafted hundreds of motions for others. I thought I would be ready for that hearing just because of all that training and experience. Before I went to prison, I even gave classes to rooms full of physicians. No amount of training or experience, even with public speaking, can prepare anyone to argue a case before a judge. It's just something you have to experience in real life.

When the judge set the hearing, I was excited to say the least. My motion was making its way through the system and I knew every detail of the case and the issues I was presenting. Then came the hearing. Now I have the judge asking me questions about the law involved in the case and the prosecutor contesting everything I am saying. I was prepared and I was able to prevail in the end. However, I did lose on two issues that I thought were really strong. Preparation was not the problem. It was not having someone there to help me pinpoint the missing elements. It's a lot to keep track of when you only have 30 minutes to argue your entire case. That is why I lost those issues.

My story does not take place during a suppression hearing and a loss for me wouldn't have been that big of a deal. I was already convicted and the sentence would remain no matter what I did. No matter, I was stressed out before and during the hearing. During a suppression hearing that stress is a thousand times greater. The moral of the story is, you have a useful role to play during a suppression hearing. More pairs of ears are far better than one.

You can follow along and make sure to note when critical facts come out. Then when the evidence component of the hearing is over and the lawyers start arguing about the law, you can provide some useful notes to your attorney. Your attorney will now be able to confidently say that specific facts came forward.

On the other side of the coin, you paying attention and taking notes can really help your lawyer cross-examine the witnesses. In our example of a police interview, imagine the officer lies (big surprise there) on the stand and says you were free to leave at any time. You can give your lawyer your narrative, right then and there, about what really happened so your lawyer can cross-examine the officer and expose his bullshit. For instance, imagine you were forced to sit on a toilet and three officers stood in the doorway with their guns clearly visible. While the officer is lying about this very fact by saying you could stroll on out of there at whim, you tell your lawyer the truth.

Armed with the truth, your lawyer is now able to get up and ask the officer very specific questions about what happened.

> "Isn't it true that you questioned my client in the home's only bathroom?"
>
> "Where was my client sitting when you interviewed him?"
>
> "Where were you standing?"
>
> "Isn't it true that your partner was present?"
>
> "Is it fair to say that you had a gun on your side while you were speaking with my client?"
>
> "How big would you say the bathroom the interview occurred in was?"
>
> "How many doors in and out of the bathroom were there?"
>
> "If my client was sitting on the toilet and you and your partner were standing there talking to him while armed with loaded guns how would he be able to leave?"

A series of questions like that would expose the bullshit cops spew all the time during suppression hearings. But defendants routinely keep these facts to themselves and then blame their lawyers for not knowing. The point is, you got to speak up when lies are being told and you have to give your lawyer the ammunition necessary to shoot back.

Suppression hearings are very stressful. Their outcome can effect the entirety of the government's case to come. Winning a suppression hearing can help you tremendously and your active participation in it is vital. Remember to be proactive during the hearing and not in the way. Take notes and give those notes to your lawyer throughout the hearing. Huddle with your lawyer during minor breaks and discuss issues you see arising such as certain facts not coming forward. Be prepared if you are going to testify. In all events, be a team member on your legal team but let your attorney do what he is trained to do.

Franks Hearing

A close relative to a suppression hearing is a "Franks hearing." In fact, they usually happen together and are commonly synonymous. However, in some jurisdictions, judges still draw a distinction and distinguishing your own claims as such helps strengthen any potential appeals.

In *Franks v. Delaware,* the Supreme Court said that a defendant is entitled to examine an applicant, called an "affiant," for the issuance of a search warrant if they can make a "substantial preliminary showing" that false information was the basis for establishing probable cause to issue a search warrant. The case involved a rape allegation where a knife and clothing were seized from the defendant's apartment. The defendant had moved to suppress the evidence as seized in violation of the Fourth Amendment through a suppression hearing. The motion that secured the suppression hearing had only alleged that the warrant itself was defective and made no claim as to the officer's original factual claims that resulted in the search warrant being issued. During the hearing, the lawyer had uncovered facts that casted doubt on the "veracity," or trustworthiness, of the affiant's claims. The lawyer tried to amend the motion to make out a claim that the affiant told an intentional lie in order to get the search warrant and wanted to question the affiant on the stand. The trial judge denied the motion.

The issue made its long way through the court system and was accepted by the Supreme Court to decide when, if ever, a defendant is allowed to question the veracity of an affiant's factual claims. The Supreme Court, of course, didn't want to waste a trial court's time with baseless claims to attack affidavits. So the Supreme Court said that a defendant is entitled to question the affiant if: (1) a fact in the affidavit is shown to be false, (2) that the affiant included the false statement intentionally or in reckless disregard for the truth, and (3) if the fact is removed from the affidavit if there is still probable cause to believe evidence of the crime would be found in the particular place named. If all three elements are met, then the judge is generally required to suppress the evidence seized under the warrant. The ultra-majority of Franks hearings lose. However, even if they don't result in suppression, they are extremely powerful and can effect the government's case in drastic ways.

Moving for a Franks hearing outright alleges that some officer of the law intentionally lied to a judge to get a search warrant. That is a bold claim and if proven is surely going to piss off any judge. No judge likes to find out they have been lied to. The cop that lied will have a hard time for the rest of their career as judges will automatically be leery of their trustworthiness. The prosecutor will also have a hard time because they play on the same team as the cops and are usually involved in reviewing search warrant applications with officers. In your own case, if there is even a close question as to whether a false statement formed the basis of probable cause, a Franks hearing will probably be in your future. It is definitely something you and your lawyer should talk about in depth.

For example, let's say that a police officer secured a warrant to search your house for drugs. In the affidavit, the officer said that he pulled your trash and found some Ziploc bags, baby formula, and an old food scale. These items mean nothing in the grand scheme of things and are certainly not illegal. But, a lot of drug dealers use those exact items in their illicit activities. The officer knows that a judge is not going to believe that you are a drug dealer just because you have three objects in your trash can. In order to get around that, and to hurry things up, the officer tells the judge that the Ziploc bags that were pulled had cocaine residue in them. If that is true, then the officer's claim has merit and a search warrant should issue. After the cops raid your house, find some cocaine in your house and you are arrested, you start to think hard and really believe that there was little to no chance that the trash had any cocaine in it. Perhaps you don't use Ziploc bags for your own illicit activities. It doesn't matter that the officer actually found cocaine in your house.

What matters here is whether he actually found cocaine in Ziploc bags found in your trash. You then tell your lawyer who there is little to no chance that any cocaine residue was found in the trash pull. As a result, your attorney demands to inspect the trash pull items and have them tested. If the prosecution says the trash pull evidence is no longer available for inspection or your lawyer's test yields no evidence of cocaine, then the affiant probably lied in the affidavit. Because the finding of cocaine was absolutely vital to a finding of probable cause, if that "fact" is removed from the affidavit then no probable cause exists and the evidence should be suppressed.

These hearings are hard to win but can be of high importance even if you don't win. They allow your lawyer to grill the police officer before a trial occurs. The officer could easily get trapped in a flurry of cross-examination questions that show he is inept and that his investigation was shoddy. If you are able to make out the required preliminary showing that a police officer lied in securing a search warrant, win or lose you should probably pursue it. In my opinion, any time you can destroy a police officer's credibility in front of a judge, you should. But, as with any other decision, whether to pursue such a hearing is a decision that you and your lawyer must make together.

☐

Curcio Hearing

You are generally allowed to waive all of your rights. Indeed, when you plead guilty you waive your rights to a trial by jury and self-incrimination. Probably the most important right protected by the United States Constitution is the right to choose whom represents you if you can afford to choose. There are times that defendants, for whatever reason, believe that a specific lawyer can get them a more favorable result than anyone else. It is your choice to make. But, if the judge becomes aware that a conflict of interest could be present, the judge will want to make sure you know about the conflict and want to keep that lawyer on the case.

These hearings are usually quick. The judge will want to ask you if you know about the conflict and what you want to do. If you already told your current lawyer who you want a new lawyer, then the hearing will probably not take place since it is a moot issue. But, if you are planning on keeping your lawyer, the judge must be sure that you understand you can't waive the right to conflict free counsel and then later complain about your lawyer being conflicted.

If you are called to a Curcio hearing, be prepared to answer questions from the judge. It is not a good idea to lie about anything. If you know about the conflict, then say you do. If you didn't have any idea about it, then you should say so.

So, why would you want to keep the lawyer if he has a conflict of interest? I can't think of a single valid reason to keep a lawyer who is potentially conflicted.

The point is that you have the right to choose your lawyer. Ultimately, if you decide to stay with the lawyer, you will not be able to later claim that the conflict was a problem for you. Preventing you from complaining later that your lawyer was conflicted thus violating your right to conflict free representation is the precise reason why judges hold Curcio hearings in the first place. If you find out later that your lawyer was laboring under a conflict of interest, you had zero idea about it until it was too late and there was no Curcio hearing concerning the issue, then you would not be prevented from bringing the claim later. But know this. If you find out that your lawyer has a potential or real conflict and you don't say anything until later, the claim could be deemed waived and forfeited.

Faretta Hearing

When you want to represent yourself and act as your own lawyer, there needs to be a hearing to determine whether you understand the many pitfalls of self-representation, that you actually want to represent yourself, and that you are competent to stand trial. The procedure is designed to ensure that you are fully aware and capable of representing yourself. This hearing is so important that if you request it and the judge fails to give it to you the conviction could be set aside as a result.

What does representing yourself mean? Well, it means you are the captain of the defense. You will be responsible for making all motions, presenting all possible defenses, advancing arguments, conducting legal research, following all the rules, and meeting deadlines. Sounds simple, but it isn't.

In *Faretta v. California,* the Supreme Court of the United States held that a criminal defendant has a fundamental right to represent himself. In order to exercise that right, the defendant must clearly express the desire to proceed pro se to the judge. But the judge is not required to grant the request in all circumstances. However, if you make such a request the judge must usually hold a hearing to determine whether you are competent to stand trial and able to represent yourself in a minimal manner. This is called a Faretta Hearing or a Faretta Inquiry.

Most importantly, the judge is going to try and scare the hell out of you. Seems backwards, but they are supposed to make sure that you are really ok with it before the train leaves the station. You should be scared if you want to represent yourself because it would be like trying to fly a jet without any flight training whatsoever. It has long been said that a "lawyer who represents himself has a fool for a client." Even lawyers who are well versed in legal research have a difficult time representing themselves. Not the least of those difficulties is the inability to respond to arguments in a cool headed manner. It is really hard to sit there, listen to a prosecutor bash you and then stand up and calmly prove to the judge that the prosecutor is wrong. The number of rules you will have to learn and understand in order to represent yourself number in the hundreds. Sure, you can open the Federal Rules of Criminal Procedure and have a decent idea what the basic rules are. But you will really struggle when there are multiple interpretations of any single rule, which is the case for literally every rule in law. If, after the judge scares you by explaining that it takes lawyers years to become adept with legal research and debate, you still want to represent yourself, you probably will be allowed to.

The judge must also satisfy himself that you are competent to stand trial. The judge will conduct a mini competency hearing in order to make sure you are competent to stand trial. To do that, the judge will ask you to explain the charges against you, the potential defenses you believe are available to you, the potential penalties if you lose at trial, and basic questions about courtroom procedure. If you get through that, you will more than likely be permitted to represent yourself.

If you request to proceed pro se on the "eve of trial" a judge will probably deny your request. It takes a long time to develop trial strategy and when defendants ask to represent themselves so late in the game it is usually a ruse to delay the trial. Judges have a responsibility to move trials along and if you have sat there for the last two years without a problem and two weeks before trial try and ask a judge to let you go it alone the judge will, at a minimum, be pissed. The Court of Appeals would probably agree with a judge that decided to deny such a request unless you are able to show "good cause." Good cause means a really good reason. For instance, if your lawyer threatens your life or something crazy like that, a judge would allow you to fire your lawyer and proceed pro se if that was your wish. But if you show up and simply tell the judge that your lawyer hasn't spent enough time with you, or that you believe your lawyer sucks, the judge will not be so accommodating.

There are times that Faretta Hearings are forced upon defendants. It is rare, but you need to understand what could cause this to happen. If you are one of those defendants who is making it impossible for any attorney to work with you (after being given at least one replacement), and you constantly interfere with the attorney's duties, the judge would be well within their rights to warn you that the only other option is to proceed without a lawyer. If you decide to continue down the destructive path, a judge is not going to force members of the bar down your throat. True, you did not say that you want to proceed pro se, but your actions are saying that your choice is to proceed on your own. That means be careful in how much you resist your lawyer's advice and weigh your options.

The Faretta Hearing is a necessary step if you want to proceed pro se. The penultimate reason for this is that no court wants to hear complaints from a defendant that they didn't understand how bad of an idea it was to waive their right to counsel. It is extremely rare for a pro se defendant to win anything and the reason is they lack experience with court procedure and rules. But if you are positive that you want to proceed pro se then simply answer the judge's questions and ask to proceed pro se as early in the case as possible. I would say that you should talk to your lawyer first, but if you are the stage of even asking for a Faretta Hearing it is unlikely that you would listen to the lawyer anyway. That is a hearing you will be truly alone for. And if you are granted your request, you will be alone for the rest of it.

Competency Hearing

Criminal defendants have a right to understand and meaningfully participate in the proceedings against them. If a defendant has a mental defect that prevents them from understanding the proceedings and cannot reasonably work with his attorney, then he is "incompetent" and cannot be subjected to a criminal prosecution. While the judge is the ultimate decision maker as to who may or may not be incompetent to stand trial, she is not a mental health professional and is not in a position to personally investigate the matter. Thus, when a question of competency arises, the judge will likely order a mental health evaluation of the defendant to determine if they are or are not competent.

First get rid of any thought that attempting to trick a court or lawyer about incompetence is a good idea. If you are a defendant and have no trouble understanding this book, then you probably have no reason to even think of asking for a competency evaluation. People try to do this and usually fail miserably.

In a phenomenal movie called One Flew Over the Cuckoo's Nest, a defendant played by Jack Nicholson decided that being incompetent was the way to go to avoid prison. So, he proceeded to trick everyone around him in to believing he was incompetent. It worked. The defendant was not prosecuted but was instead placed in a mental hospital for treatment. He thought he would skate by for the period of time necessary to seek a release. That's not what happened. Instead, the hospital decided to actually "treat" him by using electroshock therapy which turned the defendant into an invalid. Thankfully, it is extremely hard to trick the system into believing you are incompetent.

There are countless stories of defendants whom attempt to be declared incompetent without success. There are probably defendants out there who have gamed the system well enough to escape prosecution for their crimes. It is more likely that those defendants were facing relatively minor charges. The more serious the crime alleged, the more demanding the competency evaluation will become.

In one case that I evaluated, the defendant asked me to evaluate the worthiness of an appeal regarding a judge's denial of his competency hearing. The defendant asserted that he heard voices and those voices made it impossible for him to participate in the proceedings. He also claimed that the voices made it impossible for him to sleep which also interfered with his ability to participate. Finally, he claimed he didn't know the court system and the general positions of the relevant players (i.e. who is the judge?). As a result, his attorney moved for a competency hearing which the judge granted. But first, the judge wanted a full psychiatric evaluation done at the state hospital. The defendant was facing charges for kidnapping his ex-wife and children at gun point.

The defendant went to the state hospital and every time he saw the competency evaluator he appeared to be bothered by voices, tiredness and was not able to define any of the positions of court personnel. He stated that his own lawyer was there to put him in jail and the judge was there to kill him. He sounded pretty incompetent. Unfortunately for this defendant, the hospital had cameras everywhere and the various group activities that would occur were monitored by other mental health staff. In response to the voices claim, the evaluator noted that the only time there seemed to be a problem with voices was in front of the evaluator. In numerous hours of observation by others, the defendant never once seemed to be concerned with voices. With regard to the claim that he couldn't sleep, hospital count records showed that the defendant slept like a baby every single night. And, finally, he was recorded explaining the exact positions of each court player to other defendants present for their own evaluations. He was caught and was found competent. To top it off, he really pissed off the judge and prosecutor. The moral of the story is, don't try and fake it. But if you have a loved-one who is facing a criminal prosecution and you believe they are incompetent, it absolutely essential that you contact their lawyer and inform them of your belief. You should also deliver as much evidence as you have to support such a conclusion (i.e. doctor notes, hospital records, Social Security determinations, etc.).

If a competency hearing is going to happen there will probably only be one or two witnesses. The judge is not concerned with whether the defendant committed the alleged crime; that's what a trial is for. The prosecutor may want to call the expert appointed by the judge to testify. The defendant's lawyer may also want to have their own expert testify. When two experts testify and offer differing views, it will be up to the judge to decide who to believe. The point of the experts' testimony is to determine if the defendant is competent. The experts will offer their views one way or the other. Typically, if a defendant has a significant mental health disability, the judge will find them incompetent. But remember, even being a child doesn't stop prosecutions. In many jurisdictions, children as young as 14 are prosecuted as adults.

☐

Part Four

Lawyers

> *That a person who happens to be a lawyer is present at trial alongside the accused ... is not enough to satisfy the constitutional command. The Sixth Amendment recognizes the right to the assistance of counsel because it envisions counsel's playing a role that is critical to the ability of the adversarial system to produce just results. An accused is entitled to be assisted by an attorney, whether retained or appointed, who plays the role necessary to ensure that the trial is fair.*

Justice Sandra Day O'Connor
Strickland v. Washington, 466 U.S. 668, 685
May 14, 1985

Before I got an education in law, I had no idea what made up a lawyer. I quickly learned that a criminal defense lawyer must master three fundamental skills: reading, writing, and speaking. That's it. A lawyer who has not mastered these three skills will not be effective in a courtroom. It is your job to determine if your lawyer has mastered these three skills in order to ensure that they are ready, willing and able to fight your cause.

Law is filled with books. Thousands of them. Indeed, there are libraries dedicated to law. When a lawyer goes to law school, he must learn how to read these books. They are not written in a way that is decipherable to the general public. Case opinions have certain elements like *"holding"* and *"dictum"* that must be sorted out in order to be utilized properly. What you need to understand is that you do not need to go to law school to learn how to read these books. The difference between a lawyer and a layman is a lawyer is taught how to use those books efficiently. For instance, a decent criminal defense lawyer will know that his world lies primarily in **Titles 8, 18, 21, and 28** of the United States Code. It could take you days, months or even years to figure that out. Then you have to learn how to read the codes and be able to understand them.

Writing is the staple of law. Legal writing is far different than what you were taught in school. Legal writing uses strategies like IRAC (also called IFRAC) and provides the appropriate information to the reader to make a decision. In criminal law, the majority of writing is to judges through things like motions. Effective legal writing must toe the line between advocacy and being informative. It is really hard to do effectively. The most effective lawyers will be able to smoothly explain the facts of a case to a judge in writing and also push their call to action in a subtle but effective way.

Speaking may sound like a no-brainer but not everyone is a master of speaking in such a way as to convince decision makers to go one way or the other. So, for a lawyer, it is imperative they master speaking in a way politicians do. This is why lawyers are constantly accused of lying. They know how to toe that gray area of truth and fiction to be able to advance their client's case in an effective manner.

"Advocacy" is all of these skills being used together in an effective manner. It is another word for arguing. When a lawyer advocates, he is pushing the decision maker to make a finding in favor of their client. A criminal defense lawyer must advocate his client's cause before several groups of people: judges, juries, prosecutors, family members and, sometimes, the media. Each of these groups must be spoken to in a different manner to be effective. Judges are generally concerned with the law, while prosecutors are concerned with winning. Family members want to know if you are

dangerous. And, when it is appropriate (which is very rare), the media wants drama. Juries want to find out the truth. It can be quite difficult to juggle all of these groups of people during a criminal case, and the most effective criminal defense lawyer is someone who can and will.

So, how do you find out if your potential or hired lawyer has mastered these three skills? Through interviewing and inspecting their work. There is a saying in the Marine Corps: "***Inspect, don't Expect.***" You can't just sit on the sidelines and expect your case to go smoothly. You have a responsibility to ensure that your lawyer is using a mastery of these three fundamental skills to your benefit or not. It doesn't matter if you retain (pay for) a lawyer or are appointed one. You absolutely should employ these strategies discussed here to determine if your lawyer is doing his job.

Getting a Lawyer

Finding a lawyer will feel like the most urgent thing you have to do. Slow down. The gears of justice grind very slowly. There is time to find a lawyer. If you are brought to court, you will be appointed a lawyer to help you no matter what. In fact, if you are in jail and have millions of dollars to your name and are hauled into court, the judge will still appoint you a lawyer. All you have to do is tell the judge that you don't have a lawyer and you want one. If the judge asks if you are going to hire one, say, "I don't know yet. I don't have any way to find one right now." That isn't a lie either. In jail, it is impossible to find a private lawyer on your own. It does not matter how much money you have. Your physical ability to get a lawyer is greatly restricted, thus you need an attorney appointed.

In any event, you will have to eventually decide if you will hire a lawyer, stick with appointed counsel, or go it alone ("pro se"). Appointed counsel is generally free; although if it is determined that you have access to financial resources, there is a set fee schedule they use to bill from. Appointed counsel fee schedules are generally much lower than private lawyers' fees.

Let's take a look at the three types of lawyers available for federal cases:

Public Defense

The ultra-majority of criminal defendants do not have enough money to afford to pay rent let alone hire a lawyer. Even in the poorest areas in America, a decent defense will cost anywhere between $15,000 and $500,000 depending on the number and severity of the charges. Thankfully, the United States Constitution demands that all criminal defendants be provided a lawyer for their defense, even if they can't afford it. In some systems, this is done through a public defender office. In others, it is handled by non-profit organizations that receive grants from the state. Finally, there are times when a private lawyer will be appointed and paid by the state. You will hear that appointed attorneys are "public pretenders" or, even worse, working for the prosecution. And, while there are certainly lawyers out there who are not very good at their job, you need to understand how the indigent defense system works as a whole so you can work with it.

Let's begin by dispelling the fear that just because the lawyer is paid with government money they are working for the prosecutor. No matter how bad any lawyer is, it would be career suicide to surreptitiously benefit the other side by disclosing attorney-client confidences to the client's detriment. While it can theoretically happen, it is extremely unlikely that anyone appointed to represent a criminal defendant would ever use their relationship with their client to benefit the other side. Not only would they lose their license, but the case would probably be dismissed for substantial misconduct. The prosecutor definitely doesn't want that problem.

Publicly appointed lawyers do get a bad rap and are called many names, the most common of which is probably "public pretender." The reason appointed lawyers get this negative title actually has nothing to do with their abilities as lawyers, but has more to do with the fact they have too many cases to handle and are terrible communicators.

The biggest culprit of poor public defense is one of funding. It is not common to find funding with the same fervor as that given to the prosecution and police. The fact that public defense attorneys have way too many cases to handle and no money to help is a product of the government prosecuting defendants without any concern for the engine that must continue running. It is not because the lawyers are necessarily greedy (although some are). Since it is a Constitutional right to have a lawyer, courts don't look at the lawyers' case loads before appointing them to defend. This sad reality makes it an absolute necessity for indigent defendants to be on their guard and be as proactive in their defense as possible.

Most criminal defendants believe the more you pay the more likely you are to win or get the outcome you want. *In the federal system that is not necessarily true.* In state systems, public defense is usually so underfunded that paying for a lawyer is the preferred way to go. But public defenders in the federal system are paid the same as prosecutors. Their offices don't have access to the same investigative resources as prosecutors, but they are generally funded better than a private lawyer working solo. As a result, public defenders usually have access to larger teams of people such as paralegals and other assistants.

CJA Lawyer

The Criminal Justice Act directs that the court system can pay for private attorneys if the public defender is unable to take the case for whatever reason. Generally, if you are going to be assigned counsel by the court, the public defender's office is notified first and then, if they cannot take the case, they will notify the court to have a CJA lawyer assigned. Some defendants believe these lawyers are better than public defenders because they are private lawyers who take assigned cases. The thought is that since they have paying clients as well they are better lawyers. That isn't necessarily true. In fact, some believe that attorneys willing to take CJA cases may not be that great because they can't get cases without having them spoon-fed.

Many CJA lawyers are very good. And others are bad. That is the same for public defenders and private lawyers. But, if you are assigned a CJA lawyer, do not be surprised if you find it difficult to get hold of them in any regular way. That is probably the biggest complaint I have seen over the years with CJA lawyers. Their pay from the court is a fixed fee schedule which is currently set at $158 per hour with a case maximum of $12,300. This means that a lawyer has no incentive to work beyond 77 hours (about two full weeks). If they anticipate any expenses, they must request the court to release money for them.

Advantages of Appointed Counsel

The greatest advantage to appointed counsel, whether it is a public defender or a CJA lawyer, is that you don't have to pay them. They will represent you regardless of your financial situation. And, because most defendants can't afford a lawyer anyway, appointed counsel handles the lion's share of the caseload. That usually means that public defense has the most amount of experience in federal court. Another advantage of having appointed counsel is that you can be appointed counsel immediately and hire a private lawyer later on down the line. That means you get kind of a test drive without having to pay any money.

Disadvantages of Appointed Counsel

Perhaps the greatest disadvantage to appointed counsel is the sheer amount of work they handle. Because the ultra majority of criminal defendants can't afford private counsel in any way, appointed counsel are required to take on far more cases than a single person can reasonably handle. From this disadvantage flows the majority of complaints I hear from defendants:

"My lawyer doesn't visit me,"

"My lawyer doesn't spend enough time with me,"

> "My lawyer doesn't seem to listen to what I am saying,"

The number of hours it takes to prepare for an average criminal trial far exceeds 1000 hours. There are only 2080 work hours (working full time) in the year. If the lawyer must operate with a bare bones staff, or even by themselves, they cannot think of preparing for more than 2 trials in a year. If they are going to maintain 200 cases, then they must sacrifice the amount of time dedicated to each case, and also must push for the majority to plead out or win a dismissal early on.

No appointed counsel is going to get rich off your case. It is also not likely that your case will make an appointed lawyer famous through publicity. That means sacrifices will have to be made. Those sacrifices will be to the level of service that will be delivered to you. You will not likely see regular letters or have regular meetings with your appointed lawyer. Calling them will be next to impossible. Your time in court with them will feel quite rushed. It's nothing personal, it's just the way it has to be with how the system is set up for the indigent.

It is certainly possible for appointed lawyers to do a good, or even great, job with your case. Many appointed counsel represent their clients with the zeal of a big-time attorney that the rich guys would hire. Because they have to take on so many cases, it is not likely that you will get the service those who pay top dollar will get. Such is the way of life. But that does not mean appointed counsel will automatically be a bad choice. Typically, if you are planning on pleading guilty, then appointed counsel could be a great solution. There is nothing more painful than dropping tens or hundreds of thousands of dollars into a defense that will certainly end with a prison sentence. If you have access to money to hire a lawyer, I suggest that you elect to have counsel appointed instead, save your money, and see how it goes for a couple months. If you feel like the appointed counsel is not pulling a proper load or is screwing you, you can always hire one or request a new one for irreconcilable differences.

Hiring a Private Lawyer

Hiring a lawyer to represent you privately can be very difficult. Sadly, the profession of law has made itself into one of the most inaccessible professions in the country. They use terminology that isn't understandable to the public such as "Corporate Lawyer" or "Trial Lawyer" or "DUI Lawyer" or "Probate Lawyer" and so forth. Then, when you call and try and make an appointment, you have no idea what will happen. The secretary may just say that the lawyer isn't accepting new clients. The lawyer may give you a meeting but will have to first "decide" if he wants to take your case. After that, the lawyer should conduct a conflicts check but will only do so after he takes your hard earned cash. The process, though complicated, can be effectively navigated but you have to be smart. Let's start with places you may look for private attorneys.

❖ *Referrals*

Whether you are in jail or on the street, everyone and their mother will have a recommended lawyer to call. When you are in jail, you have to be very careful because many inmates are trying to show their lawyer who they are referring work in order to get better service. In such a situation, whatever good stuff the referral source is telling you about the lawyer is probably false. When you are given a lawyer's name from family, friends, associates and acquaintances on the street, the problem you run into is one of the lawyer's experience. Suffice it to say that your family, friends, associates and acquaintances probably have not faced a federal criminal case. Thus, whomever they are referring you to is not likely a criminal lawyer with experience in federal court. The point is, referrals are not generally the best source to find an effective attorney for a criminal case.

A friend may have used a lawyer in the past and had a good experience. That doesn't mean you will have a good experience. But it could. You have to take referrals with a grain of salt. Research and investigate the potential referral and also interview them. There is nothing wrong with taking a name and doing some more research on the lawyer to see if you want to hire them. Whatever you do, don't take the name and simply send money over to the lawyer.

There is one place you absolutely **NEVER** want to hear a recommendation about a lawyer from. And that's from anyone who actively works for the prosecutorial engine such as prosecutors, cops, U.S. Marshals, FBI Agents, jailers, judges, etc. There is a saying from the business world that says "if the IRS recommends your accountant, you will pay a lot in taxes." The same holds true with criminal defense lawyers: **If cops recommend your lawyer, you will spend a lot of time in prison.** If anyone in the prosecutorial world recommends a lawyer to you then you have to ask yourself why **THEY** could like the lawyer. It's probably because the lawyer makes their lives easier while the lawyer hangs the clients out to dry. This is something that could come up after you hire a lawyer. Hopefully you nailed down refunds with them, because if a cop tells you that "you have the best lawyer out there," then you will probably want to fire them and hire someone else. It's nothing personal, but your life is on the line here. You need someone who isn't trying to make friends. Yes, they need to be able to work with people in the prosecutorial world, but you want a lawyer who cops, prosecutors and even judges have a healthy fear of. Kind of like a shark. They look cool from a distance and behind the glass at Sea World, but if you are in their pool and their eyes are locked on you, you want to get away fast. You need your lawyer to be able to turn that kind of fury on. Cops who suffer a real cross examination absolutely will hate that lawyer for the rest of their lives. Prosecutors who suffer through a defense lawyer who objects to everything they say will hate working across from them. They don't give recommendations for those guys. So, don't settle for someone who the prosecutorial engine, that is trying to put you away forever, recommends.

❖ *Billboards and other Mass Advertising*

There are attorneys that take out billboards and bus stop ads to drive business their way. These lawyers want volume. They will not give you great service by any stretch of the imagination. The ultra majority of them "specialize" in simple criminal cases such as DUI or misdemeanor city court cases. If you call them and tell them you have a federal criminal case, they will probably froth at the mouth. They will give you a rate that seems on par with the profession because these lawyers are most like used car salesman. They know what you want to hear and they will tell you precisely that to get your money.

❖ *Federal Courthouse*

One of the best ways to find lawyers is to go to court and watch them in action. Courtrooms, with limited exceptions, are public places. Anyone can walk in and watch. And that is where you will find lawyers with the most experience. However, which court you go to matters. If you are facing federal criminal charges, you or your loved one should go to a federal courthouse. If you are in a courtroom and see a lawyer arguing passionately for their client, seem to interact well with the defendant sitting with them, and they seem knowledgeable when the judge asks questions, you may want to try and speak with that lawyer as he is walking out of court. Simply asking "I was wondering if I could get your card so I can make an appointment with you?" is enough to pique their interest. If they blow you off when you ask for their card, then you don't want that lawyer anyway.

❖ *The State Bar*

Every state has a licensing body, called the Bar, for lawyers. They are not permitted to give you specific recommendations, but they can help by giving you the contact information for lists of attorneys. All you have to do is contact the State Bar for the state where the case is, and ask for a list of:

- ✓ Trial Lawyers
- ✓ Criminal Defense Lawyers
- ✓ Federal Lawyers

The State Bar will send them right over to you. Once you have such a list, then your job is to go through it and find out what you can about the lawyers on the list.

The Lawyer Interview

> **Important Note**
>
> A lot of lawyers will tell their potential client that they are "federal lawyers." Or the prospective client will hear that the lawyer is the best in the area. Don't let such nonsense cloud your judgment. Assume the lawyer sitting in front of you has no idea how federal criminal law works and let him prove otherwise. If your gut says to leave, then leave.

It is very common for defendants stuck in jail to trust their families to locate and hire a lawyer. You need to rely a lot on your family and you should. But, it is not a good idea to hire a lawyer sight unseen. It is important that **YOU** can speak with the lawyer candidly throughout the course of the representation. If your family goes in and drops tens of thousands of dollars to hire someone, you will undoubtedly feel an obligation to go with that lawyer. **Don't let that happen to you.** Instead, when your family locates a good prospect, they should inform the lawyer they are interested "pending an interview with the defendant himself." It is imperative your family inform that lawyer who you will need to approve the hire **BEFORE** any money exchanges hands. If the lawyer claims that he will need his hourly rate to go and see you or set up a legal call, then it is ok to authorize your family to pay for up to 1 hour of time so he can speak with you. The lawyer doesn't necessarily need to speak with you in person though. But if you are interviewing the lawyer over a jail phone, absolutely make sure you are on an *unmonitored legal call* **that doesn't have a time limit.** The prospective lawyer can set up the call by calling the jail and speaking with the case manager. If the lawyer can't seem to set up a legal call to get hired, rest assured that lawyer will not be able to set up legal calls after you give them money. Further, if the lawyer balks to your family about waiting to hire until you have had a chance to interview, then they are definitely NOT a "good" prospect and they should move on. You and/or your family are about to drop a down payment for a house on the lawyer's desk. He should have **ZERO** problem being interviewed **BEFORE** that happens.

An interview is a two way street. It doesn't matter if you are applying for a job or hiring a lawyer. Even if the lawyer is appointed by the court for you, your first meeting with any lawyer should be an interview. An interview needs to concentrate on what your needs and expectations are and what the lawyer sitting in front of you intends to do to achieve your goals.

Start the interview off with this statement:

> *"I have not decided if I want to plead guilty and I will not be making that decision any time soon. I expect you to prepare as if we are going to trial.* **At this point I want to go to trial.**"

Most criminal lawyers have become lazy in today's plea bargain heavy world. Client's who plead guilty don't require as much work as those who elect to go to trial. For the first few months, at the very least, you should not be considering pleading guilty unless your lawyer comes with a screaming plea bargain. It does happen that lawyers tell their clients at the first meeting that "you will be pleading guilty." If your lawyer says that (or anything even close to it), end the interview and fire the lawyer instantly. Your cause is lost if that is the advice a lawyer is willing to give without knowing anything about the case from all perspectives that will be made available.

You may be thinking that this is a bad decision if you actually intend on pleading guilty. But it's not. For one reason, it doesn't matter whether you did the crime or not. The government must prove that you did it. Another reason it is a good idea to tell your lawyer who you want to proceed to trial early on as it will guide any plea bargaining meetings that your lawyer has with the prosecutor. Prosecutors are as excited for a trial as you are. They are expensive and require a significant amount of time to prepare for. There could be mistrials or even an acquittal. When a prosecutor asks your lawyer if you want to plea bargain and your lawyer says, "Well, he told me that he wants to go to trial," the prosecutor will know that the plea bargain better be worth it for you. It tells the prosecutor (and your lawyer) that you aren't a push over. Those who threaten trial, in my opinion, get better deals than those who keel over and insist on pleading guilty early on.

Moving on to the next point, after you have made it clear to the lawyer sitting in front of you that you intend on fighting for you life, you need to ask some questions. Those questions should be:

1. How many [your type] _FEDERAL_ cases have you been a lawyer on in the last five years?

There is no hard and fast rule for what the answer should be. The lower the number means less experience. If the lawyer tries to dodge this question by saying something vague (i.e. "I've done enough..." or "My fair share.") then my suggestion is to look elsewhere.

Lower numbers doesn't necessarily mean that the lawyer won't be effective. Actually, it may mean that the lawyer is hungry for cases and wants the experience. These types of lawyers can be very effective because they are hoping to make a name for themselves. If they handle a high number of the specific type of cases, then the lawyer probably specializes in your type of case. Specialization can be a double edged sword, however. The more experienced a lawyer is, the more likely that lawyer will cut corners and shoot from the hip. This can be dangerous since the law changes constantly. It is also very dangerous if your lawyer has lots of experience with your alleged crime in _state_ court but not _federal_ court. They are vastly different. Thus, if the lawyer claims to have a ton of experience, make sure to ask if that experience is in federal or state court.

2. **How many federal trials have you been lead counsel on in the last five years?**

This number will not be high. But you do not want it to be zero by any means. And you most certainly don't want the lawyer to say "enough." You need to make sure that the lawyer who will represent you is someone who can proceed to trial if you decide to go that route. It is your right after all. If the lawyer says they have never been lead on a federal trial, ask them if they will have co-counsel present at a trial to help them. If the answer is no, then you have a hard decision to make. Sometimes an inexperienced lawyer can be a blessing. Everyone starts out from nothing. If they have never been lead on a federal case, ask if they have experience in state trials. Also ask if they have sat "second chair" in any trials. That way you know they at least have some experience in the courtroom. But, make no mistake, an inexperienced lawyer can also be dangerous because he will undoubtedly make mistakes. You pay the price for those mistakes. If you find that you like talking to the lawyer in front of you and feel that you can be 100% honest with them, then you may want to keep that lawyer.

3. **How many active cases are you handling right now?**

The higher the number this is, the worse off you will be. The more expensive lawyers keep this number down. Struggling lawyers tend to take as many cases as their computer can handle. If the lawyer can't answer this question, you should be very nervous and you should tell the lawyer who. If they answer the question confidently, then you may feel they can handle the added case. But you may want to ask at what point the lawyer stops accepting cases. If they are CJA lawyers (meaning they are appointed by the court), they will likely have high case loads and be far less likely to turn down cases.

4. **Do you have any paralegals who help you?**

The answer to this question should be a resounding yes. No lawyer can handle their entire case load by themselves. The paralegal is someone who helps the lawyer comb through everything in your case. In most instances, the paralegal knows more about your case than the lawyer or even you. The lawyer sitting in front of you should be able to provide the paralegal's name to you that you can speak with if you need to. So long as the paralegal is employed by the lawyer, the attorney client privilege applies to your communications with the paralegal. Note, however, a paralegal is not allowed to give you legal advice. If a question you ask is in a grey area, they will defer your question to the lawyer. A good paralegal, though, will meet with you and interview you at least once for the lawyer's benefit. A great paralegal will also go through all of the discovery with you.

5. If I call your office from the jail, will a live person answer the phone?

There is nothing more aggravating from jail than an auto-attendant. Criminal lawyers should never have an auto-attendant because a substantial number of their clients are going to call from jail. Jail phones require a live person to press a number to accept a call from you. Now, calling on the jail phone is not a great idea and nothing of substance should be discussed on that phone because they are recorded. But, you are the client and you should be able to speak with your lawyer and/or his staff when you call. If there isn't a live person, that will never happen and you will feel like you have been abandoned.

6. Please explain to me your general investigative plan for any case?

You are looking for them to say they use a private investigator of some sort. Criminal cases are usually fact intensive. It doesn't matter if you plead guilty or go to trial. You need an investigator to beat feet and determine the truth of the story. They talk to witnesses. They go through police reports. They research whether witnesses are credible. In short, they are indispensable to a criminal case. If you are using assigned counsel or a public defender and your family wants to put some money toward the defense, it is suggested that money be used to hire a private investigator.

7. Have you ever been accused of ineffective assistance of counsel?

It may come as a surprise, but you want the answer to this question to be yes. Every good criminal defense has had at least one client claim they were ineffective and the lawyer should have no problem admitting so. This question can be verified if you have access to a law library. If the lawyer is relatively inexperienced, then he may not have suffered such a claim.

8. **Have you ever been found by any judge to have been ineffective?**

You do not want the answer to this question to be yes. It is very difficult to find a lawyer ineffective. If a lawyer is said to have been ineffective, then that means they dropped the ball really badly. They may give you a really good reason why they were found ineffective. My suggestion is if the lawyer sitting in front of you has ever been found ineffective in any criminal case, you should probably look elsewhere for a lawyer.

9. **Have you ever been sanctioned by a court? If so, why?**

This could be good or bad. Some lawyers are sanctioned (even arrested) for being over-zealous. Over-zealousness can be good or bad. Thus, the reason why is the most important part of this question. If the lawyer was sanctioned for abandoning his client, that is very very very bad. You don't want that lawyer. But is the prospective lawyer was sanctioned for continuing to argue a position even though a judge said to stop, it may be ok. It's all a matter of reasonableness. You don't want any lawyer to walk into court half-cocked and piss off your judge. But, sometimes, the judge is simply not listening and the lawyer needs to show frustration to get the judge to listen. While it rarely works, a lawyer willing to go to jail for his client's cause is not a bad thing.

The following questions are not written in any specific order. They are numbered only to keep them organized. You can ask these questions in any order. I believe you should ask them in different orders for each interview to help you be able to pay attention. If you ask the questions in the same order every time, it will be harder for you to remember the interview.

10. What is the best federal sentencing result you ever achieved and how did you make it happen?

If the lawyer sitting in front of you has any experience in criminal law, then they most certainly have been through a sentencing proceeding. Given that it is very likely that you would face a federal sentencing judge if you are reading this book, then asking about the lawyer's achievements with sentencing is perfectly reasonable. Asking about their best result will get them to open up about something that was hard won and something they are proud of. If the lawyer can't provide you with an enthusiastic story about their best sentencing achievement, then they probably aren't very excited about working in criminal law and you should be wary about hiring them.

It is possible the lawyer sitting in front of you has never been to a federal sentencing proceeding because they primarily work in the state courts. If that is the case, then allow them to tell you a story from the state courts. Just because a potential lawyer only works in state court doesn't mean they won't be good for you in a federal case. But it does mean they will have to work very hard to truly understand the federal sentencing system. More than anything, you are trying to gauge whether the lawyer sitting in front of you is someone who is excited about doing criminal defense work. You don't want someone who ran to criminal defense as a fall back and hates it.

11. What is your general approach to sentencing mitigation?

Sentencing mitigation is the process by which a lawyer convinces a judge or prosecutor that your sentence should be lower. And this is the ultimate job of any federal criminal defense lawyer. It is something that needs to happen from day one. You are telling the lawyer who you haven't decided if you would ever plead the case out, but that doesn't mean the lawyer shouldn't be trying to lessen the blows that come your way all the time. You want to hear the lawyer talk about how they will gather mitigation evidence and present it to all the powers that be (prosecutor, probation officer, and judge) throughout. The most effective sentencing mitigation strategies, which we will talk about more in depth later, includes researching sentencing statistics, investigating your upbringing, explaining "why" the offense occurred, and providing credible character support. For instance, does the lawyer usually interview family members and social friends? Work colleagues? Gather your educational records? Seek a psychologist to test you?

12. How can I participate in the defense?

This question targets whether or not the lawyer will be a team player. Too many lawyers take liberties with their power as professionals and believe they are in control of everything. That doesn't make for a good defense. You are part of the team and you need to be included in the defense. You are looking to see if the lawyer is caught off guard by the question or if they are genuinely interested in working WITH you. In the end, the lawyer will make strategy calls and you will make the calls about the ultimate course of events. But that doesn't mean your lawyer shouldn't seek your input into those strategy calls if at all possible. And it doesn't mean you shouldn't ask your lawyer about the risks and benefits of any ultimate course of action.

13. What is your favorite cartoon?

Throw this question in about halfway through the interview and ask it fast following a response to a serious answer. I ask this question in every interview I do because I want to see that the person sitting in front of me is a person. And I want to make sure they can live with their answer. I personally don't care if they say My Little Pony or the Smurfs, the goal here is to see if the lawyer answers confidently to a crazy curve ball. If they struggle with answering such a question, then they probably can't handle curve balls too well.

To get the most benefit from this question you got to ask it in a way that throws them off. Here is an example:

Defendant: *So, I am curious if I call your office from the jail if a live person will be there to answer the phone?*

Prospective lawyer: *Yes. My paralegal is always in the office and her name is Jennifer. Unless she is*

> *out sick or something, then during normal business hours she should answer the phone.*
>
> ***Defendant***: *What's your favorite cartoon?*

They shouldn't take too long to answer the question. They should be able to roll with it. And they should be confident in their answer. Hopefully it garners a little laughter too because there is nothing wrong with breaking the ice either.

Former Prosecutors

I personally do not recommend hiring a former civilian prosecutor to be your defense lawyer. I except military lawyers because they are required to do both prosecution and defense work and it is randomly assigned for each individual case. In my experience as both a defendant and an advocate, I have yet to see a former civilian prosecutor work really hard on a case. But, you may want to hire one and there is no reason not to if you are satisfied with their answers. However, a friend of mine named Doug Passon (a phenomenal documentarian and incredible Sentencing Mitigation Attorney) suggests you ask the following questions of former civilian prosecutors if you are considering hiring one:

14. Why did you switch to criminal defense?

Some former prosecutors have seen the light and experienced first hand the horrible tricks their colleagues use to gain unjust convictions and sentences and that's why they left. Others leave because there was a change in politics in the prosecutor's office (such as the head prosecutor was ousted) and they have nowhere else to go but to criminal defense. It is your job to determine which one is sitting in front of you and this question primes that subject. Now, lawyers who have worked as prosecutors are epic bullshit artists so you have to really look at them to see if they are just throwing crap at you to convince you or if they are being genuine.

15. Are there any prosecutions that you wish could have been handled differently? If so, how and why?

If the lawyer sitting in front of you tells you that they left the prosecutor's office because they were tired of unethical conduct, then they should have stories galore to tell. Perhaps it was discovering that a police officer lied in a report. Maybe it was a plea negotiation that they just went too far with. Or it could have been sitting by while another prosecutor withheld evidence. You aren't looking for any case specifics here. You are looking for contrition and candor. Everyone has regrets in their professional lives and being able to admit those in front of a prospective client is powerful. It also demonstrates that the lawyer will have zero problem shouldering blame if any is to be had.

16. What have you learned to do differently since switching to criminal defense?

With this question you are looking to see if they are human. In my experience, former civilian prosecutors are prima donna's who don't believe they have anything to learn. If they can't give you something with substance here, then my suggestion is to move on.

I realize that I am being very critical of former civilian prosecutors. I admit that I am biased with regard to this, so take what I am telling you about former civilian prosecutors with a grain of salt. You may feel the former prosecutor sitting in front of you is going to work best for you. And if you honestly believe that, then go for it.

WHAT YOU DON'T WANT TO HEAR

There are several statements that should give you cause to run for the hills if you hear them at any point during your time with the lawyer. These are:

I have friends in the prosecutor's office.

This statement insinuates that the lawyer can work out a deal because he has friends. Whether he has friends in the prosecutor's office or not will not make a deal. It just means they will answer the phone. Well, they will answer the phone for all the other lawyers out there too. This isn't the third world. Remember that. If you buy in to a lawyer's claim that he is friends with prosecutors, and you think that this is going to somehow bring you fortune, you do so at your own peril.

I used to be a prosecutor.

It doesn't matter if they were a federal or state prosecutor. Generally speaking, prosecutors are lazy. They have entire police departments that work as their investigators and they have the full force of the government budget. In federal criminal cases, the prosecutor (called an Assistant U.S. Attorney, or AUSA) has access to the entire government like, for instance, the FBI, the US Marshals, DEA, ATF, IRS (yes, the IRS and they have guns too), and even Homeland Security. They also have paralegals, second chair attorneys, and a slew of other help to get through a case. Furthermore, federal prosecutors win 97% of the time. There is nothing more effective at producing laziness than winning every time.

When prosecutors leave the prosecutor's office, for whatever reason, their options are quite limited. The only place for them is usually in criminal defense. They are there because they have no place else to go.

I guarantee that ...

Even though judges like to say that law is "objective," it isn't. Every thing is subject to interpretation. And there are as many interpretations out there as there are judges in the federal judiciary. When lawyers tell potential or current client that they "guarantee" anything will come to pass, they are absolutely lying. Nothing is guaranteed in law. Unethical lawyers will offer these "guarantees" loosely and when they don't succeed they'll just say, "oh well." Some guarantees that I have heard of are:

> *I guarantee we will win trial.*
>
> *I guarantee you will get life.*
>
> *I guarantee the judge will suppress the evidence.*
>
> *I guarantee I will answer the phone every time you call.*
>
> *I guarantee you will win the detention hearing.*
>
> *I guarantee you won't go to prison.*

I guarantee the prosecutor will find a witness to testify against you.

And the list goes on. If you hear any lawyer say they "guarantee" anything then it is highly advisable to seek other counsel. If you have been appointed counsel and you hear some crazy guarantee (although I have never heard of a public defender stating any guarantees), you may want to contact the chief public defender in your district and ask them to look into the matter. Lawyers who make willy-nilly guarantees are just looking to take your money and run. They will not work for you in the way that is necessary to succeed.

I never lost a case at trial.

If the lawyer you are talking to is a real trial lawyer, then he or she has lost at least one case in their career. If a lawyer claims to have never lost a case at trial, then they are either lying or haven't taken enough cases to trial to seriously make that claim. Trials are unpredictable. It doesn't matter how strong any case may be, the jury can go either way. Trying to predict what a jury does in deliberations is impossible.

I don't work with snitches.

Many lawyers will tell this to their clients in an effort to sound like they comply with some retarded written jail code. Snitches are common in the state and federal criminal systems. If the lawyer sitting in front of you is telling you that they don't work with snitches, they are lying to you. The fact remains that a lawyer has a duty to act in his client's best interests. And if the client has information that could set him free, then the lawyer is duty bound to try and use that. It is that simple. Lawyers don't get to just jump off cases because someone decides to work for the government. This doesn't mean that a lawyer may agree with any decision to snitch. They may not. But, lawyers disagree with numerous things that criminal defendants have done or could do. That doesn't mean they won't work with them as a rule. I am not advocating for anyone to work for the government, but my position shouldn't stop your decision one way or the other if you have truthful and reliable information to provide and it could let you out of jail.

I'm gonna sue the cops for doing this to you.

This is a sales pitch. The lawyer shouldn't be thinking about potential civil suits regarding violations of your rights when you are trying to save your own skin. Right now, your life is on the line. Further, it is incredibly difficult to sue the police for charging people with crimes. Is it possible? Sure. But it is speculative until you win your criminal case. In fact, if you don't win your criminal case, it is likely you will **NOT** be able to sue the police or anyone else under the "Preiser/Heck Rule." That rule states that if a civil claim could cast doubt on a criminal conviction, then it is necessary to first get the conviction **overturned**. If you have any civil claims, then you should be looking for a separate lawyer to deal with that. In fact, if you mention it to a prospective or current lawyer, their answer *should* be to contact a different lawyer.

I'm gonna get you probation.

If you are charged with a felony in the federal system, it is virtually certain that you will *not* get probation. In fact, over 95% of federal criminal defendants go to prison. To make such a bold claim at the early stages of the case is preposterous. Until the lawyer has reviewed the discovery, investigated your version of events, and read the law as it relates to your situation, he can't make any such claim. If he does, that is a sign he isn't going to be a good advocate for you. You need a realist as your lawyer and not a magician.

If only you ....

The least effective lawyers will blame everyone else for the problems with the case. They will say things like:

> *If only you didn't talk to the police we would have won at trial.*
>
> *If only your first lawyer filed a suppression motion we would have won.*
>
> *If only your family had more money we could get the experts we need.*
>
> *If only...*

If a lawyer you are speaking with ever tries to temper their own work with blaming others, then you should find someone else. For instance, if you confessed to the police, a good lawyer wouldn't care about that since it is so common. Rather than blame you, a good lawyer will come out with a strategy of how to get it thrown out or use it against the government in some way. Blaming the past for future performance is not effective and it is a sign of a terrible lawyer. So, don't let them get away with this. Call someone else.

Remember, it is easy for someone to point to past mistakes (a bad lawyer previously, a bad decision made, etc.) and blame them. If that's all they got, then they are telling you they have no idea how to deal with these "complications." You should demand the lawyer tell you how they are going to deal with those issues. But, if I were listening to such garbage,

I would thank the lawyer for his time and move on to the next candidate. It's that simple.

You're gonna get life if you ...

Lawyers tend to scare the bejesus out of their clients with threats of life in prison. While over 95% of criminal defendants will go to prison, life is not a common sentence. It happens. People even can and do get hundreds of years but not "life." But those sentences are not the general rule. Most federal defendants will see the light of day once again. If your lawyer is threatening you with a potential life sentence, then pull out the Guidelines, calculate them for your case, and see where they land. If you want a trial, and your lawyer says, you are gonna get life if you go to trial, then calculate the Guidelines as if you would blow trial. If those don't show a 360-Life sentence or more, then it is extremely _un_likely that you would get a life sentence. "You're gonna get life if you demand a speedy trial." "You're gonna get life if you don't debrief with the prosecutor." "You're gonna get life if you don't plead guilty now." These are just a few other examples of the life threat.

We're going to waive your speedy trial rights.

I know we have spoken about speedy trial rights quite a bit and for good reason. It is the one thing that holds the government to the fire and forces them to get on with it. With very few exceptions, demanding a speedy trial is a helpful tool. Even if a judge orders the case delayed, it doesn't need to happen with your consent. You never need to make the prosecution's life easier. They are trying to take your freedom away for God's sake. Don't just take it up the ass with a lawyer who is just going to provide you lube. You want your lawyer to be a barrier to the chastity of your butt.

I will get you <u>under</u> the mandatory minimum ...

Mandatory minimums are called "mandatory" because there is no choice in the matter. If you are convicted of a crime that has a mandatory minimum, then that is the lowest possible sentence that you can get unless one of two situations applies. If a lawyer makes this claim, then they better be able to provide a specific plan for doing so. That's because there are only two ways in the federal system to get less than the mandatory minimum penalty: snitch or debrief. Defendants who provide "substantial assistance" to the prosecution of another can be given less than the mandatory minimum, but *only* when the **PROSECUTOR** files a special motion asking for it. With debriefing, it is a lot like snitching but has very specific rules to apply. If a lawyer is saying this to you before you engage him as your lawyer, then it is a completely bullshit statement. He couldn't possibly know if this is possible without first engaging in plea discussions with the prosecution.

You can't get the discovery.

If a lawyer says this early in the representation, you should fire them instantly. You can't fight a case without reviewing the discovery personally. And, as we discussed earlier, your lawyer should be fighting to prevent any orders that prohibit your access to discovery.

I am connected to the President of the United States.

I have only ever heard of one person being told this and it was well known anyway. He hired Alan Dershowitz to help with a clemency application. The guy thought a pardon was in the bag during the Trump presidency because of the connection Dershowitz had with Trump. And do you know where that guy is now? He is **still in prison** (for the next decade or so). If any lawyer claims they are connected with any political power you should totally ignore it. Even if they are telling the truth, that doesn't mean anything with regard to your criminal case. I personally could never trust anyone who drops names as a way to sound more powerful and that includes lawyers. So, I suggest if a lawyer makes any such claim to you, then move on.

I never let my clients testify.

If a lawyer says this, then they are admitting that they interfere with fundamental decisions that belong solely to the defendant. It is true that most defendants don't testify if they go to trial. And it is usually good advice. But, it is a decision that you get to make and it shouldn't be made by a lawyer at the earliest stages of the case. If a lawyer is willing to admit that he doesn't let his clients testify, then he is essentially telling you that he will act as your parent and not your representative.

We don't want to piss off the prosecutor.

First of all, the prosecutor has no like for you. While negotiating a plea bargain will require some give and take that doesn't mean your lawyer should just roll over on command for the prosecutor. And a lawyer who is willing to do that is not an effective advocate. When lawyers tell you that their plan is to not piss off the prosecutor, you can expect that you will see more time in prison because he will let the prosecutor take their time to build a more solid case to bury you. Never forget, the prosecutor is trying to take your freedom away and you don't need to make their lives easier.

If you don't do [x], I will leave the case and you'll be on your own.

This is something that may be said by a lawyer during the course of representation. It is unlikely they will say anything like this at the earliest stages of the case. But, if you ever hear a lawyer threaten to leave a case if you don't take a specific course of action, then tell them to get off the case and get a new lawyer. You will *not* be left alone. If you can't afford a new lawyer, your old lawyer **must** file a motion to have free counsel appointed to you. There is a big difference between a threat and a disagreement about strategy. If you both disagree on something, then you guys may be able to come to a middle ground resolution. We are only concerned with a lawyer threatening you here.

By way of example, this is the opposite of a lawyer saying that if you are hell-bent on him taking a course of action that he believes is unethical and believes he should resign from the case. In those situations, there is an "irreconcilable difference" and the lawyer would be right to leave. That isn't a threat. It's the reality of hiring a professional to help you. Imagine you went to a surgeon and said, "hey, while you are there, I want you to take out my heart and not put it back." The surgeon would tell you no, and would tell you to find someone else because there is no way that doing precisely as you ask would be ethical (or legal for that matter).

I'll accept commissary for payment.

Jails and prisons are places of significant opportunity. Everything is for sale. And that includes legal assistance. If you are taking advice from jailhouse lawyers in return for commissary purchases then you are not likely getting good advice. It is even worse if you are thinking about firing your lawyer and "using" a jailhouse lawyer to advance your defense. Don't get me wrong, there are jailhouse lawyers out there who know what they are doing and do a great job. But, the vast majority of those whom call themselves jailhouse lawyers have zero idea what they are doing and have no idea what the law really means. More than anything, the majority of self-declared jailhouse lawyers have a gift of gab and nothing more. I am not saying that all jailhouse lawyers are bad or even offer bad advice. You need to make sure what they are telling you is accurate though. Hint: If the person you are talking to can't show you where in the law what they are talking about is, then chances are they really don't know what they are talking about.

If you hear any of these things (at any time during the interview or through the representation, you should probably thank the lawyer for his time, get up and call someone else. If you haven't heard any of these things at any point, then it's time to talk about terms.

Vetting a Lawyer

Just because the lawyer **told** you how they will work for you doesn't mean you can't see if they are full of shit. It does happen and there are ways to figure out if they told you the truth.

First, go to your local law library (or the prison law library) and do a search for the lawyer's name. Make sure to isolate your search for federal cases only. If you can't find it in any of the federal data bases, then their experience in federal court is either non-existent or very limited. The law library databases put will note the names of lawyers who argue cases at the beginning of millions of case opinions from judges. If a lawyer claims to have won many suppression motions and you can't find their name in any case opinion, you should seriously question whether they are telling you the truth. Federal judges love writing opinions and law library databases make them available. It may be that the lawyer isn't lying. He may have won a ton of motions in state court, but that isn't going to help you very much. Federal court is its own beast and you want someone who can navigate it well.

Second, ask the lawyer to give you a date and time they are scheduled to be in court to argue something. It can be literally anything. Tell them you want to watch them in action. It doesn't matter if you go or your mother goes. You want the lawyer to know that you are grading them before you pay. If they seem frustrated by your due diligence, then you should find someone else. Simply giving you a court hearing date and time is not hard and should be given without question.

Third, ask the lawyer to provide you with three case names and numbers for the federal court you are in that he was lead counsel on. Case names/numbers are not confidential. Tell him you want at least one case name/number where he was lead counsel at a trial. Once you have these, you (or someone you have helping you) want to go to the federal courthouse and request the docket sheets for those cases. Looking at the docket sheets, you should be able to answer these questions:

How long ago was the case?

If the time since the last case in federal court was over a year, you should seriously question whether the lawyer is right to represent you. Having old experience is better than no experience. The risk is that the lawyer does not believe they need to update themselves as to changes in rules and laws since their last case. Perhaps the lawyer is a hard worker and always makes sure. All too often, however, lawyers shoot from the hip using their "old" experiences as the guidepost. That can be very dangerous for you.

Are there motions that don't involve asking for more time?

If the lawyer files motions in the cases, that don't simply ask for more time, it is a clue the lawyer does work. If all you see are motions for extensions of time (also called "adjournment"), then you should be concerned that the lawyer will put your case on the backburner too.

How often does the lawyer request extensions of time?

Requesting extensions is a routine part of law. There isn't enough time in the day to handle every case on time. But, how often does the lawyer request an extension? Lawyers who request extensions a lot either have terrible time management skills or have way too many cases to handle.

What were the charges?

The severity of the charges the lawyer has handled previously is an indicator of the lawyer's experience level. Lawyers who only handle immigration cases, for instance, are usually not equipped to effectively handle a federal felony drug conspiracy. The greatest indicator of the lawyer's experience with severe charges is to look at how much time the cases he handled involved. You are looking to see if the lawyer has handled charges that are at least similar to yours.

How many days was the trial?

If you are planning on going to trial, you want to make sure that the lawyer is going to have a real trial. If the trials you are seeing only last a day, then it is likely the lawyer didn't prepare well for those cases and only asked for a one day trial. Felony trials should take at least three days and that's for a single defendant. The more defendants there are the longer the trial should be. Lawyers who only ask for a one day trial have no intention of challenging the prosecution's case every step of the way.

Looking at the docket sheets for some cases is far better than getting "recommendations." If you ask a lawyer for recommendations (if you ask anyone for that matter), you will only be given the names of people who will speak very highly about the lawyer no matter what. Beyond the three cases the lawyer provides you to look up, you can also run a search on the public access terminal at the federal court (or on PACER online) for the lawyer's name. Every case the lawyer entered an appearance in will be displayed. In fact, you can click on each of those cases and look at the docket sheet. Thus, if the lawyer claims to have a ton of experience in federal court and their name is not found or only matches a couple of cases, you know the lawyer is lying to you, then seek to hire someone.

Lawyer's Fees

How does the lawyer charge you or your family? Some lawyers charge a flat rate. Others charge by the hour. In criminal work, there is no such thing as a contingency. There is little to no chance that at the end of the case that you will have a viable lawsuit. Even if you think you do, though, you shouldn't be thinking about that right now. Your life is on the line. If you win, then you can go and look for a civil lawyer to handle the lawsuits if there are any.

HOURLY

Lawyers who charge an hourly rate only get paid for work done. Generally speaking, they will ask for a retainer (an amount prepaid) that is kept in a trust account. Each month, they will issue a bill outlining their hours of work on the case and bill against that retainer. The hourly rate does not usually cover expenses. Most hourly lawyers will nickel and dime everything. If you ask for a photocopy, you will pay for that. Well, not only do you pay for the copy itself, but also the time it took someone to make the copy.

Generally speaking lawyers who do hourly based fees set a standard interval by which to determine time. That means if they work for 1-9 minutes on your case, they may charge a minimum of 10 minutes. That way, if they work for 1 hour and 16 minutes, they can charge 1 hour and 20 minutes for their time.

The biggest benefit to hourly rates is that you only pay for work done. If your lawyer forgets about you and you decide to fire him as a result, any unused funds are given back to you. But, there is a gigantic risk that your defense fees could get out of control. What you don't want is a lawyer to pad the case with fake hours. This happens constantly. It is less common in smaller practices, but it can happen. In order to ensure that you aren't charged for work not done, it is vital for you to get a monthly hours sheet. Make the lawyer prove the work done. When you get the sheet, go through it. If it says they wrote a motion, and you haven't seen the motion, demand the lawyer give you a copy to prove the hours. On the other hand, if your lawyer is doing the work, and proving to you that it is being done, then you should pay him the agreed upon rate.

Where the cost can get out of control is during a trial. These require days of preparation and usually involve more than just the attorney. You will be paying hourly rates for paralegals and legal secretaries that are involved in the trial process too. To illustrate, if you have a three day trial that lasts seven hours each day, you can expect to pay:

Lawyer = $300 per hour

Paralegal = $100 per hour

Legal Secretary = $50 per hour

Total hourly = $450

Total hours = 21

Total Cost = $9450

And that's just for the actual trial. That doesn't include the all-nighters your lawyer will bill you for so he can draft motions required during trial.

If your lawyer has different fees, the number can go up or down accordingly. But the point should be clear. Hourly can be very expensive.

FLAT RATE

A flat rate is a non-refundable fee that is paid up front. Some lawyers will permit a payment plan for this. Obviously, the biggest benefit to a flat rate is the locked in amount you will pay. But is it? No. The answer is definitely no. First, expenses are not going to be included in this. Second, the flat rate will only cover part one of the representation. If you decide to go to trial, that will be another flat rate fee.

There are a lot of downsides to flat rate fees. Not the least of which is the lawyer is not incentivized and may not do the work. The less work he does on the case, the more he makes per hour. The less he relies on his staff is less money that he needs to pay from the fee to them. That usually means they operate a bare bones staff to begin with. Finally, flat rate lawyers need to take more cases to fill up their pockets. If your case drones on for several years, the lawyer will probably not want to do the work necessary to justify the fee.

That doesn't mean a flat rate cannot work. It can. There are lawyers out there who work very hard regardless of the fee. But, you have to be wary of the flat rate in any event. One way to ensure a flat rate lawyer stays honest is to require them to provide you with a monthly work log demonstrating what they did over the previous month.

If you decide to work with a flat rate lawyer, it is absolutely vital that you get them to agree to certain work milestones during the representation. If they meet those milestones, then they are worth the fee. If they don't meet those milestones, then you likely wasted your money. But if you get it in writing that they will meet those milestones, then you have a contract and a potential basis to sue them later for a refund.

FREE

Federal Public Defender's Office

Did you know you can use the public defender's office to represent you even if you aren't poor? Rule 44(a) of the Federal Rules of Criminal Procedure directs that the court *must* appoint you a lawyer if you are "unable" to secure counsel to represent you. If you are in jail, it is really difficult to find a lawyer and no judge will question it if you say you are "unable." In most cases, they have the greatest amount of experience in the federal court system since that is the only place they work. In fact, if you show up to court for your first appearance without a lawyer, a public defender will be assigned to you immediately. If you have the funds to pay them, they will inform you that they will bill you for services. If you don't have the funds, they won't bill you.

The old adage you get what you pay for is only partially true. I can't tell you how many people have told me they wish they just used the public defender's office. Most of them noticed that defendants represented by the public defender's office resolved their cases faster and with better results. Some of the most effective lawyers you will find are public defenders. Many of them have a special disdain for prosecutors. Most of them genuinely enjoy being defense lawyers.

FREE

Criminal Justice Act Appointment

Whether you get a public defender or Criminal Justice Act (CJA) appointed attorney is up to the court and public defender's office. **You don't get to choose one way or the other.** CJA appointments are necessary because the public defenders office could have a conflict of interest, or simply has too many cases to handle. CJA attorneys accept cases for a flat rate that is paid by the court system. If you get a CJA lawyer and he tries to get you to pay him, you need to inform the court right away. The CJA lawyer isn't supposed to use the appointment process to try and extort defendants. But it does happen. Sometimes a

CJA lawyer will tell a client that if he pays, he will get better representation. That isn't how this works, and telling the judge would be the right move. It is virtually guaranteed that you would get a new lawyer and he will get into a lot of trouble.

Contract

When you engage a lawyer to represent you, it is absolutely imperative that you nail down the terms of the representation. All too often, clients get up without knowing exactly what to expect their lawyer to do and feel as though their lawyer didn't do their job.

If you plan on paying a lawyer, you *need* to get a written contract from them. It doesn't matter if they are hourly or flat rate. If you have a free lawyer, you will not get a written contract. The written contract keeps everyone honest. It has existed for hundreds of years for a reason. If the lawyer has a contract already prepared, make sure you read every single line of it. If you don't understand something in it, ask. If the lawyer is evasive in answering your questions, then you probably want to find a different lawyer. There are certain elements you want to see in the contract which will be different depending on the type of fee arrangement you have.

The contract, at a minimum, should provide you with the information to answer the following:

❖ **How much must be paid up front?**

If you have a flat rate arrangement, you want to determine if there is a payment plan or if the entire amount must be paid up front. If you are paying hourly, you want to determine what the retainer expectation is and at what point you will be asked for a further retainer.

❖ **Are you required to pay for ancillary things like postage, copies, travel expenses, or paralegal time?**

If this isn't in the contract, then you shouldn't have to pay for it. Bringing it up could be a bad idea because it could signal the lawyer to start charging for those things. If you are in an hourly arrangement, it is virtually guaranteed there will be a fee schedule. In that case, you should ask for a detailed fee schedule. A fee schedule will detail every type of lawyer, assistant, office fees, and the like.

❖ **How long does the fee last?**

In a flat fee arrangement, it is common for the fee to only cover the portions of the case up to trial. That means if you decide to go to trial, you will be expected to pay more. You want the lawyer to commit to that number up front. It is not uncommon for a trial fee to be equal to the fee for all of the time before the trial. That means if the lawyer charges you $35,000 flat rate up front, he will likely expect to be paid $35,000 for the trial. You also want to make sure that the fees you pay will include preparation for and conducting sentencing. The fact remains that it is likely you will face a sentencing court. So you need to make sure this is spelled out. It is uncommon for a lawyer to charge an extra flat fee for sentencing.

- ❖ **(If a flat fee) Can I get a monthly accounting of work done?**

Just because there is a flat fee arrangement doesn't mean you shouldn't get a regular update of the work done on the case. This is one of the best ways to ensure that your lawyer is actually working for you. If you have a flat fee arrangement do not feel bad about asking for this.

- ❖ **Is the fee refundable if the contract is terminated?**

If you are in an hourly arrangement, whatever monies are left over will be returned to you. This question is thus more applicable to flat fee arrangements. It is uncommon for this to be spelled out in a contract. That means you need to request that such a clause be put into the contract. It is unreasonable to believe that the entire amount would be refunded unless the lawyer totally drops the ball. If the lawyer insists that the fee is non-refundable, and there is no negotiating that, then you should seriously consider going to a different lawyer. You *could* suggest the following clause be put into the contract:

> *In the event the attorney-client relationship terminates for any reason whatsoever, the attorney agrees to provide, within 30 days of the termination, a detailed statement of work done on the case. If the contract is terminated prior to the filing of any substantive documents (i.e. motions) on the judicial record, the client shall be entitled to a refund of 75% of the fee paid. If the contract is terminated after substantive filings, but before a guilty plea agreement is presented or a guilty plea entered, the client shall be entitled to a refund of 50% of the fee paid. If the contract is terminated after a guilty plea agreement is presented, or after a guilty plea is entered but before a sentencing hearing, the client shall be entitled to a refund of 25% of the fee paid. Likewise, in the event the contract is terminated without the entry of a guilty plea or filing of an accepted plea agreement and after the court schedules a final pretrial conference,*

> the client shall be entitled to a refund of 25% of the fee paid. At any other time following the events agreed to herein, the fee shall be considered non-refundable.

If the lawyer hums and haws at this proposal, you should say that you are expected to pay a lot of money and you want to have protection built into the contract from poor performance. The proposal offered above is quite reasonable and if a lawyer is afraid of it, it should be a clue that the lawyer has little intention of doing the work necessary for you on the case. Ergo, you should probably look for someone else. If the lawyer himself proposes a refund agreement of some sort, you want to make sure it incentivizes work. That is the entire point of the agreement. If you can't figure out what the incentive is, like the milestones we suggest above, then there probably is no incentive.

After you have figured all of that out, you are going to want to request the lawyer put the following into every contract regardless of the fee arrangement:

Access to Client Files

I can't tell you the amount of times people have tried get the files from their lawyer and can't. It is really helpful to have the exact procedure you need to follow to get your files if you ever want to. You also want to be able to get the file from your lawyer after the case is over since this will be vital to investigate for ineffective assistance of counsel claims. So, make sure there is a specific procedure spelled out for you to follow and have that put into the contract.

Copies of Court Filings

I have yet to meet a defendant who doesn't want to see what is being filed **BEFORE** it gets filed. It doesn't matter if you don't understand it. The only way to keep tabs on your lawyer is by inspecting his work. No lawyer should have any qualms with agreeing to giving you a copy of something and talking about it before it gets filed on the record. Maybe the lawyer messed up some facts. Who knows? But if it gets filed and it is wrong, you are the one who will pay the ultimate price. If a lawyer refuses to agree to provide you with filings before they get filed as part of the contact, you should look him right in the eye and ask: **is it common for you to file documents without the client's input?** No lawyer should be afraid of that because there should be no reason at all to mess this up.

No Waivers of Rights Without Express Authorization

Lawyers have a tendency to waive things without getting the client's express authorization. While some waivers require your specific voice (like waiving a trial by pleading guilty), there are a ton more that don't. The most common is waiver of time limits. Now, the lawyer needs to be able to work with his opponent on some level so allowing them some leeway here is necessary. The amount of leeway is what you want to confine. You also want to make sure things aren't getting waived without you knowing about it.

Presentation of Plea Agreements

It is very sad that attorneys put their clients under the gun to read and agree to a plea agreement. Plea agreements are complicated contracts and they require careful analysis and consideration. Even if you eventually reject it, you want to have time to consider the agreement. Therefore, you want to make sure that your lawyer has a contractual duty to give you an appropriate amount of time to consider any plea agreement.

Access to Discovery

Probably the most frustrating thing a defendant deals with is accessing and reviewing all of the discovery. Lawyers have a number of reasons for not giving the discovery to a client. The biggest reason for keeping the discovery away from a client is to make sure nobody can see it and use it against the client. Having the discovery in your possession, especially in a jail environment, can be dangerous for a number of reasons. But, it is impossible to defend against a charge without looking at what the government has on you. And it is not possible to review the discovery with the lawyer present because it will take many hours to review. There are times that protective orders are put in place because the discovery contains information about informants that the government doesn't want you to have. It is likely the judge will agree with the government. But that doesn't mean your lawyer should agree to blanket protective orders either. If there is going to be a protective order, it should be confined to the information that is being protected and nothing else. In any case, you probably are going to want to make sure the lawyer is required to give you all the discovery he can legally give you.

Having all of these issues resolved at the beginning by putting your expectations into a contract will alleviate a lot of problems. If the lawyer fails to comply with the agreement, then he is breach. That means you would have cause to sue him and potentially recover your money. Everything that you are proposing to the lawyer is not unreasonable and any lawyer who doesn't agree is probably not a criminal defense lawyer you want to work with.

Inspecting a Lawyer's Work

Inspecting your lawyer's work is going to become the most important job you have. If the lawyer isn't doing his job, you pay the ultimate price. The lawyer still goes home. In order to inspect the lawyer's work you will have to employ a number of tactics to ensure the lawyer is doing everything he can to advocate for you.

Request Service of all Documents

You want the lawyer to send you copies of literally everything. Emails to or from the prosecutor, filings in court, and investigative reports generated by the defense team are just a few of the things they should be sending to you. If he gives you some reason he can't give you something, then you need to demand he show it to you in person and prove to you why he can't mail it to you. The only reason a lawyer couldn't share something with you is if he is ordered to keep it from you by a judge. If that happens, then he would have an order signed by a judge stating exactly that. And, if he has such an order in his hand, you can and should demand he object to the order as an interference with your right to defend yourself.

Now, how do you know if the lawyer is sending you everything. It is impossible to verify every little thing the lawyer does. For instance, if he emails the prosecutor, the only record is usually the email. But, that's not entirely true. If the lawyer bills you for an email sent on a specific day (or, in the flat fee/appointed counsel case, logs an email on their hours sheet) and you haven't seen that email, then you should demand he show you the email. If he refuses, then he either owes you a refund or a helluva explanation as to why the hours are logged the way they are. Hiding things from you is certainly a reason to ask for or hire a new lawyer (depending on your situation).

When you get the documents, you need to read them. Even if you are having a hard time following the legalese, you need to make sure that the factual information contained in the document is in line with your version of events. You also need to make sure the lawyer is not making any waivers for you that you don't want. For instance, you could get a brief in the mail and in a footnote notice that the lawyer concedes a fact. If you didn't authorize the lawyer to concede the fact, then you and him need to have a very serious conversation about it. Facts must be proven by the government. It's that simple. When you concede facts, you make their life easier. Some facts can be conceded because they are too obvious not to concede. But, that doesn't mean it should be a surprise to you. The same goes for waivers of things like time limits. You shouldn't be blindsided by these things. If these things are not a surprise to you, then all is well and good. But **if you are surprised, that is a problem.**

If you notice something in a document that rubs you the wrong way, you need to inform the lawyer immediately. You should demand the lawyer correct the information immediately. You need to memorialize your complaint and demand in writing and you need to save a copy of the writing. You can't just say you called the lawyer and have no other proof. If you are in jail, the jail should provide you with copies by request. If they refuse to copy your documents, then literally write it again, word for word. If you can send it certified mail, you should do so. If the lawyer refuses to fix the errors, that letter could become important evidence for years to come.

Request Copies of the Docket Sheet

The docket sheet is usually a public document that anyone can access. Your lawyer can print one off in about a second. You and/or your family can sign up for a federal PACER account (https://pacer.psc.uscourts.gov/) to access the docket sheets for nearly every federal case in the country. That includes yours. A docket sheet is an index of the entire case file. Anything that is filed on the case is listed there unless it is under seal. Cases usually start at document "1" and go from there. If you see documents being skipped, then you should question why they are being skipped. Sometimes the clerk's office skips a number for whatever reason. But if you see a lot of skips, that is usually indicative of sealed documents. If you haven't been told about those documents, then you should question your lawyer.

One of the best ways to keep a lawyer honest is to require that he or she produce a copy of the docket sheet to you at least once per month. If they know they are going to be giving you a copy, then they will be aware that you are paying attention to everything. Unless they are just absolute morons, they will take less liberty with your case than with those who don't pay so much attention.

If you are in jail, and you have nobody to help you and the lawyer refuses to give you the docket sheet, you can always send a letter asking the Clerk of the Court to send you a copy. You don't want to say anything in that letter other than, "I am the defendant in this case, and I would like a copy of the docket sheet mailed to me." Other than that, give them the mailing address for the jail and provide them with a case number.

Pay Close Attention During Hearings

There should never be a time that the lawyer has a hearing in your case without you present. You should tell your lawyer you will never waive your personal presence in court. If, for some crazy reason, you aren't in court with your lawyer (like the jail forgot to bring you or something), then you need to tell the lawyer to object that you aren't present and to demand you be produced for the hearing. If the judge insists on going through with the hearing, then tell the lawyer you want a transcript of the hearing made immediately and provided to you. If you are appointed counsel, then the transcript should be provided to you without cost. If you retain a lawyer, the transcript will cost $3.65 per page (standard processing) to prepare and another $0.10 per page to give a copy to you. It is absolutely worth the cost to get this so you can make sure your lawyer didn't say something completely wrong or waive your rights in any way.

I will give you an example from my own life. I had a collateral state case that I vehemently contested. I informed my lawyers there were no circumstances where I would plead the case out. Either we would get a dismissal or we would go to trial. There was no ambiguity in my demand. Because I was in federal custody at the time, I couldn't be produced to state court because someone didn't file any special paperwork. My lawyers did it alone. They told me that everything went fine and that I would get a trial. After I fired those lawyers about 18 months later, my new lawyer went to the state court and found out that my old lawyers told the prosecutor and judge I would plead guilty in the case! Had I demanded a transcript be produced immediately, I would have fired those lawyers much faster than I did, and I would have corrected the record. Luckily, my new lawyer was quite effective and we achieved the dismissal I wanted.

If you are at a hearing and you hear your lawyer say something that is false or he inappropriately waives any of your rights, then you need to inform the lawyer immediately. If the lawyer is standing at the podium and you are sitting at counsel's table, then simply stand up and say, "Your honor, can I please speak with my lawyer for a second?" Your lawyer will be given a minute or two to confer with you and you should tell him what he said that was wrong. He should then immediately correct the record. If he is an especially horrible lawyer and refuses to correct the record, you can correct the record yourself.

Finally, if there is something that is said at the hearing that you don't understand, you need to ask the lawyer to explain it to you. The rule of thumb is to act like a dumb blonde. Do not try and give an explanation in your question. Just ask the lawyer to explain it. "What does _____ mean?" It is usually a good idea to wait for the end of the hearing to ask the lawyer questions. You don't want him to divide his attention between you and the hearing itself. You save non-urgent questions until the hearing is over. If you had a long hearing, it is not unusual for the Marshals to let you talk with your lawyer at counsel's table at the conclusion of the hearing. All that has to happen is your lawyer ask them for a few minutes before they take you. If there is a hearing immediately following yours, then they will say there isn't enough time. At which point tell your lawyer you want him to meet with you in the attorney booths in the courthouse (yes, they have them).

Random Checks

The random check is the most effective tool to make sure an employee is doing their job. And, make no mistake, the lawyer is your employee. Yes, he is a highly educated employee. But, an employee none-the-less. In order to conduct random checks you can do several things. First, ask the lawyer to give you copies of something that you already have. It will remind the lawyer who you are paying attention and that you care deeply about your own case. Second, during visits throw out some random questions about your case but off the primary topic. For instance, if your lawyer is talking to you about suppression motions in your meeting with him, then throw in a question about his investigation and trial preparation. An example would be, "Oh. I was going to ask you how the investigation is going?" You want to make sure you are able to tick off points that the lawyer previously said would be done. Did the lawyer tell you an expert of some sort would be needed? Then the lawyer should be able to give you a name and even their resume. Did the lawyer tell you that the investigator planned on interviewing someone? Then you should get a date and time of the interview and even a transcript of the interview. By the time your case is over, your lawyer should have a very large file for you that he developed. If the lawyer only ever produces discovery that the prosecutor provided him, then you are in big trouble.

Speaking of discovery, there is one other random check that you can and should do. Make sure the lawyer has been reviewing the discovery by asking questions about it. This is very easy to do. Every time the lawyer comes to see you, make sure you have at least one question regarding the discovery. It can be anything from who was interviewed by the government, who the government seems to want to use as witnesses, or even who the lead agent on your case is. The only way your lawyer would know any of that information is to have read the discovery and digested it. Don't be swindled by "that's not important" or "we are going a different direction" remarks that lawyers tend to make when they don't know something. They either know it or they don't. Simple as that. If they don't know it, you are looking to see that they admit they don't know. If they admit they don't know, then you can start educating them and see if they are receptive to what you have to say. Remember, the lawyer needs to know your story *and* the government's story to be an effective advocate for you.

Part Five

Defense Tactics

Just because your lawyer is in control of "strategy" doesn't mean you should just sit by and let them do as they please. You need to learn some of the strategies out there to work _with_ your lawyer. Here, we are going to discuss some important strategies including types of defenses and plea bargaining.

Trial Strategies

It is true that a lawyer is granted a substantial amount of discretion to determine the specifics of your defense strategy. But that doesn't mean you shouldn't give your input and to do that you need to understand some common strategies employed in criminal cases. When determining a viable defense strategy, it is important to understand the strengths and weaknesses of the government's case because that will be the single most important factor in determining the strategy to employ. In this section we are going to explore some common defense strategies that defendants want to employ throughout their case. The general problem is they find out about these defense strategies long after the case is over and then try and convince others that the lawyer should have used such strategy in your case. Invariably, a court will shoot down your argument because the lawyer is the one who decides the strategies to employ to advance your ultimate position. So, make sure and advocate for the strategies you want to see your lawyer employ **early in the process.** This is not something you will be able to get back later.

Strategy: Choose a Trial Defense as Early as Possible, Even if You Plan on Pleading Guilty

There are several well accepted defenses to criminal charges that lawyers refer to when developing a defendant's case. No-Presentation, Alibi, Impossibility, Insanity, Character Defense, Duress or Justification, and Entrapment are some of the most common. Some of these must be disclosed to the prosecutor early on and others do not.

We are going to review a few of these defenses below, but first I want to stress why this "strategy" is indispensable for you to win anything. It doesn't matter if you are guilty as hell. You and your lawyer need to have a strategy to deal with the charges and it is best if you are both on the same page with this as early as possible. While it isn't applied in the federal system, some jurisdictions mandate a trial for certain offenses and a plea bargain cannot be negotiated. Even if you want to negotiate a plea bargain at any point, you need to prepare a defense so your lawyer can show the prosecutor that you have a case they should be scared of. It's that simple. You need to have some ammo to load into your gun, no matter how small it may be, to shoot back. And make no mistake, a small gun can kill the tank if employed strategically.

There are a lot of types of defenses lawyers learn in law school and the ones presented below list are not even close to exhaustive. These are just some common defenses employed.

COMMON DEFENSES

No-Presentation

No-Presentation defenses are where you sit at the defendant's table and not introduce anything from your side. A no-presentation defense does not mean that your lawyer has no work to do for you either. Rather than trying to convince the jury that you didn't do something, your lawyer's job is to poke holes ("reasonable doubt") all through the government's case. Your lawyer will still have to cross-examine all of their witnesses and challenge any evidence that the government wants to present.

You are probably thinking that this is a weak defense strategy and in many ways you would be right. What normal person wants to sit in the jury box and not hear from the other side? But, it may make the jury's job much more complicated if you present a case. Your lawyer may want to remind the jury that the prosecution did not meet the elements of the crime and must set you free without confusing them with a defense. If you have a fairly educated jury, they may really like you for making it so easy for them to make a decision. And the jury liking you is definitely a major priority.

As weak as the defense sounds, it can be quite effective. One of the most powerful ways to implement a no-presentation strategy is to put forth the investigative effort to discredit each and every witness the government plans on calling. The weaker their witnesses become, the better for you. And, make no mistake, if a prosecutor is afraid that their witnesses won't be believed, it can go a long way to getting you a fabulous plea deal.

An example of a no-presentation defense can be found in the hit-comedy *My Cousin Vinney*. In the end, the movie also implemented an impossibility defense (that the car the boys drove was not the same as the car involved). But the bulk of the hilarious trial centered on discrediting every witness (old lady had bad vision, fat guy cooking couldn't tell the actual amount of time, the expert didn't know everything about vehicle suspension, etc.). Vinney was a terrible lawyer. However, the point is very simple. Discredit witnesses, and a prosecutor could be afraid to bring the case to trial.

While you and your lawyer are strategizing, it is important to discuss if the prosecution will have significant trouble proving an aspect of the case. If you guys notice something, then that will become a big bargaining chip for a plea agreement if that is what you want. Or it will allow you and your lawyer to focus your investigation and case development on a winnable strategy.

Impossibility

If it was impossible for you to have committed a crime then you are probably going to want to present all of the evidence that shows such impossibility. There are a couple of different impossibility defenses which we will divide into "alibi" and "other impossibilities." Alibis are evidence that you present to show you were somewhere else at the time of the crime. Other impossibilities could be hundreds of different scenarios and you need to think outside the box to determine if that is your situation.

Alibis

Contrary to popular opinion, an alibi is not actually a "defense" per se. Rather, it is evidence that casts reasonable doubt on the government's case. But, there are significant strategy considerations when dealing with alibis that you should understand. In a nutshell, presenting an alibi is the same as showing it was physically impossible for you to have committed the crime by showing you were not in the area on the date and time of the alleged criminal acts.

As a general rule, you will not see a trial case that empanels a jury where a serious alibi question exists. The government does not usually bring cases they believe are total losers. So, if you have an airtight alibi you may want to bring it to the government's attention at the earliest possible opportunity. An airtight alibi would be you were so far away that there is no possible way you could have been at the crime scene and you have credible and conclusive evidence to support that conclusion. Credible evidence would be a security camera, witnesses, receipts, etc. For instance, if you have security footage showing you in a hotel at 6am in New York and you are alleged to have committed a robbery in Tampa, Florida at the same time, then it would cast significant doubt as to the government's case no matter how many witnesses are put on the stand because it would have been physically impossible to have been in both places at the same exact time.

The ultra majority of alibi cases are ones that have weaknesses that the prosecution will exploit. A common one is, "I was at home in bed with my wife." Your wife can certainly testify that you were there and never left at all that night and there is nothing wrong with that. But the prosecution is going to point out that your wife would have, at some point, slept, used the restroom, walked into another room, or even went out in the backyard. If your wife can withstand the onslaught that will surely come, then her testimony may be sufficient for the jury to set you free. But, that is a gigantic gamble to play and you have to understand that there are significant risks to trying to present an alibi defense.

Furthermore, alibis are something that usually have to be disclosed well in advance of trial. In the federal system, the rule does not force the defendant to disclose the alibi to the government until the government demands it be produced. Put differently, if the government doesn't ask, you don't have to tell. Make no mistake, the government is going to ask as a matter of course. As soon as you are arraigned, they will probably file a document demanding that your lawyer disclose any potential alibi evidence you intend on presenting. If that happens, you only have 14 days to produce the information and the names, addresses, and telephone numbers of the witnesses supporting the alibi. So if you think you may have an alibi, then you need to make sure your lawyer listens to you as early as possible.

The general rule for you is to have a serious talk with your lawyer as to any alibi you may have. Do not try and fabricate an alibi because it will get found out. Although it is much harder in today's surveillance intensive world to pull off, the courts and prosecution are aware of the relative ease in developing a fabricated alibi. If you convince someone to lie for you, they will probably be charged with a number of crimes as well. But if you have a legitimate alibi, then put it forward.

Entrapment

Most defendants believe they were entrapped by the government. And with good reason. It's because they were. Entrapment occurs where the government invents the crime or is the one to put it into motion. This is extremely common in drug interdiction, prostitution, and child molestation cases. What makes this defense very complicated is that the government is allowed to break the law in order to enforce it. That doesn't mean you shouldn't be prepared to mount an entrapment defense.

The first requirement in developing an entrapment defense is determining if government agents put the crime into motion. The government can be anything from undercover cops to paid informants. Each jurisdiction throughout the country has differing opinions as to who can be a government agent. For instance, private citizens who entrap you without any direction from a government official is not legal entrapment. There are some pretty famous examples of the private world engaging in criminal detection through the use of trapping techniques. A really famous one was Dateline's "To Catch a Predator." In that show, the host would put out ads on the Internet purporting to be a child, or someone who has a child, who was willing to engage in sexual activity. They would wait for someone to answer the ad and when that happened, they would set up a meeting with the unsuspecting criminal. The criminal would arrive at a location and be confronted with cameras and questioning from the network about their activities. The network would contact the police and the offender would be arrested. In that situation, the government did not direct anything.

One of the most common types of entrapment is where the government "employs" an informant to set up drug buys from their friends or acquaintances. Usually, the police will bust the informant and make a deal with them: "work for us or go to jail." They usually choose to work for the cops. They get to stay out of jail and in some cases will even get money. These types of guys are generally considered agents for the purposes of an entrapment defense.

The point being that it is often hard to tell the difference just from paper and an investigation is going to be necessary to determine if the actors involved were government agents. But, if you know that you didn't come up with the idea for the crime, it is likely a good idea to have a conversation with your lawyer about this possible defense strategy. You will have to detail all the who, what, where, when, and how details for your lawyer and from there your lawyer should engage in an investigation to determine if the government was involved in designing the criminal plan. If you are able to prove that, then you will need to develop all of the evidence possible showing that you weren't predisposed to committing the crime.

Predisposition to committing the crime is the second element of entrapment. If you were predisposed to commit the crime then, no matter how much the government was involved in developing the crime, you can't be entrapped. There are a number of factors that a jury would be instructed to consider when trying to determine if you are predisposed to committing the crime. Often times, the prosecution will introduce evidence of "other bad acts" showing that you have no problem committing the same crime. But that isn't the only way for the government to get out from under the entrapment rug.

Imagine a defendant who went to a place called "Drug Park." While he was there, he approached someone, handed them money, and apparently received a small package in return. The man with the package is an undercover police officer and immediately takes the buyer into custody. It is clear as day that the government is the one who set up the criminal activity and it was most certainly a government agent conducting the sting. The defendant tries to assert entrapment. The government admits that it set up the whole situation but shows predisposition through several pieces of evidence: the defendant's knowledge of the park's criminal purpose, that the officer never approached the defendant, and the time it took for the defendant to enter the park and purchase the product. In order to show all of this, the government has a video of the transaction which shows the defendant entering the park and within five minutes approaches the area where drugs are being sold and approaches the agent. The tape goes on to show the defendant handing money to the agent and the agent handing him a package. There is no indication on the video that anyone suggested the defendant go over and talk to the agent or to purchase the drugs. Then the government calls a few witnesses to the stand who will testify as to the general knowledge that "Drug Park" is the place to buy drugs. They may even call a witness who will (perhaps falsely) claim that the defendant has purchased drugs from him the past. Thus, they are able to show knowledge of the drug trade there. Finally, the government will make sure that the jury sees it took less than five minutes for the defendant to purchase the drugs.

The key is showing that the government overbore your will to make a rational decision under the circumstances. Let's wrinkle the government's case up a little. The defendant told his lawyer who he received a phone call stating that his son is in debt to a major gang and if the defendant didn't go and buy them some drugs they would kill his son. The lawyer pulls the guy's phone records and sees that a call was made to him shortly before he went to the park and seeks discovery on the phone number. The lawyer also doesn't trust the government to be honest so he issues a subpoena to the phone company to find out who the number belongs to. When the lawyer finds out that the cell phone that contacted the defendant is registered to the city he starts putting two and two together. The lawyer puts the defendant on the stand who tells his story and also puts a few witnesses on the stand confirming that the defendant has been helping his son battle addiction for years. The jury could believe that the defendant's will was overborne by the government in calling him and falsely claiming that his son was in debt and danger of death.

Entrapment defenses are limited only by imagination. They require a significant amount of planning and investigation. But when it is clear the government entrapped someone, it is a great strategy to employ. And remember, even if you don't intend on taking the case to trial, this is something that could be used to push for a better deal from the prosecution.

Strategy: Reject and Renegotiate a Plea Offer

It is true that you have no right to be offered anything from the government. But that doesn't mean you should take any offer they throw at you either. The ultra-majority of initial offers from the government will have little to really offer you. If you have been paying attention throughout this book, then you have been pressing your rights at every stage. Doing just that should push a sane prosecutor to be concerned you will press the case at trial. The more concerned about that they are, the more negotiation power you have. If you have been pushing hard by mounting an effective defense throughout, then you have negotiation power and you should use it.

Negotiation is an art form. Hopefully you have a lawyer who is decent at it. Your lawyer is going to have to advocate for what you want while being amenable to what the prosecution wants. It's a hard job to say the least. Because it is an art form, there are a million ways to do it. You shouldn't push your lawyer to use one style over another. Their style is what they need to use. People who use their own style to negotiate tend to negotiate more effectively. People who try and copy other's styles tend to lose negotiations.

Once you have decided that the offer you are looking at isn't good enough, but you have also decided that you are willing to take something, then you are in a position to craft a counter-offer. In the contracting world, it is usually understood that a counter-offer is a categorical rejection of an offer. So, if you decide to "counter-offer" and think that is going to protect the first offer, think again. If you counter, the government can revoke its original offer (although it doesn't have to).

Ask yourself what you want. Now, if you are facing a federal indictment and your Guidelines range says that you should go to prison for a decade, don't think of asking for probation. A counter offer like that is essentially a big F-You to the prosecutor and says you have no intention of ever negotiating with them. If you are on a war path to a trial, and you would only accept probation, then by all means offer it. Just understand that the prosecutor isn't going to take it seriously. But, hey. Maybe they will?!

Obviously, the first thing you want to make sure of is that you spend less time in prison. As a result, pretty much every negotiation will center on that. But don't develop tunnel vision. There are other aspects of the plea bargain that can be used.

For instance, let's say the government comes in with an offer for 10 years in return for a guilty plea to conspiracy to distribute 100 grams or more of heroin in violation of 21 U.S.C. § 841(a)(1)(B). That's the mandatory minimum, so not bad. You may want to try and get the prosecutor to drop it down to the

5-year mandatory minimum instead. So what can you give up? You could offer an increase term of supervised release when you get out in return for bringing you down to the 5-40 provision of the statute. Or, rather than ask for a locked in sentence, you could ask the prosecutor to lower it to the 5-40 and put a cap of 10 years on your sentence exposure. That would allow you to try and convince the judge to go down to 5, but prevents you from going over the 10. Prosecutors agree to things like this all the time. Remember, you are saving the prosecution a lot of time, money, and effort to just give them the conviction and prison time.

Let's do another example. Let's say the government presents Herb-the-Perv with an offer for one count of attempted production of child pornography and agrees to not bring any further charges. It's a 15-30 year sentence exposure and not bad for the weirdo Herb the Perv. But, is that all he can get. Herb's lawyer calls up the prosecutor and says, "how about Herb pleads to one count of enticement of a minor and we stipulate to a 15-year penalty. Herb will agree to 15 years of supervised release to follow too." What does this get Herb if it is accepted? Well, a locked in 15-year penalty for starters. But why on earth would he plead to a more serious charge that has a life maximum? Because he would get First Step Act time credits for that charge in prison but not for the attempted production. The prosecutor gets to tell the world they got him on a more serious charge, got the time, and put him away. Herb gets out in 11 years with good conduct time and First Step Act credits for time off and halfway house placement. If he agreed to the first offer, Herb could face more than 15-years and wouldn`t get any First Step Act credits while in prison. Thus, he would serve about 13-years. That two years is a big difference.

The point is, you need to try and be creative about what you all are willing to do. Great lawyers already know what the prosecutors want. Decent lawyers will at least take your ideas and craft a reasonable counter offer.

IF YOU DECIDE TO NEGOTIATE WITH THE PROSECUTION AND THEY AGREE TO YOUR TERMS THEN DO NOT BE THAT GUY WHO BACKS OUT. It makes you and your lawyer look really bad and rest assured the prosecutor will complain in front of everyone who will listen that you wasted everyone`s time (including the judge).

Strategy: If you are indigent, request your lawyer file an application for funds to be used for investigators and experts.

The Criminal Justice Act allows a judge to release funds for your defense that would reasonably be sought by a private lawyer with a fully funded client. The motion is filed "ex parte" which means the government won't know it is even being requested. I am of the opinion that every criminal defendant needs to have an investigator to tear through all the discovery and find witnesses. It doesn't matter if you will ultimately plead guilty because a proper defense investigation is vital to do literally everything in a criminal case (like plea bargain, go to trial, evaluate the veracity of officers' claims, etc.). Federal Public Defenders usually have an investigator or two on their staff so they don't need to do this. But if you have a CJA lawyer, they can **and definitely should ask** for the money to get at least one investigator.

Likewise, your lawyer could ask for funds to get an expert in your case. Experts could be needed for a variety of reasons. The most common is a psychologist to do a psych evaluation to determine if you are a danger to the community. If you are charged with any violent crime or sexual offense, then your lawyer *absolutely* needs to request funds for this. Whether you need an expert or not is something that you and your lawyer need to discuss. But, if the lawyer ever mentions that you should have an expert and says something like, "too bad you are indigent...," then point out the Criminal Justice Act allows for funds for adequate representation which includes funds for investigators, experts, and other necessities.

Your lawyer can apply for funds for pretty much anything that is reasonable to the defense. Does that mean the judge will grant the request? No. But it does open up potential appellate issues about the adequacy of your representation. If your lawyer refuses to seek funds for these things and there is a reasonable basis to pursue further investigations, then you should probably consider requesting replacement counsel.

Strategy: Move To Suppress The Police Interview(s)

There are a number of reasons that an interview can be thrown out. If you are "in custody" and the police don't inform you of your rights, then you have a very strong case to move for suppression. Looking for ways to show you were "in custody" is a powerful way to move for suppression if your statement was given in an untraditional area like: your sofa, a police car, your bathroom, your front yard, or anywhere else that isn't a police station. You'd be surprised how often police screw this up.

To prove you were in custody, you would have to show that you were in a position that "a reasonable person" would have seen as not free to leave. If you were in handcuffs, inside a locked police car, surrounded by armed police, or in any other situation that regular people would assume they couldn't leave from and the police questioned you without reading your rights, that is a basis to suppress for failing to provide you the Miranda warning.

Another reason to move for suppression of a confession is if you asked for a lawyer. If, at any point, you clearly and unequivocally asked for a lawyer (regardless of being informed of your rights), and they press on with questioning, the confession can be suppressed. Once you ask for a lawyer, the police absolutely MUST stop asking you questions. It's that simple. Too often, a suspect will ask for a lawyer and the police will say, "you don't want to do that. I can't help you if you ask for a lawyer." The key here is showing that you *clearly* asked for a **LAWYER**. If you said, "I don't know, I think I need to speak with someone first," then you didn't invoke your right to a lawyer. You would have to say, "I want a lawyer," or "I want to talk to an attorney," or something along those lines. The key is clarity.

What happens if you told the initial officers you wanted a lawyer, they didn't ask you any questions, and transported you to the police station. Then they put you in an interview room and a new cop comes in and asks you if you want to talk. Rather than pressing your right to a lawyer, you decide to talk. The new cop tells you what your rights are and you sign a waiver form. Is the resulting confession illegal or not? The answer is not easy. I haven't ever found a case where this was litigated to an appellate court, but I would believe that you would have a basis to push for suppression. It could go either way, but the fact that you told one cop that you want a lawyer and the other just ignored it could convince a judge that the cops are gaming the constitution. This is where having a good lawyer is helpful. You may not win, but if the government is scared that you would win, this strategy could push a better offer your way.

Strategy: Move For Suppression Of Evidence

There are two types of evidence suppression cases. Ones that involve a warrant and ones that don't. If there was a warrant, then the suppression motion needs to concentrate on the warrant itself and the resulting search and seizure conducted under that warrant. If there wasn't a warrant, then the motion needs to concentrate on the potential "exigencies" of the situation. Let's look at both.

WARRANT BASED SEIZURE

The Fourth Amendment generally demands that the government have a warrant issued by a "neutral and detached" person to be able to take property from someone. The warrant must do two things:

- describe with particularity the thing(s) to be seized
- describe with particularity the place(s) to be searched

Most cops comply with describing the place to searched with particularity. If they are going to search a house, they will "describe" the lot the house sits on, the color of the house, any numbers to identify the house, and the like. The law allows them to search all items within the property that they describe. This means cars, luggage, closets, basements, bathrooms, bedrooms, etc.

What most cops take liberty with are the "things" to be seized. If they want to take something, it must be authorized. Now, unless the items are protected by the First Amendment, "particularity" doesn't require them to describe each individual item exactly. Rather, they are allowed to seek categories of items. But, the items must be supported by the probable cause presented in the affidavit. What you want to do is go down the list of the items they ask to take and try and come up with a rational reason why the item can connect to the crime. Then have a conversation with your lawyer if there are any items or categories that don't make sense to the crime. For instance, if they are searching for drug trafficking evidence and get authorization to search for and seize children's underwear, then it makes no sense. What does children's underwear have to do with drug trafficking? Nothing that I can think of.

If there is a particularity challenge, then you are going to move to suppress the evidence on the basis that the warrant itself is invalid. Invalid warrants happen, and if they are really bad, the judge may throw the evidence out of the trial.

Next, you need to determine if the officers seized items *not* authorized by the warrant. List each and every item that isn't arguably authorized because this goes to the question of whether the officers acted with "good faith." If they acted with good faith, then they cannot have exceeded the scope of the warrant. This will help your particularity challenge.

If you don't have a particularity challenge and the officers exceed the scope of the warrant, you can still move for suppression but you are alleging that the officers ignored the warrant as opposed to the warrant being invalid. It is way worse when they ignore the warrant. For instance, let's say the warrant allows them to take all evidence of money laundering (computers, cash, checkbooks, bank statements, money counters, etc.) but makes absolutely no mention of firearms in the house. In America, firearms are not illegal to possess except under certain defined circumstances. If they take all the guns, without your permission or without the warrant's authorization, then they are likely exceeding the warrant. No amount of justification can support them taking the guns. As an example, their claim that the guns were taken for "safety purposes" shouldn't hold water. The guns can remain locked in your house or you can arrange to have them taken by someone else. The point is, the police do not have authorization to take them and that is potentially a basis to get everything thrown out.

WARRANTLESS SEIZURES

If the cops take anything from you without a warrant, or the police entered your home without a warrant, and you didn't consent to the search and seizure, then you have a strong case for suppression and you should move for it. The police aren't allowed to just enter where they want and take what they want whenever they want. That is the entire purpose of the Fourth Amendment. If the police act without a warrant, then the government must prove that an exigent circumstance was present to authorize the search and seizure. There are not many exigent circumstances. Before I get into those, here's a true-story example of a warrantless search and seizure that resulted in the guy getting a dismissal.

In county jail, a 19-year old kid ended up in there after being arrested for possession of marijuana. Not really a big deal on the grand scheme of things, but he was charged with felony possession. He had priors and was facing some time in prison as a result. The police report said the marijuana was found on the floor-board of the vehicle by the driver's door. I thought about it and it became clear that there were only two ways the officer could have seen the drug: if the door was open or the officer reached his or her head into the window. The police report stated that the drugs were in "plain view" which is one of those exceptions allowed. Plain view means that the officer could see it without accessing an area they would need a warrant to access. After questioning the young-man, I found out that while he was in the driver seat, the officer reached her head through the window and looked down at the floor. That is not a plain view exception issue. We filed a motion to suppress immediately. He didn't have a lawyer yet because the state system moved way slower than the federal system with that. The judge immediately got him a lawyer, a hearing occurred, and the case was tossed. The judge found the officer violated the Fourth Amendment by poking her head through the driver's window. He was released because the prosecutor could not justify why an officer poked her head through the window.

The exceptions to the warrant requirement are few and well defined. They are:

- consent
- search incident to arrest
- community caretaking exception
- inventory search
- plain view doctrine
- imminent destruction of evidence
- protection of third parties or officers
- fleeing felon

If there isn't a warrant and you challenge the search and seizure, the government must prove one of these exceptions applied. It isn't that easy to prove unless you signed a consent form. And, even if one of the exceptions applies, that doesn't mean the search is valid. For instance, let's say the police ran into a house on fire to get people out. When they get in, they find that the fire is confined to one room and a person is in there. The person says, "nobody else is in the house, I live alone." The police get the person out. Rather than listen to the person's claim they live alone, they go and search room by room and find a kilo of heroin on the nightstand. There was no reason for the police to continue their search. They had no reason to believe the person was lying about being the only one there. That means, even though there was an emergency, the continued search was not legal. You will have to research each of these exceptions to see if they apply to your case and how the government may attempt to prove their application.

How to Write a Motion and Brief

A "motion" is a request asking the judge to take a specific course of action. A "brief" supports the motion by presenting the relevant facts and law in an attempt to convince the judge your position is the right one. As a general rule, if you file a motion, then the other side (the government) must be given an opportunity to respond. And, with limited exceptions, you can "reply" to the government's response. There are some simple rules you need to follow if you want to file an effective motion and brief.

Pencil, Typing, or Pen

When you write a motion and brief in a pro se capacity, you can pretty write it using anything and on any type of paper. It is said that there are defendants who won their freedom from death row using a pencil and toilet paper. That doesn't mean you shouldn't use your best penmanship (print, don't write in cursive). If all you have is a pencil and some paper, then go ahead and write your motion using the pencil. If you have access to a pen, great. It's even better if you can access a typewriter (if you are in a Federal Detention Center they have those). But don't fret too much if you can't access a typewriter or word processor. Just be neat. Don't cross/scratch things out (rewrite it if you have to) and don't spill anything on the paper (like coffee or food). It is best to use white paper. If you don't have access to that, then don't worry. Just write it on clean paper.

Copies

Always make a copy of anything you are going to send to the court. If there isn't any photocopier access at your facility, then hand-write a copy (word-for-word). You will need the copy to reply to the government's response and you may need the copy if the document gets lost in the mail (or thrown away by the jail).

The Caption

The very first thing you have to do is make a "caption." The caption tells the clerk of the court where to file the document when they get it by providing: the name of the court, the names of the parties, the case number(s), and the title of the document. Most federal district courts use the format of the state system where the court sits. But, it isn't necessary to be that precise for your caption. So long as you provide the required information, then you are in the clear. Here is a caption example.

The Title

The title is included in the caption. But it bears mentioning that you want the title to clearly identify what the document is about. If you are trying to represent yourself for the whole thing, then you should entitle the document "Motion to Proceed Pro Se" or "Motion to Represent Myself." If you are trying to get a new lawyer, then you would say, "Motion for Replacement Counsel Due." The key is to state that you making a "motion" and what that motion ultimately seeks to have done. You don't need to get creative. Just be clear.

Writing in the Third or First Person

When lawyers write motions and briefs, they write them in reference to the client. Thus, the documents are always written in the third person. Writing in the third person when you are talking about yourself is very hard to do consistently. You don't need to do this. You can write in the first person to ensure you are clear. The judge isn't going to grant or deny your motion just because you didn't write in the third person.

The Motion

The very first paragraph of your document is the actual "motion" and a simple explanation of what is to come. You want to make sure your thesis statement (the main idea) is clearly stated. You want the judge to fully understand what you want as early as possible. Here are a couple of examples of openings:

Third Person

John Abner, Defendant pro se, respectfully requests the Court replace his defense counsel. Mr. Abner and defense counsel have irreconcilable differences regarding the ultimate course of this case. As a result, Mr. Abner requires a new defense lawyer who will respect his decisions about the fundamental objectives of the case.

First Person

I am writing to request the Court replace my lawyer. We are having irreconcilable differences and the relationship between us has soured to the point of no longer working. As I explain below, the law supports my request. Accordingly, I respectfully request the Court release my current defense lawyer and appoint me a new one.

The Brief

There is a method used in law that makes writing briefs much easier. It is called "IF-RAC." This stands for "issue," "facts," "rule," "analysis," and "conclusion." Following this format will ensure that your brief is clear and understandable to everyone who must read it.

Issue: The "issue" is usually presented as a question. It is the question you are asking the judge to answer. *"Is replacing defense counsel necessary and appropriate?"* It is effective to just write out the question under a heading called "Issue."

Facts: In this section, you want to present the *relevant* facts. Do not go on a diatribe regarding the entire case unless your motion requires you to do so (such as for a Motion to Suppress or a Motion to Dismiss). If a fact you present in this section does not reasonably tie back to the issue you present, then you don't need it. Remember, what you write in here could tip off the prosecution as to your strategies and what you intend on contesting. Doing that will just make sure the prosecution changes up their game.

Sticking with our example of replacing a lawyer, the facts that you present need to establish that there is an irreconcilable difference between the two of you or that communication has broken down so much that you guys can't be expected to work together any longer. This means don't present facts about the case itself. You only have to present facts that show the irreconcilable differences. Here is an example (using the first person as John Abner):

> *I am being represented by Jeremy Dewey from the law firm "Dewey, Fukem, and Howe." Over the last several weeks, I have met with Mr. Dewey three times. And at each of those meetings, Mr. Dewey just yells at me. I mean that literally. At the last visit, the jail officers had to come in and ask if everything was ok. Mr. Dewey was red in the face and screaming. At that meeting, I tried to tell Mr. Dewey that I want to go to trial. Mr. Dewey informed me that he "won't take the case to trial under any circumstance." I know I have a fundamental right to have a trial and I want to do that. Because Mr. Dewey is telling me he refuses to prepare for trial, I require a new assigned lawyer who will prepare my case for trial as is my right.*

It is far easier to write a narrative form of the facts than to try and do it like lawyers do. A judge can understand this. And, so long as John signs the document "under the penalty of perjury" then the facts will be accepted as his testimony for the purposes of the motion. **FOR THIS REASON, DO NOT LIE OR FIB ABOUT THE FACTS. TELL THE TRUTH NO MATTER HOW BAD THEY SEEM.** If you lie about the facts in any motion or brief that you write, you will find a very angry judge who will do very little to help you along while you try and navigate these choppy waters. Be honest and credible and the judge will respect you for that.

Rule: This deals with the rules of law that apply to the case. This is where you present the judge your legal argument that supports a decision in your favor. Continuing on with John, he did some research and found out that the standard to get a new lawyer appointed is that there needs to be "irreconcilable differences" or "a breakdown of communication." He has jotted down the relevant case from his circuit talking about this and writes the following in this section:

> *I have researched the legal landscape for this issue and found that the standard for replacing counsel asks whether there is an "irreconcilable difference" or "a complete breakdown of communication." If a defendant presents facts that support a finding of either of these scenarios, then there is a "justifiable" reason to replace counsel. See United States v. Grady, 997 F.2d 421, 424 (8th Cir. 1993).*

Analysis: This is where you make an argument by applying the law to your factual situation. I didn't spend a lot of time researching this example, so please **DO NOT JUST COPY IT.** Since defendants have a fundamental right to decide if the case will go to trial, then it follows a lawyer must prepare for trial if the defendant wants that to happen. Therefore, John writes this (still in the first person):

> *I believe that the facts here fall under both of these categories. First, our differences about whether I will get a trial is not a mere trial strategy disagreement but an issue of fundamental importance to me. The Supreme Court has made clear in numerous cases that whether to proceed to trial is the defendant's decision, not the lawyer's. See Jones v. Barnes, 463 U.S. 745, 751 (1983). Mr. Dewey apparently can't get past the fact that I want him to prepare a defense for trial. It doesn't matter if Mr. Dewey disagrees with my decision to go to trial or even if he thinks I could lose. It is a decision I get to make and he must abide by it. It is obvious to me that Mr. Dewey is refusing to prepare my case for trial which will certainly result in my being rendered ineffective assistance of counsel. Mr. Dewey's failure to even acknowledge that this decision is mine to make shows that there is a "complete breakdown of communication" between us. We will not be able to plan anything if every meeting is going to begin with, "I won't take this case to trial." Accordingly, I request that I be given a new lawyer to represent me.*

Conclusion: The conclusion should summarize your facts and argument and reassert exactly what you want the judge to do. There is a little legal trick that lawyers use and you should to. That's saying, "and all other relief the Court deems proper under the circumstances." Writing that at the end of your conclusion makes sure that if the judge disagrees with your specifically requested relief, but otherwise agrees with you, then there is an out for the judge to give you something. In John's case, he concludes:

> *I am aware that I have a right to decide if the case will go to trial. And it follows that a lawyer should prepare for trial and not just yell at his client that the case will never see a trial court. A lawyer who makes such a statement clearly has no intention of providing effective assistance of counsel as commanded by the Sixth Amendment. As a result, I reasonably believe there are irreconcilable differences and a breakdown of communication sufficient to warrant the substitution of counsel. Accordingly, I respectfully request that the Court please assign me a new lawyer who will be willing to at least discuss strategies that will result in a trial. Thank you.*

The very last thing you need to put in the motion is a signature block. Make sure you put the address for you at the jail (if you are in jail) so the Court can communicate with you. If you mail your motion and you are transferred, you **MUST NOTIFY THE COURT OF YOUR NEW ADDRESS**. What I did in such situations is drop a quick letter in the mail from where I was departing stating that I was "being transferred and the location is presently unknown. As soon as I find out the location and relevant address information, I will immediately notify the Court." Such a letter will put the court on notice and it only takes a second to write, put in an envelope and drop in the mail on the way out of the jail.

Motion to Proceed Pro Se

If you want to represent yourself in court you can do it. Do not wait until the day before trial to do this. It will not give you more time. If you want to proceed pro se, then do so as soon as you have made the decision to. Before we get into an actual motion, You need to understand the risks associated with doing so. Let's discuss those risks a little.

1. Lack of Law Library Access

It will be your responsibility to research the law as it relates to literally everything in your case. This includes being able to research the application of the Federal Rules of Criminal Procedure, the Federal Rules of Evidence, the local rules for the district court, jury instructions, and statutes. And that's the easy stuff. You will also be responsible for researching cases and providing argument as to your basis of application for the law. To do all of this, you need access to a law library.

Lawyers pay a lot of money to have access to comprehensive electronic law libraries through LexisNexis or Westlaw. These law libraries give real time updates to lawyers. *They are very expensive* and usually not something a pro se criminal defendant can afford. Furthermore, you can only even think of purchasing such access if you aren't in jail.

If you are in jail and decide to represent yourself, you need to recognize that you **DON'T HAVE A RIGHT TO ACCESS A LAW LIBRARY**. There are cases out there that talk about a prisoner's right of access to the courts. Those cases have to do with civil rights issues while you are locked up and doesn't provide you any protection with regard to representing yourself. If the jail you are at doesn't have a law library, then you will really have a tough job ahead of you. If the jail provides a law library of some sort, it is likely that it is incomplete.

Some jails still provide book based libraries. Book law libraries use "digests" and other research tools to locate relevant cases. This is a very hard way to do research and it is extremely unlikely a book based law library in a jail will have everything you need.

Federal Detention Centers that are run by the Federal Bureau of Prisons have an electronic law library system that is arguably sufficient for researching federal law. They do not provide any information about state law (except for DC and military). But you will have access to a multitude of cases and all the rules. They are provided through a LexisNexis program. The biggest issue with the BOP's law library is the update cycle. It doesn't happen in real time. So if there is a case that could help you that comes out, you may not even be able to read it until the update cycle completes once every couple of months.

If you are on the street, you can access some free law library resources. This includes:

Google Scholar scholar.google.com
Syracuse Law School TRAC system trac.syr.edu
Casetext (they have a 14 day free trial) casetext.com

Accessing a law library is only the tip of the iceberg. You will have to master how to use the system available to you. And you don't have that much time to do it. Legal research mastery takes a lifetime. Lawyers spend all three years of law school learning the basics of legal research. Then they spend their entire careers honing those skills. Is it possible to master legal research as a pro se litigant?

Sure. It just take a lot of time and dedication. You may have the dedication necessary, but you may not have the time.

2. Lack of Understanding of the Law and Procedural Rules

Access to a law library is only as good as your ability to comprehend everything you are reading. Legal reading is very different than any other reading you have ever done. If you are going to represent yourself, you will have to truly understand the law because if you get it wrong, the judge will just shoot you down. You will also have to follow the rules in the court. True, the judge is supposed to give you some leeway, but that doesn't mean you aren't bound by the rules. You are bound to them just like a lawyer is. Your failure to follow the rules can result in sanctions that can drastically hurt your case. Oh, and for every rule there is in law, there are a hundred cases that have interpreted each of them in one way or another. The same goes for every type of objection, every statute, every line in the Constitution, and every Supreme Court case.

3. Lack of Ability to Advocate

You will be responsible for advancing your arguments in a way that doesn't waste the judge's time. If you waste the judge's time, they will ignore you or simply tell you to move on. You being dumbfounded isn't going to help you. Advocacy is very difficult to pull off effectively. It is a thousand times harder when you are trying to advocate for yourself.

I read of an example where someone wanted to represent themselves. They filed a motion that said they wanted to represent themselves and the judge said, "sure, fine." The guy then filed a motion to suppress (which made little legal sense). The judge graciously held a hearing to hear arguments about the motion to suppress. The guy stands up and begins to try and educate the judge about the formation of the Constitution and the Fourth Amendment. What was even more nuts is the guy got the history wrong too. The judge told the defendant to move on. The defendant refused to move on. He kept going down the road of trying to educate a federal judge about the history of the Constitution. Suffice it to say that the motion to suppress was denied (very quickly) and, after he blew trial, he got 20 years in prison and is still there.

4. <u>Waiver of Ineffective Assistance of Counsel Claims</u>

If you decide to represent yourself, you will waive any later claim that you were deprived the effective assistance of counsel. That's because you were your own counsel and you can't be upset that you were bad at it.

5. <u>Jury's Don't Like Pro Se Parties</u>

We can talk about the need for a jury to be unbiased. But none of that really matters. Nobody likes to have their time wasted. A jury is selected from largely unwilling citizens. They are forced to sit there and decide if you are guilty of the crime charged. The absolute last thing they want to do is have their own time wasted. They want the case to end. Simple as that. Because pro se parties don't understand the rules very well, have a hard time effectively advocating their position, and are emotionally tied to the case, there will be significant delays that wouldn't be there if a trained lawyer was involved. Thus, you will start off the case in the hole because the jury doesn't like the fact that you are representing yourself.

6. Stand-By Counsel

Judges do not like when a pro se party goes it alone only to realize that it was a gigantic mistake. They also don't like when there are issues on the fly that you need to have answered but don't have any help. To make sure these problems don't arise, it is common for a judge to appoint "stand-by counsel" to be there just in case. Stand-by counsel is **_not_** your lawyer and has no duty to really do anything for you. Most often, they are there to help make sure any documents you want to file get filed. They are there to answer procedural questions you may have. They are **_not_** there to strategize with you. And there is nothing you can do to get rid of them. Finally, the stand-by counsel is usually the lawyer you already hate. That means if you want that lawyer gone forever, you are still going to have to file a motion to get that lawyer off the case (which you will have to show irreconcilable differences, a breakdown of communication, or a conflict of interest). Getting rid of that lawyer will **_not_** sway the judge's opinion of whether to have a stand-by counsel available for you.

With all that known, if you want to represent yourself, then you can file a motion asking for to proceed pro se. Here is a form motion you can copy to help you get there.

MOTION

Third Person

Comes Now, [Defendant's Name], Defendant pro se, with a Motion to Proceed Pro Se in the above captioned action. Defendant understands that there are many risks associated with proceeding pro se and accepts those risks. In Faretta v. California, 422 U.S. 806 (1975), the Supreme Court held that a defendant has a right to represent himself and fully reject counsel. The Court is required to hold a hearing to determine if the waiver is knowing and voluntary and further must ensure that the Defendant understands the risks of self-representation. Accordingly, Defendant respectfully requests the Court set a Faretta hearing and, after such hearing, grant this motion so Defendant can proceed pro se in this action. Defendant further requests the Court grant him all other relief deemed appropriate under the circumstances.

First Person

I am requesting to proceed pro se in my case. I understands that there are many risks associated with proceeding pro se and I accept those risks. In Faretta v. California, 422 U.S. 806 (1975), the Supreme Court held that a defendant has a right to represent himself and fully reject counsel. The Court is required to hold a hearing to determine if the waiver is knowing and voluntary and further must ensure that the defendant understands the risks of self-representation. Accordingly, I respectfully request the Court set a Faretta hearing and, after such hearing, grant this motion so I can proceed pro se in this action. I further request the Court grant me all other relief deemed appropriate under the circumstances.

Speedy Trial Demand

The right to a trial is a fundamental right that a lawyer cannot take away from you without your explicit consent. But, the right to a speedy trial is something that _can_ be waived by your silence or your lawyer's actions. That is why it is generally advisable to invoke your right to a speedy trial early so there is no confusion at all. Lawyers tend to waive defendants' speedy trial rights by asking for extensions or by failing to contest extensions requested by the prosecution. And defendants who have no idea what is going on usually just sit there and allow it to happen. We have spoken about the right to a speedy trial in general terms earlier in this book, but not as a specific strategy to employ.

The strategy is simple. Regardless of whether you are guilty or innocent of the crimes alleged, the right to a speedy trial forces the government to get off its ass and prove you committed the crimes. For federal cases, the Speedy Trial Act requires the government to take you to trial no later than 70 days following the arraignment. If you are arrested under a criminal complaint and there isn't an indictment secured yet, then the government has 30 days to get the indictment and then has 70 days to take you to trial. Pressing your speedy trial rights under this law prevents the government from gallivanting all around the world trying to develop more evidence to use against you. Instead of having time to bury you they have to prepare for a trial.

You may be thinking that invoking your right to a speedy trial would put pressure on your lawyer to prepare quickly as well and you would be right. But it is far easier to invoke your right to a speedy trial and then revoke your demand than it is to waive it and then try and get it back. That means you can demand a speedy trial and if you and your lawyer agree more time is needed then you will get it. Furthermore, putting some pressure on your lawyer isn't necessarily a bad thing either. The more the lawyer feels that you are invested in your defense the more most lawyers will work on the case. An invested client makes for an interesting case. The vast majority of criminal defendants just sit there and let the lawyer do as he pleases. This is boring for anyone. If you and the lawyer become united regarding your speedy trial rights, you will see your lawyer light up. Well, unless he really sucks. In that case, you may need to get a new lawyer.

There are some things that stop the speedy trial clock. One of these is the filing of pretrial motions that must be resolved before trial starts like motions to suppress and motions to dismiss. The filing of a motion doesn't mean that everyone can take years to get to you though. If you demanded a speedy trial, then the court should schedule time to hear your motions in a reasonable amount of time. While the judge is deciding your motion the clock stays stopped until a decision is made. Again, this is not something the judge should take too long to do but it can take a while. Thus, it is highly unlikely you would have a trial within 70 days in any event. But, when you demand your speedy trial a trial will be scheduled at the 70 day mark and the judge will set a time limit for motions to be filed. If you want to keep your speedy trial, you need to make sure your lawyer abides by these time limits strictly.

Another thing that can stop the clock is that the government can request a designation that the case is "complex." The complex case designation is something that prosecutors overuse in order to stop the 70-day time limit permanently. But the complex case status is not an automatic thing that gets granted unless your lawyer allows it. In order to stave off this designation you need to make sure your lawyer opposes the request. To do that, at the beginning of the case you need to make sure your lawyer knows that you will not tolerate a waiver of speedy trial rights for any reason and that you expect your lawyer to oppose any requests for continuances and complex case designation. If your lawyer pushes back on you about this make sure and remind him that this decision, to have a speedy trial, is a fundamental right that he must push for if that is your wish.

If you are not given a speedy trial within the time limits the case can be dismissed and you released from custody. But the only way to have this happen is if there is no evidence that you are the one delaying the trial. If you turn around and feel you need to fire your lawyer, then you would be the one who is implicitly requesting more time so a new lawyer can prepare. The judge isn't going to dismiss the case for those occurrences.

That doesn't mean you shouldn't be willing to allow your lawyer a continuance when there is a benefit of some sort coming to you. If you are hoping for a plea bargain, for instance, pushing for a speedy trial is something that can push the government to give you one. But if you are unwilling to give the lawyer and prosecutor a reasonable amount of time to talk about it, then there won't be a plea bargain. Remember that word though. **REASONABLE** is the key. Let's say your lawyer says that the prosecutor is interested in talking about a plea bargain but needs one week to get the proper authorizations. That is a reasonable request and you could easily agree to a one week continuance of the trial date. But if they try and tell you that they need three months, that isn't reasonable and you would be well justified to tell them to pound sand.

Throughout my federal case I waived my speedy trial rights routinely and had no idea the benefit of pursuing a speedy trial. And I regret it. Rather than invoke my rights, I just sat by while my lawyers sought delay after delay. They kept saying the prosecutor would give me a deal. Turns out that "deal" was horrendous and the delays just allowed the government time to put a wired snitch into my cell. Had I demanded a speedy trial, I am certain my case would have resolved more favorably for me.

After I got to federal prison, the State of Arizona sought to prosecute me for a bullshit case that carried with it a 27-year mandatory minimum consecutive to my federal term. Because of the 27-year mandatory minimum and the fact that winning a case in Arizona is very difficult to do, I really had no intention of taking the case to trial. But I also had no intention of pleading guilty. I would only agree to plead no contest and I would never agree to admit that I did anything. When I got to Arizona I had invoked my right to speedy trial during literally every court hearing and I made sure to tell my lawyer who I demanded a speedy trial. During one of the hearings we asserted that under one of the rules the Arizona courts had, they had only 30 days to take me to trial and that clock was already ticking. Everyone in the courtroom tried to get me to waive my speedy trial rights by scaring me. The prosecution was up in arms. My lawyer just sat there with a grin on his face because he knew, like I did, that I was the one with the power. The prosecutor approached my lawyer and requested a one week continuance to get the powers that be together. My lawyer informed the prosecutor right then and there that one week is all we would give and they had better come with a screaming offer if they expected me to do anything. In the end, I got a probation sentence that will never happen and I pled no-contest to a reduced charge. That speedy trial demand scared the hell out of the prosecution and gave me the upper hand

Now that we have gone over the benefits of the strategy, here are the two most effective ways to ensure your speedy trial rights are properly asserted.

Letter to Lawyer

Write a letter to your lawyer, and make sure you keep a copy of it, that says:

> *I want to make sure that you understand that I demand to have all my speedy trial rights, under the Constitution, the Speedy Trial Act, or any other applicable law, protected. I expect you, as my lawyer,* **to make sure the record adequately reflects that I do not, under any circumstance, waive these rights and in fact expressly demand a speedy trial.** *Moreover, I expect that you will oppose any and all requests for extensions of time including any requests for declaring my case complex under the Speedy Trial Act. If you require any extensions for any reason, then I request that you confer with me before requesting any extensions from the court or the prosecution. Thank you.*

If is possible, send the letter to your lawyer via certified mail and to make sure your family/friend keeps a copy and the certified mail tracking number to prove the lawyer received the letter. It will help protect you if you ever need to challenge your lawyer's conduct later. Remember, there is nothing wrong with agreeing to some delays if they are necessary (such as your lawyer is sick, you want to pursue pretrial motions that create some minor delays, etc.). The key here is to make sure your lawyer doesn't just walk into court and inadvertently waive your rights without your knowledge or consent.

Following this letter, your lawyer should file something on the court record specifically asserting your right to a speedy trial. If they don't do that (and prove it to you), then you may want to file your own notice.

Notice to the Court
(only do this of the lawyer doesn't file a provable notice)

A "Notice" is a document, that looks a lot like a motion (with a caption, signature line, etc), that is used to notify the court and parties of something. These ensure that something you want known is on the record if it is ever an issue later. In this case, you would draft a "Notice of Speedy Trial Demand" so the record clearly and unequivocally shows that you demand your speedy trial rights remain inviolate. That document should say:

> *I am the defendant in the above captioned case. I hereby notify the Court and the Government that I fully invoke all of my rights to a speedy trial as provided by the United States Constitution and the Speedy Trial Act.*

Make sure and put a caption and signature line. Then mail it to the court. You should also mail a copy to your lawyer too.

That's it. If that is on the record and speedy trial rights get waived without you present, you will have protected the record if there is an appeal later. Remember, asserting your speedy trial rights doesn't mean that you can't later waive them. You most certainly can. But make sure you are getting something in return for the waiver (such as a plea agreement for way less time)

Fighting for Bail

If you want to get bail, you need to prepare as if you are going to trial. Make no mistake, a bail hearing is like a mini-trial. You want to make sure that your lawyer is going to have at least one witness called and is going to fight to **PROVE** that you are not a flight risk or a danger to the community if you are monitored while on bail.

In some cases, the crime charged can create a presumption that the defendant is not suitable for bail. This means that you are required to prove, by a preponderance of the evidence, that you aren't a danger or a flight risk. Rather than go through the crimes where a presumption applies, let's make this really easy. **EVERYONE SHOULD APPROACH BAIL HEARINGS AS IF THE PRESUMPTION APPLIES AGAINST THEM.** If you do that, then you are going to have a hearing that really fights for your freedom. So, how do you prove all this?

Remember, detention hearings are scheduled pretty quickly. That means your lawyer isn't going to have a lot of time to prepare for it. It is on you to make sure that your lawyer has all the information they need to prove you are not a danger or a flight risk.

First, you need to decide if you would be happy with going to a halfway house pending disposition of the case. Halfway houses allow you to work in the community and access a number of other community resources, but your movements will be greatly restricted. If you violate any of the halfway house's rules, you will be hauled back into court and potentially placed in jail. And, it is likely you will feel like the restrictions are so onerous that you should get credit towards any future sentence imposed. Well, you don't get any credit whatsoever. If you decide that you are ok with going to a halfway house, then cool. But if you aren't you need to tell your lawyer ASAP. The judge will be really pissed if you go through an entire bail hearing where they grant you halfway house just to be told you don't want it. If you aren't ok with going to halfway house, then your lawyer should craft his arguments in such a way to push harder for you to go home.

Next, you need to work on proving that you aren't a flight risk. The first and last concern for the court is to determine whether you will show up for court. Federal crimes come with stiff penalties. And those penalties make everyone assume that you will just take off and go to some non-extradition country to avoid prosecution. It is well known that it is quite rare for defendants to take off. But showing that you will reduce that risk goes a long way to show that you are serious. To that end, provide your lawyer with answers to the following:

Would you agree to wear and pay for a GPS monitor?

If you aren't going to a halfway house, it is likely that you will be ordered to wear one of these anyway. If you come right out of the gate and state that you will wear one AND PAY FOR IT, you will go a long way to convincing the judge that you aren't a flight risk.

Would you agree to live with a specific person who takes responsibility for you?

This is called a "third party custodian." The more related to the person you are the better. That's because it is presumed you are less likely to screw over your own family than your friends. If there is someone who (i) has no felony convictions, (ii) is an upstanding member of society, (iii) is willing to remove items from their home as requested by probation (i.e. firearms, computers for computer offenders, etc.), and (iv) has significant ties to the community, then you should provide your lawyer with their name, address and telephone number. If there isn't anyone to take responsibility for you, then the needle ticks closer to halfway house placement than home placement. But that doesn't mean if you don't have anyone that you can't argue for staying home. It's just harder.

What conditions would you agree to?

While you are out on bail, there are a number of required conditions that will be placed on you to restrict your freedom. There are also discretionary conditions the court could impose beyond those that are required by the statute. For instance, if you are alleged to have committed a computer based or internet based offense, there will likely be a restriction on access to the internet and internet capable devices (including cell phones). If you are willing to pay for the probation office's monitoring software, then the condition could be loosened.

Another condition that is common is a curfew condition. This is especially so for drug offenders and other offenses that are commonly committed at night. You may also not be allowed to go to a bar, drink alcohol, or take any medications not prescribed by a physician. Your lawyer should be able to provide you with a list of the common conditions that are imposed on defendants when granted bail by contacting probation.

What are your ties to the community?

You need to tell your lawyer about any jobs that you have (and hopefully still have), any property you own, the names of friends and all family in the area, and all the other reasons you have to stick around. Provide your lawyer a list of these things so they can reference it easily. There is no such thing as being too detailed with this. The more you can prove community ties, the greater likelihood you have of proving you aren't a flight risk.

What is your financial condition?

If you are financially stable in that you have savings, stock accounts, and access to cash flow, it shows that you can take care of yourself while you are out on bail. This reduces the likelihood that you would resort to criminal activity to support yourself thereby showing the court that you aren't a potential danger to the community. If you are bordering on bankruptcy, it is going to make the judge a little nervous. Nobody is financially perfect in the criminal justice community. So don't try and show yourself as perfect. Just be honest with your lawyer about your finances so they have the information if they need it.

What are your philanthropic activities?

While you are on bail, it is unlikely that you will be engaged in too much philanthropy. But showing the court that you support your community in some appreciable way helps show that you have no desire to leave it and further are not a danger to it. If you are alleged to have committed a crime through philanthropy (such as defrauding a non-profit or abusing kids by accessing a non-profit), then you probably don't want to point to anything in particular. However, you should still speak with your lawyer about this because they may be able to craft an argument showing that, despite the allegation, your philanthropic endeavors are positive indicators of your community worth.

Do you have other any pending criminal or civil court issues?

If you have any outstanding traffic tickets or warrants for failure to appear, you want to make sure your lawyer knows about those things. If they are catching you totally by surprise, then you and your lawyer may want to try and delay the detention hearing until you can get those things straightened out. And by "straightened out," I mean dismissed. Further, if you have any pending civil issues, such as a lawsuit against you, you need to explain it to your criminal defense lawyer. Finally, if you have a criminal history, do not let your lawyer get blindsided by it. Negative issues need to be dealt with up front if you have any hope of being granted bail.

In my own case, the prosecutor made an argument that I would never show up for court because I had a failure to appear warrant for a traffic ticket. The prosecutor told the magistrate that my failure to appear showed I have "no respect for the duty of a magistrate" to hear civil traffic issues. And, according to the prosecutor, if I don't respect a state magistrate, then why would I respect a federal judge? It was an outlandish argument, but it is one that the magistrate bought. The magistrate in the federal detention hearing even repeated the comment to stress that he believed I had no respect for magistrates specifically. My lawyer had no idea how to deal with this.

DEFENSE MOTION FOR RELEASE

After your lawyer has all the information you can give them, they need to draft and file a Motion for Release Pending Trial. In many state systems, lawyers will just walk in to court and have arguments for about five minutes so a judge can decide. That is not the case in the federal system and if your lawyer doesn't want to file a formal written motion and brief, you should be wary of their representation of you. Federal judges like to stew over things and the vast majority of bail and sentencing decisions are made while the judge is in his office (or on the throne!). If your lawyer doesn't file a formal motion and brief, then the judge has nothing to consider **_before_** a hearing kicks off. The motion and brief should outline everything that proves you are not a flight risk or a danger to the community. It should bring forward the law on bail for the judge to consider. And it should give the judge something to really think about. If all the judge has is a Motion for Detention (guess who files that?), then that is what will be on the top of their mind throughout. Even if your lawyer needs an extra week to draft this, it is better for you to allow them that week than to skip this.

DEFENSE RESPONSE TO MOTION FOR DETENTION

If the government files a motion for detention, your lawyer needs to provide a *written* response to it. In fact, you have a right to file such a response. Too many lawyers just figure they can deal with it all at the hearing. No! No! No! Your lawyer needs to make sure and temper whatever blows the government throws and also needs to show where the government is full of crap. They routinely stretch the facts, or even invent them, to help their detention case. For these reasons, it is required that your lawyer draft a response to the government's arguments and rendition of facts. In order to respond properly, your lawyer absolutely must let you read and review the document. If you notice anything that is false, you need to put a big star on it and explain to your lawyer how it is false. Any time your lawyer can destroy the prosecutor's credibility to the judge, he should. They walk into court with a presumption of being credible just because they are prosecutors and it is sickening because they usually b.s. their way through everything. Make sure your lawyer takes the opportunity to ruin the prosecutor a little.

You may be wondering if attacking the prosecutor is such a good idea. Hell, your lawyer may question the strategy of casting the prosecutor in a negative light. Remember, that person is trying to take your freedom away (potentially forever) and has zero care for who you are or what your freedom means to you and your family. Using every public opportunity to make the prosecutor's life a living hell seems like that is precisely the job they signed up for. Moreover, if your lawyer is the one questioning whether to destroy the prosecutor's credibility, then you should be questioning if they are there to defend you or to make the prosecutor happy. You definitely do not want a lawyer who cares one iota about the prosecutor's happiness.

Now, you and your lawyer have enough information to actually fight for Bail. Remember that you don't get any credit for time served while you are on house arrest, in a halfway house, or in any other environment than a jail or prison during this time.

Correcting the Record

Even though you are the employer and the lawyer is the employee, lawyers tend to take significant liberties with nearly every facet of your case. Sure, that's why you hired them. But, what happens when the lawyer makes a claim that is false, misleading, or otherwise not in line with your instructions? What happens when that claim is made to the judge on the case? These kinds of problems can be disastrous for you and their effects can linger for many years. If your lawyer refuses to correct the record, then you will have to do something to protect your rights. That may include getting a new lawyer.

The record is **your** friend. It is one way to keep everyone in the courtroom honest. Everything that is said in court is recorded in some way (whether it be by tape recording or someone sitting there typing everything out). Every document that goes in front of a judge is saved in the court file and will remain there for many years. If you ever want to file an appeal, the appeal court will rely solely on the record in the district court to determine if you should win your appeal. If it isn't on the record, then as far as the appeal court is concerned it never happened. If something is said on the record that you try and contradict later, the record will control. It doesn't matter how much you yell and holler. If you don't get the correct information on the record, you will never be able to contradict it. For instance, if the record says that you said you were guilty, there is nothing you can do to change anyone's mind that you are guilty. And, yes, prisoners try and do precisely that every day.

Let me tell you two true stories about this very issue. The first one involves a guy who didn't commit the crime. In fact, all the evidence showed that there was no possible way for the guy to have committed the crime. But, his lawyer came to him with a plea agreement and told the guy that if he lost at trial he would get life. The guy took the deal and walked into court and said that he was "in fact, Guilty." He got the benefit of the deal which was 3 years in prison and most of the charges were dropped. After good time credits and taking the drug program, he would be out in about a year and a half. When the guy got to prison he had buyer's remorse. He came to me and requested that we file a motion attacking his conviction and say that he is innocent and his lawyer pressured him. But the record told a very different story. Indeed, the judge specifically asked him if he was pressured to plead guilty. His answer was a very clear "no." The judge also asked a lot of questions to make sure that he knew that nobody in the world could make him plead guilty. He stated his understanding. Finally, the judge asked if he understood that there is generally no backing out of the deal. He voiced his agreement. So, when we filed the motion to attack the conviction and tried to assert that he was innocent, the prosecutor and judge concentrated on those in court statements and didn't care about any of the evidence that demonstrated he was innocent. The judge essentially ruled that, because the guy went into court and voluntarily pleaded guilty, there was nothing that could be done. In this type of case, the record was tainted by the defendant himself, and not his attorney. But the point should be clear. If you are going to lie on the record, even to take a deal, then that lie will become the truth forever. It is next to impossible to overturn the conviction in such instances.

The second story involves a guy who got smart. His lawyer was not doing a damn thing to help him. After the first meeting, the lawyer instructed the guy to plead guilty to armed bank robbery. The guy kept saying he didn't do it and that he wanted to go to trial. The lawyer just wouldn't listen. So, this guy decided to send a letter to the judge and ask for a new lawyer. He didn't use the words "irreconcilable differences" in his letter so the judge denied the request without a hearing. The guy went to trial and lost. He was sentenced to 13 years in prison and started the appeal process. His old lawyer was still on the case and that became a big problem. The lawyer dragged his feet for years and then filed an "Anders Brief" which is a brief that says there are no issues for an appeal court to consider. In layman terms, it meant the lawyer was conceding the appeal. But there was an issue for the appeals court to consider: the letter requesting a new lawyer and its denial. I pointed out to the Court of Appeals that the guy requested a new lawyer and in his letter said the lawyer was "evasive and uncooperative" with the defendant, it was the same as saying irreconcilable differences and he should have gotten a new lawyer. The Court of Appeals denied the Anders Brief, ordered a new lawyer, requested the new lawyer brief the letter issue, and even reprimanded the old lawyer by preventing him from taking any more cases in that court.

Just one simple letter to a judge is the basis for giving this guy a brand new trial. The government has fought this letter tooth and nail but they don't have a leg to stand on because they didn't say anything about it in the district court. It just went ignored by literally everyone. The moral of the story is that this guy protected the record. He made sure the record very clearly showed that he wanted a new lawyer and stated his reason for it. The second the district court denied his letter request, it created an appealable issue.

Think of correcting the record as putting bullets to the side in case you need them later on. Once you notify a court there is a problem they should deal with it. If they don't deal with it, or they deal with it incorrectly, then there is an issue for appeal preserved for you.

Failing to speak the truth is a sin in a courtroom that no judge should forgive. The whole purpose of court is to bring the truth forward and apply the law to it. If your lawyer is someone who is loose with the truth, then you not only need a new lawyer, but you need to ensure that the record properly reflects that truth. Lawyers are not witnesses to the case so they can't introduce facts without evidence. Thus, when a lawyer fails to speak the truth, it is usually regarding a legal position. The legal positions you are always worried about are: waivers of your rights, concessions of facts, and stipulating the authenticity of evidence. In a civil case, it is routine to concede facts and stipulate that certain evidence is authentic. But, in a criminal case, the Constitution places the duty to prove each and every detail of the case beyond a reasonable doubt on the government. So, why would you want to make their life easier? Unless you and your lawyer discussed a strategy that involves waivers, concessions or stipulations, then you absolutely do not want to make their life any easier. The government is trying to take away your freedom. Don't help them do it.

If your lawyer says something that is patently false, waives your right to something, concedes facts that you were unaware of, or stipulates to the authenticity of evidence without first consulting with you then you need to follow these steps to ensure that the record is protected:

Step One: Stand up and wait until the judge recognizes you. As soon as the judge asks you what you need, simply state, "Your Honor. Can I please speak with my lawyer for a minute?" If the Marshals in the courtroom prevent you from standing up, don't fight them or anything (that's a really bad idea). Simply speak up and say, "Excuse me your Honor. Can I please speak with my lawyer for a minute?"

Step Two: When your lawyer comes over, tell him what he said that was wrong. For instance, if your lawyer just said that you intend on pleading guilty, but you have not made a decision either way, then you need to tell your lawyer, "I never said I would plead guilty. I want you to make it clear on the record that I never made any such decision." If your lawyer just messed up some key fact, then tell him what was wrong about what he said. If he starts conceding facts and helping the government prove their case, you should tell him to withdraw that concession unless you were previously aware that the concession would be made.

Step Three: If your lawyer corrects the record then all is well. Sit down and allow the hearing to go forward. If your lawyer tells you that he isn't going to correct the record, or it becomes apparent that he is not going to correct the record, then you need to correct the record. To do that, you simply (stand up or speak up depending on your first interaction with the Marshals) ask the judge if you could say something. "Your Honor. Can I say something on the record really quickly?"

Step Four: If the judge tells you that you are not allowed to say something on the record, then just sit down and go to Step Six-B. If the judge tell you to "proceed" or "go ahead" or anything else that says you can speak, then you need to say, "Your Honor, my attorney stated that I intend to plead guilty. I would like the record to reflect that I never made any decision about pleading guilty and at this point I am still invoking all my constitutional rights."

Step Five: If you are noticing a pattern that demonstrates your lawyer is not advocating properly for you (i.e. he keeps lying or conceding issues that you don't agree with), then you need to also state, "Your Honor. My attorney and I seem to have irreconcilable differences on major issues regarding the course of this case. For instance, my attorney keeps telling the [court/prosecutor] information that is simply not correct. I specifically instructed my lawyer who I will not waive any of my constitutional rights, but he keeps asserting on the record that I am waiving things. Since we are having irreconcilable differences, I respectfully ask the court to appoint me new counsel." This step can also be done by filing a motion if you don't feel comfortable saying all this with the lawyer standing next to you.

DO NOT ABUSE THIS. If you keep firing lawyers, the judge will eventually force you to represent yourself. It also will not work if all you are trying to do is delay a trial. If your lawyer legitimately is not doing what he is supposed to be doing and you can prove it, then you absolutely should request a new lawyer. Even if you have a paid lawyer, you can ask the judge to appoint one because of irreconcilable differences. If you want to hire another lawyer instead, you can do it quietly and the new lawyer will take care of letting the court know. Since you don't have to pay for an appointed lawyer though, it may be better to just ask for appointed counsel until you can find another retained lawyer. That way, at least someone is available to defend you.

Step Six-A: Wait a second to see if the judge has any questions of you. If the judge starts talking to lawyers in the room, then it should be ok to sit down. But, if the judge acknowledges you and the judge starts asking you questions, answer them honestly. If the judge does not acknowledge you then sit down. What you said is now on the permanent record and that is the goal. If there is an appeal or later proceeding where you want to point to this disagreement, you can. In your pretrial notebook, make sure to note the date and time that you said what you said so you can point the judge to it if you ever need to later.

Step Six-B: If the judge refuses to let you speak on the record, you need to file a motion to correct the record. However, before you do that, you should have another talk with your lawyer to see if he will correct it. You should stress to your lawyer who you are upset about what he said in court and you want the record to be corrected immediately. You should also instruct the lawyer to give you a file stamped copy of the document he files correcting the record. If your lawyer refuses to correct the record or refuses to prove that he corrected the record in a reasonable amount of time, then - and only then - should you file something with the court.

Step Seven: If you haven't fired your lawyer, then you need to have a "coming to Jesus" meeting with him. You need to make sure the lawyer understands what he did wrong and what he is expected to do to prevent it from happening in the future. More than anything, the lawyer needs to understand that you are aware he can be fired and a new lawyer be appointed. If you paid the lawyer, and you followed everything about getting a written contract, then the lawyer will know that you can - and will - seek to have your money returned for breach of contract at the very least.

If you intend on correcting the record in writing, you need to follow some very simple rules to make sure you don't later hurt yourself. Remember, everything said on the record, whether written or spoken, is saved forever. And what is said there is far more powerful than anything said in any other forum.

Rule 1
Only say what is absolutely necessary to achieve your goal.

If you are trying to get a new lawyer because of irreconcilable differences, you do not want to go into the details of your defense. It is probably the most violated rule by defendants and it serves to haunt them for years to come. If your lawyer is telling you that you have absolutely no defense and that he won't take your case to trial no matter what you say, then all you need to say is just that. You do not need to go into the details of the strengths or weaknesses of your case. If you do mention these things, all you are doing is telling the prosecutor your strategies and intentions.

Similarly, if you are just trying to make sure the record is clear as to some intention (like, you don't waive a specific right) then you simply state that and nothing more. "I wanted to make sure the record clearly reflected that I am not waiving my right to [INSERT WHAT YOU DON'T WANT TO WAIVE HERE]." Nothing else needs to be said.

Rule 2
Do not lie.

Whenever you write something to the judge, whether it is a motion or a letter to ensure the record is reflected properly, you should put the following phrase at the beginning:

> "I declare under the penalty of perjury that the following statements I make are true and correct."

At the end of your motion, letter, or other written document, you should write:

> "I declare the above statements are true and correct under the penalty of perjury."

What this says is that you are willing to be prosecuted if they find out you are lying. If you don't lie, then you have nothing to worry about. Everything you put in the document between those phrases is now "sworn" testimony to the judge.

A lot of defendants have asked me what the harm in putting little white lies in a document is. It seems pretty harmless. But, it absolutely destroys your credibility with the judge if it is found out. And make no mistake, if the prosecution can prove you lied, they will do it. They want to bury you and lying only helps them do that.

Little white lies, especially those that are obviously false, also serve to have your requests denied by the judge. If they can't believe you on things that are provable, then why in the world should they listen when you have a he-said-she-said claim? When you make a claim that your lawyer, for instance, is not representing you appropriately and you say "irreconcilable differences" but you throw in some lie to try and make the lawyer seem worse than they are, the judge will probably deny your request. If the judge grants your request, your own lawyer will probably start defending himself to the judge and now you have made yet another enemy. **<u>DO NOT LIE.</u>**

Does that mean you have to say everything? Hell no. That is why you need to keep your statements to a judge short and sweet.

Rule 3
Be courteous and professional.

Discourtesy and unprofessionalism are a sure fire way to get a judge to turn against you. Being courteous to your lawyer, the prosecutor and the judge shows respect for the system that you are dealing with. Sure, the system has a long way to go to be properly fair, but it is still a great system of law. Courtesy and professionalism also does not mean that you aren't fighting back.

In history, even warriors had times of significant courtesy for each other. Indeed, during the Civil War, General Robert E. Lee and General Ulysses S. Grant met and discussed the terms of the South's surrender. They didn't walk in to the negotiation and bash each other. They were both obviously very much divided as to their loyalties, but they were professional. That professionalism saved the lives of thousands of people and allowed for our country to begin healing.

It seems most defendants confuse zeal with anger. Zeal means that you are passionate about your position but you don't exude hate to the person standing next to you. They may be lying about you. They may even hate you. In the end, professionalism is the name of the game.

Rule 4
Don't pretend to be a lawyer.

Perhaps the worst mistake a criminal defendant can make is to pretend he is a lawyer by attempting to use legalese (Latin and French phrases) when they have zero idea what those foreign phrases even mean. Federal district judges are lawyers. They are usually very good lawyers. They may not agree with certain positions, but they know the law. And they know it well. The most annoying thing a judge must do is try and decipher a criminal defendant's writings when those writings incorrectly use legal jargon. What's more is that most judges hate that jargon anyway because it is tedious.

I remember reading a pro se motion to a court that began:

> "*Comes now, the defendant, pro se, in propria persona, and sui juris...*"

I am certain that any judge who read that line had visions of homicide, or even suicide, because all the guy said in plain English was, "I am the defendant representing myself, representing myself, and representing myself..." Yes, those words all say the same thing, just in Latin and French. As it turns out, the guy who wrote that line was selling legal assistance to inmates and did not do a very good job.

When defendants use tons of legal jargon, they take away from the meat of the issue. Imagine trying to read your favorite novel and it alternating from Latin to English and back to Latin. You would spend so much time trying to translate the Latin that you would likely forget the plot altogether. When you are advocating some position to a judge, it is very bad to make them have to figure out what you want. And you definitely don't want them contemplating their own demise when reading it!

Instead, just speak plain English. Use proper grammar. And check your spelling. Doing just that has won several people their lives from death row. If you aren't a great speller and you don't have a spell checker, then have someone proofread it for you. The key with any writing is to be understandable to the reader. Just because you believe you said it, doesn't mean that the reader will see your point. Having someone read it and simply tell you what they think your writing is about will tell you if your writing is clear.

Rule 5
Don't be scared.

Your life is on the line and if you feel you need to say something, then you should say it. That doesn't mean go off half-cocked and start cursing the judge, prosecutor and anyone else you can think of. But, if you have something to say that is directly relevant and is necessary to protect you, then by all means say it. There is little, if anything, a judge can do to you for speaking up when there is an injustice that you want to prevent. I mean, you are already indicted, being prosecuted and likely sitting in jail at this point. They can't take away your birthday. So, don't be scared. Speak up.

☐

Plea Bargaining

Whatever might be the situation in an ideal world, the fact is that the guilty plea and the often concomitant plea bargain are important components of this country's criminal justice system. Properly administered, they can benefit all concerned. The defendant avoids extended pretrial incarceration and the anxieties and uncertainties of a trial; he gains a speedy disposition of his case, the chance to acknowledge his guilt, and a prompt start in realizing whatever potential there may be for rehabilitation. Judges and prosecutors conserve vital and scarce resources. The public is protected from the risks posed by those charged with criminal offenses who are at large on bail while awaiting completion of criminal proceedings.

Justice Potter Stewart
United States Supreme Court
Blackledge v. Allison, 431 U.S. 63
May 2, 1977

WARNING: CRIMINAL DEFENDANTS DO NOT HAVE A RIGHT TO BE OFFERED A PLEA BARGAIN. MANY INMATES TELL OTHERS THAT YOU SHOULD ALWAYS REJECT THE FIRST OFFER. BE VERY CAREFUL WHEN YOU DECIDE TO REJECT AN OFFER. THE GOVERNMENT MAY NOT COME BACK WITH ANY OTHERS. IN THE FEDERAL SYSTEM, PROSECUTORS WILL PLAY HARDER BALL THAN STATE PROSECUTORS. WEIGH EVERY OFFER SERIOUSLY BEFORE DECIDING TO REJECT THEM!

Plea bargaining is a significant part of a criminal defense. The ultra majority of federal criminal cases end by a guilty plea and, if you can get the government to stipulate to a specific sentence or charges, then you should do it. Right? Well, not always. A plea bargain is a contract between you and the government. The government expects you to plead guilty and you expect something in return for pleading guilty. If you get very little in return, then you probably don't want to sign the agreement. But, if you are getting a good deal, then you probably want to sign the agreement.

Sadly, criminal defendants tend to have zero idea what makes up a good agreement or a bad agreement. Instead, the depend on their attorney to advise them about the terms of the agreement. And they almost always do so to their own detriment. Here, we will discuss what makes up a proper plea bargain contract, how to understand that plea bargain contract and how to determine if you are getting something worth *your* while. We are also going to discuss ways to protect yourself from bad lawyering and shifty prosecutors.

What are contracts generally?

Contracts have been a fact of the business world for centuries. Back in the 1960's the United States Supreme Court evaluated whether contracts were permitted in criminal cases and expressly held that they are. And while the plea agreement is technically a contract, certain rules are placed upon the government to ensure that you are properly protected.

In order for a contract to be valid there must be four elements: offer, acceptance, consideration and performance. If any of these elements are missing, there is no contract. Interestingly, criminal attorneys on both sides of the aisle honestly have little idea of what makes a proper contract. Business lawyers have read criminal plea agreements and are appalled at what they have in them. What's of utmost concern to you, is "consideration." Consideration is the principle that the parties must make some valuable exchange. In the criminal world, the defendant gives up all of his constitutional rights to a public jury trial, placing the ultimate burden of proof on the government and avoid self incrimination. The prosecution will make some concession of some sort. The problem is the prosecutor and defense lawyer will push you to believe that some concessions are worth a lot when they are not.

Considering a plea agreement.

Most times a lawyer will come to their client and say the government made "an offer" that he should consider. Any time an offer is made, the lawyer absolutely must tell you about it no matter what your position is. The problem with most "offers" is they aren't necessarily in writing. Writing is key because nobody can contest what the words on the paper say. If the offer is merely verbal, everyone's understanding is contestable. If your lawyer comes to you and says there is "an offer" from the government, then you should ask to see whatever they wrote. If they sent an email making an offer, then tell your lawyer you want to see the email. If nothing is in writing, but what the lawyer says sounds good, then you should say, "I am interested assuming what you are telling me is accurate. I will need to see it in writing before I can confirm whether I will accept however."

Some lawyers will pressure you by saying "it's take it or leave it" and "the prosecutor is going to mad if I ask for it in writing." Don't listen to such garbage. If the prosecutor is really that dense, then ask your lawyer to schedule a Frye Hearing. At the Frye Hearing tell the judge that you wanted to consider the offer but you were told that it could not be provided in writing prior to acceptance. No judge in his right mind would argue with you that a refusal to reduce the offer to writing is ridiculous. The benefit of a Frye Hearing is that the judge will be told the exact terms of the plea bargain offer and then you can seriously consider it. Just ask the judge if you can think about it because you were unaware of the specific terms of the offer. The judge will probably give you a few hours to a couple of days to consider the offer.

There is one exception to this rule and that's if trial is about to occur. It does happen that a prosecutor will make an offer just before a jury is selected or even after one is empaneled. In that situation, if you are interested, just have your lawyer jot down the offer on a piece of paper so both you and the prosecutor can sign it. If the offer is serious, then there will be no objection to that piece of paper being filed on the public record.

Understanding the Written Contract

Prosecutors invariably draft the plea agreement. They all contain legalese which confuses the most educated people. That doesn't mean you should just sign it. You should seek to *understand literally every single term* the contract has in it.

First things first. **READ THE CONTRACT.** Read it word-for-word, line-for-line, and page-for-page. Any word, phrase or sentence that you do not understand should be written down so you can ask your lawyer to explain the word. **DO NOT FEEL RUSHED. Do not accept that you only have a few minutes to consider the agreement.** While a contract can have a time limit put on it, if that time limit is ridiculous, then you should reject the offer as not understandable and tell your lawyer precisely that. One way to give you some time with the agreement is to ask your lawyer to schedule a *Frye* Hearing of they put pressure on you.

What type of plea agreement do you have?

Next, you need to determine what type of plea agreement it is. In federal procedure, there are three (3) types of plea agreements. All plea agreements are governed by Federal Rule of Criminal Procedure 11(c).

The first type of plea agreement is one where the government agrees to dismiss or not to bring further charges. This type of plea agreement is actually contained in almost every plea agreement because it is routine for the government to agree not to bring any further charges out of the facts that gave rise to the case in the first place. Aside from that blanket statement, the government can simply agree to not bring specific charges or will move to dismiss already brought charges to reduce your overall exposure. These agreements, however, do not provide that much protection to the defendant since the judge is allowed to consider uncharged or dismissed conduct when fashioning sentence. The biggest benefit from this type of agreement is that your statutory minimums and maximums *could* be contained. I say "*could*" because if you are charged with three counts that all have a potential maximum of **LIFE** and the government agrees to dismiss two counts, it is not likely a good agreement standing alone to accept it as you are still facing life and you only have one of those to give.

The second type of agreement is called a "non-binding agreement." What that means is that if you sign it, the government's promises only bind the prosecution and *not the judge*. So, if the prosecutor agrees to make a recommendation that you should get a specific sentence, or that you should get a full acceptance of responsibility reduction, or that you should fall in to a specific range of sentences, <u>**it is only a RECOMMENDATION**</u>. The judge can reject it outright and sentence you within the statutory minimum or maximum as the judge sees fit. The benefit of such an agreement is that the government is bound to voice its recommendation and cannot contradict it. But the government can, and will, give the judge all the bad facts it wants about you which, in and of itself, could push the judge to impose a higher sentence. The other benefit of this type of agreement is it allows you to argue for a lower sentence than the recommendation the government agreed to give. The downside of these agreements is that you can't get out of it if the judge rejects it. In many ways, it is better to just enter an open plea rather than take a non-binding plea because all you get is a recommendation anyway. If you reject the plea, the only difference is that the prosecutor will argue for whatever sentence they want to argue for.

The third type of agreement is called a "binding agreement." That means if you sign it and the judge accepts the agreement, the judge *must* give you everything agreed to in the contract. If the judge rejects it, then the judge must allow you to withdraw your guilty plea and set the case for trial if you want to. It is quite rare for a judge to reject these types of plea agreements but it does happen. It usually happens when the judge perceives your conduct as far more serious than the government does and the judge isn't going to let such a low sentence be imposed. In that case, you *may* be better off demanding the trial. The other reason a judge may reject the agreement is if the sentence is too harsh. In that situation, you may want to proceed with sentencing. Suffice it to say that the judge will let everyone know why it is rejected.

What are you getting?

You need to take out a sheet of paper and write down everything that you are getting in return for accepting the plea. If there is going to be a dismissal of charges, write down those charges. Write down what counts you will be pleading to. Make sure to put their minimum and maximum sentences so you know what you are facing under the plea agreement too.

All too often, defendants are given a plea agreement that says the defendant will get a three point reduction from the Guidelines for entering into the agreement. Is that a deal? Hell no. If you plead guilty, you are probably going to get at least two points for acceptance of responsibility. The third point is something the government moves for if you save them time and money. The vast majority of people who plead guilty without a plea agreement get a reduction for acceptance of responsibility. That means the stipulation for acceptance of responsibility means next to nothing. Defense lawyers will try and push their clients to take an agreement that dismisses charges so there is "only" one count and "gives" the three point reduction. After the defendant is sentenced, he finds out that his guideline range was the same either way. He got nothing special but a waiver of his trial and appeal rights. He could have entered an open plea and been able to at least file an appeal.

You want to see things of serious value be given to you in the written agreement. Things of value include:

- ✓ reduced sentence
- ✓ reduced sentencing range
- ✓ reduced charge to plead guilty to
- ✓ lower potential mandatory minimum that previously available
- ✓ The Safety Valve

✓ agreement to not pursue any other charges

Things that are said to be of value but really aren't include:

➢ An agreement to ask for the **low-end** of the calculated guidelines range but **not** agree to lock in any specific range (over 90% of all sentences imposed give the low-end of the guidelines range anyway and when the range isn't locked in, it can spiral out of control; the low end of life is life by the way),

➢ Acceptance of Responsibility Points (they are awarded regardless of an agreement but you sometimes have to fight for them by specifically asking the judge for it).

The Safety Valve

If you intend on pleading guilty to a drug offense and certain other conditions apply, the court may impose a sentence below the mandatory minimum. This only applies to drug offenses and the other criteria must be met for this to apply. Since the Guidelines have not been updated since 2018, the First Step Act amendment that applies to the safety valve is not discussed in the Guidelines. The U.S. Sentencing Commission is currently in talks to amend the Guidelines and we expect those later this year (2023). What we discuss below does not mention the Guidelines because of this. You need to check the Guidelines if you are reading this after November of 2023 to see if any of the criteria were updated or changed at all.

Lawyers generally tell their clients that they got an "offer" for the safety valve. **<u>YOU DON'T NEED A PLEA AGREEMENT TO GET THE SAFETY VALVE.</u>** Congress made it a law, not a bargaining chip. That means if the government isn't giving you more than the safety valve, then it may be a good idea to reject it. If the government "offers" you a safety valve and agrees to lock in a sentence below the mandatory minimum through a C-Plea or at least agrees to a Guidelines range below the mandatory minimum, then it could be good to accept. There are pitfalls to accepting an agreement for a safety valve though.

The safety valve has five criteria. Well, its six if you count the fact that the crime **MUST BE A DRUG OFFENSE.** You cannot plead guilty to anything else. For instance, if you plead to a drug crime and a firearms offense, then you can't get the safety valve. The other five criteria are:

✓ You can't have more than 4 criminal history points, but you don't count any 1-point offenses, and you can't have a countable 3-point or 2-point offense at all (if they are too old to be counted, then for this, you are good);

✓ You can't be found by the court to have used violence or even a "credible threat of violence," and you can't be found to have possessed a firearm at all or other dangerous weapon (this means that if you get 2 points for a weapon, you won't qualify)

✓ Your offense could not have resulted in death or serious bodily injury to anyone (if they prove someone died from your drug crime, then you won't qualify)

✓ You can't be given leader, organizer, manager or supervisor points

✓ You **MUST** provide all truthful information known by you about your offense

Many defendants see the part about providing information to the government and cringe. Most defendants do not want to be snitches. And, with few exceptions, getting a safety valve does not make you a snitch. You are only required to provide information about **your** offenses. That doesn't mean you need to provide any specific names of people or anything unless you were part of a conspiracy. If you are pleading guilty to a conspiracy, you are going to implicate your buddies in the conspiracy anyway because they are usually named in the indictment. What you say during the "debrief" with the government cannot be used to further enhance your sentence either. Finally, even if you only have information in your possession that the government already has, you still can qualify for the safety valve.

The debrief is the most contested part of this whole process. Even if you have an agreement with the government, they may come out and say you lied or didn't provide all relevant information. Sadly, most lawyers do not get the debriefing transcribed and they should to avoid this very problem. The debrief should happen with a court reporter physically present or at least on tape to ensure the government can't claim you are lying. If they are not ok with that, then tell your lawyer to ask the judge to have a hearing to conduct the debrief. Your lawyer should be able to easily argue that the government routinely claims defendants are not completely truthful and it is on the defendant to prove he met the requirement. The only way to prove this is with a record. If the judge won`t give a hearing and the prosecutor won`t allow the debrief to be recorded word-for-word, then tell you may want to ask your lawyer to detail for you exactly how you guys will *prove* that you told the truth and that you provided all relevant information. If your lawyer tells you that you don`t have to worry about proving this, you should probably fire him on the spot. It is well established that the **DEFENDANT** bears the burden of proof as to the elements of a safety valve application.

Cooperation Agreements and 5K1.1 Motions

There are a number of defendants who will choose to "cooperate" with the government in prosecuting other individuals. While I don't personally condone this conduct, the fact remains that there are people out there who will do it. And, if you decide that you want to provide information to the government to help prosecute someone else, there are some things you need to know.

Snitches have a number of names in prison. They are called "case jumper," "informant," "snitch," and "rat." In legal terms, A case jumper is someone who helps the government prosecute someone from a totally different case. An informant is someone who is working with the government to set up someone (like in drug buys). And a snitch is someone who starts singing after committing a crime to save their own skin. The biggest problem with cooperators is they usually lie in order to get the deal they are after. If you are one of the people who plans on telling a bunch of lies to get your own ass out of trouble, then know this: Karma is a fickle bitch. That isn't a threat by any means. **You** will have to survive in prison and pray that politically motivated prisoners never find out that you are "hot." In today's cell phone laden world, even prisoners find out about cooperators in a matter of minutes. And, make no mistake, they don't care about the rules either. You also may have to testify in front of the very people you decide to tell on. The prosecutor can fill your head with all manner of lies as to how you will be protected. But that only can go so far and it certainly won't stop your target, or his friends, or his family, from figuring out who you are if there is a trial. Most snitches operate under the assumption that there won't be a trial. While that is a fairly safe assumption given that 95% of cases end with a plea, the fact remains that the prosecutor **cannot** promise a case won't see a trial if they intend on charging a crime. As you know now, only the defendant can decide if he will plead guilty.

In all events, if you are going to take a deal to cooperate then you need to be really careful and read the deal meticulously. If there is something you think you are getting, then you need to make sure it is in the written deal explicitly. Beyond the typical things to watch out for in a plea agreement, you also need to watch out for the government's use of "discretionary" language. Your lawyer won't even point this stuff out to you but it will haunt you. Discretionary language involves using words like, "In the sole discretion of the government..." or "as determined by the government..." or something to that effect. The government uses this language to renege on the deal every day of the week and they do it without any remorse. Be very careful of language that says they will be the sole decision maker as to whether they will file the 5K1.1 motion too. It is routine for prosecutors to use that language to screw you over.

You have to take apart the contract and really figure out all the ways the government can get out of it. If they put a clause in the contract that allows them to withhold the promised motion if they decide if you are lying, then rest assured they will say you are lying. There is nothing in the contract to protect you from such a decision, so why wouldn't they. The government has their cake and eats it too!

You would think that I am trying to scare you out of cooperating. Maybe I am, but I have helped a number of people who have suffered through this very problem. If I were in this position, I would insist on the lawyer getting some more assurances that a motion would be filed or to have a third-party involved in deciding if the information is "false" or an intentional lie. I would also insist that there is some language in the agreement that doesn't allow the government to suggest what the "truth" is in order to meet their own goals.

I realize that the demands I would put on the table or not ones that prosecutors would like by any means and it could mean the end of the deal. Since I haven't ever been in that situation, it is easy for me to say. But the point should be clear. If you are going to make a deal with the devil, then make sure you are a devil about the details. The government will use every loophole it puts into its own contract and will hang you out to dry.

Finally, if you cooperate, do yourself a favor and don't advertise it to people in the prison system. I thought this would go without saying, but I have seen people walk in and talk about cooperating as if there is nothing to it. Their prison bids are not comfortable. Even if the guy doesn't get jumped, he will be run out of every housing unit he goes to, will learn to live in the SHU, and learn a lot about the BOP's transfer process.

If you get stuck in a situation where the government reneges on the deal, you need to demand your lawyer press every objection he can to preserve your appeal rights. If he looks at you like, "oh well," then don't hesitate to stand up and tell the judge,

> *"Your honor. We had a deal and I upheld my end of that deal and now the government gets to just throw it away. I can't understand that and I believe it is a violation of my rights. My lawyer is standing here looking like there is nothing wrong here and that is a problem. I want the record to reflect that I object to the government's refusal to stand by their deal and I request the Court order the government to abide by the agreement."*

If you decide to cooperate with the government, make sure to avoid the pitfall of trusting the government. Read everything. Question everything. Remain honest. And insist that there are protections built into your agreement. If you do all that, then you shouldn't have too much to worry about.

Immigration Consequences of Convictions

Regardless of whether you have a plea agreement, enter an open plea, or go to trial, if you aren't a U.S. Citizen then your status will likely be **REVOKED** by immigration authorities. That means if you have are a resident alien (have a green card), it will be revoked and you will have to be deported. There is very little that can keep you in the United States. While it is possible, you need to understand that there is an extraordinarily high probability that the U.S. Immigration judge will order you deported.

If you are a citizen, but you procured that citizenship through falsities or fraud, it can be revoked and you can be deported. This is a lot harder to do than with other immigration statuses. The government has to prove it and if they can, you will likely be charged with the criminal counterparts for this. If you are a naturalized citizen and you didn't game the system to get your citizenship, then it is extremely *un*likely that you will lose your citizenship.

If you are hell-bent on staying in the United States and you aren't a citizen, you may want to consider going to trial because that is your only real chance at staying. If you win and you have a green card then you won't be deported (although it could still happen, it's just harder). If you plead guilty in any way, your immigration case is effectively lost. You can try and convince the immigration judge that you are in danger if you go back to your home country and get asylum status, but know that the immigration judge will not be too swayed by such a claim. They will look at you and say, "well you should have thought about that before you decided to bring crime to America." For more information about immigration defenses, you should contact an immigration lawyer.

Finally, if you are deported and decide to illegally re-enter the United States after being convicted of a felony or after being previously deported, it is a virtual certainty that you will spend some time in prison. The Guidelines provide hefty enhancements for people who were already deported.

What are you waiving as part of the deal?

Appeal Waivers

Every plea agreement offered by the government will have a number of "waivers" in them. For instance, it is a foregone conclusion that you will "waive" your right to appeal the conviction. And, it is also likely you will not be able to appeal a sentence that is imposed in accordance with the agreement itself. There are some problems that have started shining through various appeals regarding waivers and there are ways you can prevent them.

A great number of plea agreements state that the prosecution and defendant agree that the prosecution will recommend the court impose a sentence at the low-end of the calculated Guidelines range. Lawyers point to the "low-end" language and push that it is a good deal. While it **could** be a good deal, you need to read this language like a prosecutor. What I am talking about is the word "calculated." Guess what the low-end of offense level 41 is? **324 months**! The problem is you don't know what the PSR is going to say about the final offense level (and make no mistake, the government will push for the highest offense level possible) and putting your life in the hands of a "low-end" promise is not good enough for you to waive your constitutional rights. But that is exactly what the waiver will expect you to do.

We are going to spend a lot of time talking about objecting to the presentencing report. But an objection is only as powerful as your ability to appeal it. The waivers that prosecutors usually put into the plea agreement make a blanket statement that you will not appeal anything involving the conviction or sentence. Courts have held that such a waiver even waives the ability to appeal any objections to later issues. And that is a major problem. You absolutely do not want to waive your right to challenge anything that happens from the time your plea agreement is signed until sentencing. This includes: objections to the presentence report, objections to the Guidelines calculations (unless they are specifically stipulated in the agreement), objectionable prosecutor conduct following the plea, and any judicial decisions rendered following the entry of the guilty plea. How do you get this into the agreement? Good question.

You may want to tell your lawyer who you will not sign an agreement unless these exceptions to the appeal waiver are spelled out fully. Your lawyer will undoubtedly tell you that they have never seen such a carve-out in a plea agreement. And you should respond, "that's all well and good. But I do not want to put myself to the complete mercy of the judge without some appellate protection. As a lawyer you should agree that waiving the right to appeal something that hasn't even happened yet (like the guidelines calculations) is crazy." The fact remains that if a prosecutor really wants to end the case with a plea agreement, and you aren't being ridiculous, then you have the upper hand to negotiate this reasonable change. **IF YOUR LAWYER TELLS YOU THAT THE PROSECUTOR REFUSES TO**

CHANGE THE LANGUAGE, THEN REQUEST YOUR LAWYER SET UP A FRYE HEARING.

The Frye hearing should be set up under the guise of ensuring your knowledge of the offer is on the record. Your lawyer should **not** tell the prosecutor that you plan on telling the judge your reason for rejecting the plea. Instead, your lawyer should tell the prosecutor that he wants to make sure he is personally insulated from any Frye claims. The prosecutor will surely not object to having that on the record. Then when you and your lawyer are at the hearing, you pounce and explain to the judge why exactly you won't accept the agreement. The entire purpose, then, of the Frye hearing is to put the prosecutor on blast for being unreasonable. If I were the one standing there, I would say:

> *"Your Honor. I actually want to accept this plea agreement, but I made a request that I am being told is not possible. The contract says that I will waive all my appellate rights including the right to appeal anything that happens from this day forward. I have no problem waiving issues that have already come to pass, but waiving future issues requires me to become a time-traveler and determine if anything could become a problem later. So, I requested that the waiver include exceptions to allow me to appeal: the court's final adjudication*

> *of the Guidelines, PSR issues, and any other decisions the court may make in this case from this day forward. So, if the prosecutor is willing to be reasonable about the waiver language, I would accept the plea agreement."*

Saying something like that puts the ball in the prosecutor's court. The prosecutor may shift the blame to your lawyer and claim that your lawyer never made any such counter-offer and then agree to requested language. If they blame your lawyer, understand that they are just trying to save face in front of a federal judge. It doesn't mean your lawyer didn't actually make the counter-offer. (So, don't be too judgmental).

If the prosecutor decides that there is no wiggle room for the waiver language, I would reject the plea agreement and plead "open" (i.e. without the plea agreement). **Pleading open allows you to appeal ALL SENTENCING ISSUES.** (This may *not* be the best course of action if the agreement involves charges being dismissed because those charges won't be dismissed. So make sure and talk to your lawyer about the risks of pleading open if you decide to go that way). Since the judge is sitting there at that time, it will become known that the only reason you are not accepting the agreement itself is to protect a reasonable amount of your appellate rights, and you can keep pointing that out to the judge in every proceeding later. For instance, if you go to trial and lose, you can tell the judge, "We are only at trial because the government wouldn't agree to a reasonable exception to the appellate waiver." Suffice it to say, I would rather face the bullet shooting out of a gun while wearing a bullet-proof vest than to take the blast without any protection whatsoever. The appeal court is like a bullet-proof vest. Don't just throw it away and risk a direct shot without any help whatsoever.

Collateral Attack Waivers

You will undoubtedly see a waiver of some of your collateral attack rights. The problem is most of these waivers are written to reference the United States Code and don't necessarily spell out that you are waiving your collateral attack rights. "Collateral attack" is the process by which you challenge your conviction through "habeas corpus." These claims are advanced through 28 U.S.C. § 2255 and, very rarely, under 28 U.S.C. § 2241. If you see a waiver of "collateral attack" rights or waivers of the 2241 or 2255 statutes, you may want to make sure to inform your lawyer you **WILL NOT WAIVE YOUR RIGHT "TO RAISE INEFFECTIVE ASSISTANCE**

OF COUNSEL CLAIMS, PROSECUTORIAL MISCONDUCT CLAIMS, OR FUTURE CHANGES IN SUPREME COURT LAW." Your lawyer will probably tell you that you don't waive those things even if the waiver is written expansively. **DO NOT LISTEN TO IT.** Your response should be very simple,

> *"If it is something that doesn't get waived in your opinion, then nobody will have a problem making sure the language expressly says I am not waiving those rights."*

If the prosecution refuses to carve out these three measly exceptions to the waiver, you should ask yourself what they are hiding. There should be no reason they wouldn't agree to this unless they committed misconduct or are terrified that your lawyer is horrible or that the Supreme Court will one day let you go. If there is even a possibility those issues are present, it would make me want the exceptions to be spelled out more. I would demand it and inform the lawyer who a failure to provide that language would be a deal breaker.

If you do not make sure you protect the right to raise ineffective assistance of counsel or prosecutorial misconduct claims, you are potentially leaving yourself unable to access things that could change later. What happens if the Supreme Court renders a decision that makes your conviction unconstitutional? If you make an unqualified waiver of your § 2255 rights, then you will NOT have any way to bring a claim into court later. The idea is to protect yourself. Don't just accept the boilerplate put into the plea agreement. If you do, then when you are sitting in jail and file something just to see it rejected because of your waiver, then you only have yourself to blame.

410 Waivers

It has become commonplace for prosecutors to include something called a "410 Waiver." They are very good at not defining this. You should seriously consider whether you will accept an agreement that has a 410 Waiver in it. The reason is because Rule 410 of the Federal Rules of Evidence is *extremely powerful and protects you*. It prevents the prosecution from telling a jury about any guilty pleas you made or agreements you accepted that were later vacated. A lot can happen after you enter into a plea agreement. You may find out your lawyer lied to you about a key piece of evidence. Or you may decide that you really wanted a trial and felt pressured to take the plea. These are reasons that a judge *could* let you out of the plea agreement and set your case for trial. If you entered into a 410 Waiver and it was found to be knowing and voluntary, then you will really hate life. The prosecutor is going to stand up and immediately tell the jury that you **CONFESSED TO THE CRIME IN FRONT OF A JUDGE.** And, because you waived your rights under Rule 410, you will have no recourse. Rest assured, the jury will find you guilty if the prosecutor puts your plea comments into the record.

The best case I ever read that speaks about this issue was United States v. Jim, 839 F. Supp. 2d 1157 (2012), from the District of New Mexico. There, Judge Browning evaluated the 410 Waiver in the defendant's agreement and found that everything the defendant said at court, to the probation officer and in the plea agreement were admissible in the trial. He was convicted and **sentenced to 30 years** in prison. The 410 Waiver was used to its fullest extent and the Tenth Circuit upheld Judge Browning's decision without any serious question.

Compassionate Release Waivers

The law regarding compassionate release has changed drastically. And I am willing to bet that prosecutors will start seeking waivers that limit your access to compassionate release. 18 U.S.C. § 3582(c)(1)(A) governs "compassionate release." The phrase "compassionate release" is now a misnomer because it is no longer limited to four specific issues determined by the BOP. The First Step Act of 2018 expanded the application of the statute greatly and it has been used to even convince judges that harsh conditions of confinement during the pandemic was sufficient to warrant some relief. If you notice that you are waiving any rights under § 3582, then you probably are going to want to seek to have that removed. You don't want to be sitting in prison years from now with a potential issue to bring in front of the court and simply be told, "Sorry, you waived that in your plea agreement." You don't know the future, and to waive such speculative rights is absurd. Don't be afraid to tell your lawyer who you don't want to waive those statutory rights.

FOIA Waivers

More and more prosecutors are asking defendants to waive their rights under the Freedom of Information Act ("FOIA") and Privacy Act. And most defendants do it without even thinking about it. Seriously consider this because it is your only real way of discovering if there was prosecutorial misconduct in your case. There is no legitimate reason for a prosecutor to expect you to waive your right to request your files from the FBI, Homeland Security, the United States Attorney's Office, or any other federal agency. The whole reason these laws exist is to make sure the public can inspect the government's work (FOIA) and to make sure records about any specific person is accurate (Privacy Act). Being a stickler on this language could one day save you. It may not. But why should you waive your right to inspect the files? I don't believe you should.

What are you facing without the deal?

Next you need to determine what you realistically face if you don't take the plea offer and proceed to trial or simply plead without an agreement. In order to do that, you must determine your guidelines range. Determining the guidelines range is a nuanced process. There are three ways in which you can determine your guidelines range. The first, and best option, is to request the preparation of a presentence report in anticipation of a guilty plea. The second, and most common, is to have your lawyer provide you with his estimates. And the third is that you do it yourself if you have access to the Guidelines Manual. These are not mutually exclusive either. You should use all of these options. You will want to *compare the Guidelines range if you were to plead guilty (get acceptance of responsibility points) or go to trial (do not get acceptance of responsibility points).*

A pre-plea presentence investigation report is prepared by a probation officer. Federal probation officers spend their entire careers learning the Guidelines Manual. Most of them could school a lawyer for days on its application and judges have a tendency to listen to a probation officer's calculation. Remember, at this stage you are trying to get a relative idea of what your Guidelines range is so you can determine if the plea offer you are considering is worth anything. If you accept the plea, or are later found guilty, a full report will be created for the purposes of sentencing.

Getting your lawyer's recommendation is also an important step. Although, most lawyers shoot from the hip and do not provide the detailed analysis of the Guidelines range that a probation officer will do. Their recommendation is important in that it tells you if your lawyer has any idea what's going on and if he is someone who knows how federal sentencing works. If your lawyer's estimate is way off, then you know what's up with his work. Perhaps it is time to get a new lawyer.

Calculating the Guidelines yourself requires a lot of time and dedication. But you can do it. Be the devil's advocate. Do not just assume you are right on something. If there is a possibility the government can prove an enhancement, then assume it is proved when you are estimating your exposure.

If all your estimates are different, it is probably best to take the probation officer's calculation. Now, there will be an opportunity to object and reduce the Guidelines range later. When you are considering whether the plea you are accepting is worth your time it is best to err on the side of caution and assume you will lose every objection.

After you determine an estimated Guidelines range, you need to have your lawyer get all the available sentencing statistics regarding your offense. If your lawyer looks at you like you have three heads when you ask for this, simply tell them to go to Sentencing Commission Sourcebooks (the web address is https://www.ussc.gov/research/) for help. It doesn't matter if you have a public defender or a private lawyer. They should get this for you. These numbers are gold. They tell you the National, Circuit and District average and median sentences imposed over the course of more than ten years. You will see the median and average sentences for each of these categories. It is common for these numbers to be a little different. The median will isolate the outliers or those that received extreme sentences one way or another. The average includes all the outliers in its calculation. Statistics are not a guarantee that you will receive any certain sentence. But they do provide you with a really good idea of what judges generally think in your situation.

Now you have all the information you need to determine whether you have a good plea offer. But the work has really just begun because you must analyze all of that information so you can make an educated decision.

Remember, when it comes to pleading guilty, **NOBODY CAN MAKE YOU DO IT.** It doesn't matter if the bargain offered is made of platinum. If you don't want it and you want a trial, that is your right. Even if you have no chance of winning at trial, it is your right to be tried before a jury. Do not feel compelled to accept anything. But you also have to remember that the prosecution is under no obligation to make any other offers and once you reject an offer it is likely gone forever.

Part Six

Sentencing

It is highly likely that if you are reading this book you will face sentencing of some manner. Regardless of whether you accepted a plea agreement, are found guilty at trial or just plead guilty without an agreement, you need to be prepared for sentencing. In fact, your preparation for sentencing will need as thorough as, or even more than, trial. That's because this is the only time you will get to show the judge that you are a person and not just some criminal monster.

Sentencing is comprised of several phases: Presentence Report, Objections, Sentencing Memorandum, and Presentation. Each of these phases is vital and you must make sure that your lawyer is handling them. If you are standing before the sentencing judge when you realize none of this happened, it is way too late.

Presentence Report

Unless you are facing the death penalty, as soon as you are found guilty the judge is going to order the preparation of a "presentence report" or simply "PSR." This report is the single most relied on document by a judge in fashioning your sentence. If you entered into a C-plea, for instance, the judge will use the report to determine if the agreed upon sentence is fair on both sides. If you entered any other type of plea, the judge is going to rely principally on that report to determine the actual sentence to give you. The PSR is also the single document the Bureau of Prisons will rely upon to determine literally everything for you while you are incarcerated. For instance, if the PSR doesn't explicitly state that you graduated high school, no matter how many degrees you have amassed, you will be required to either try and verify your diploma (very difficult) or enroll and complete the GED program. The PSR will also determine if you will ever be eligible for a minimum security camp and what your base security level should be scored as. Suffice it to say that the PSR is something that you need to read cover-to-cover several times and demand corrections if necessary.

The PSR is developed in stages. If done properly, your PSR will be complete. All too often though, attorneys do not put the proper amount of effort into ensuring the PSR is accurate. The absolute minimum stage that will occur is an interview by a PSR writer who is a probation officer. Everything else is up to you to ensure your attorney completes. These are: opening letter to the probation officer, interview, follow up letter to the probation officer, disclosure of first draft, objections, response to government objections, final disclosure before sentencing, and formal objections. This is so important, we are going to go over each of these stages in depth.

Stage One
Letter to the Probation Officer

The first stage is the simplest form of advocacy that can be employed but, sadly, most attorneys do not use it. You should demand that your lawyer take this step because it serves to temper the prosecution's version of events, humanize you early in the process, and advocate for a specific sentencing recommendation at the earliest possible time.

Probably the most important element of the letter is the defense's Guidelines calculation along with specific rationales why certain calculations do or do not apply. If there is an enhancement you believe could be applied, you need to give your reasons why it shouldn't apply. If you can't come up with a reason, then conceding that it does apply will go a long way to convincing the probation officer that you are at least reasonable. If you and your lawyer can't come up with a specific Guidelines calculation with rationales, then you need to either fire your lawyer immediately or hire a federal sentencing mitigation specialist to help. But this is something you should have known way before the PSR was ordered prepared. No matter if you go to trial or plead guilty, you and your lawyer should have been estimating your Guidelines range throughout.

The letter also needs to provide the defense's version of events. This is different than your personal allocution. Instead, the defense needs to ensure the presentence report writer sees the case from the defense's eyes, not the prosecution's. To do this, the defense needs to make sure to put together a narrative supported by relevant evidence. To do that, your lawyer should sift through all of the discovery sent over and also use his own investigation to paint a better picture of you and the offense. Of course, it is easier said than done to convince a lawyer to do all this work. That means you need to also sift through the discovery and specifically inquire as to your attorney's investigation to help develop a reasonable and convincing version of events. Make no mistake, the government is going to perform this step in rapid fashion and paint you as a monster. The only way to temper the government's picture is to provide a reasonable and convincing version of events.

Next, the letter should have is some sort of statement from you for allocution. All too often, the lawyer will say that you will make your statement at sentencing. And while making a statement at sentencing can be (and is) powerful, it is just as powerful to make one to the probation officer as early as possible too. This statement should be well thought out and written by you, the defendant. Your attorney should not write a statement for you because it will appear you don't care and their language will make it obvious that you didn't write it. That doesn't mean your lawyer can't guide you. But, your lawyer should not write it for you. It needs to be in your words and your handwriting. Your lawyer will take that statement and quote from it in the probation letter and attach your statement to that letter for the probation officer's review. You need to find a way to show meaningful contrition in that letter. That means don't just say you are sorry for the sake of being sorry. Be specific about what you are sorry about and why. If you are sorry that your family has been put through hell because of your conduct, then say so. If you are sorry because, at the time, you didn't care that your best friend was also getting addicted to drugs because of you, it needs to be said. If there is a specific victim that can be identified in some concrete way, apologize to that victim. Do not be the guy (and there are many) that says, "I am sorry to my family and all the victims. I am sorry to you judge." That is not an allocution worth anything. If that's all you got, it may be better to just stay silent.

The letter to the probation officer should also discuss and attach character letters from your supporters. You do not want to have a letter campaign. The number of letters you get is not helpful and indeed may cause more damage. Instead, you want quality letters that discuss you as a person by providing specific examples. A single letter with specific examples is far more powerful than a hundred that simply say you are a good guy. Alan Ellis, the preeminent federal sentencing specialist suggests a letter from someone giving an anecdote of a positive experience about you (perhaps they witnessed you pull someone out of a burning car or saw you volunteering at your local food bank or remember you being an extraordinarily helpful person) will go a really long way to humanize you to the probation officer and, subsequently, the judge.

If you and your lawyer have decided that a psychological evaluation is necessary in your case and that evaluation was favorable to your case, you need to make sure that is also discussed in the letter and attached to it. This is a delicate subject and should be considered a strategy choice. For instance, if you are charged with a sexual offense, providing a psychosexual evaluation that discusses your risk towards groups of people and of recidivism is expected. But if that evaluation says that you are the most dangerous person in the world, then you probably do not want to put that in. One topic that can be especially helpful if you have a psychological evaluation done is your substance abuse history. If you have a "verifiable" substance abuse disorder within one year from the date of your arrest, you may qualify for a substantial reduction (1 year) in your federal sentence by entering into the drug program. A psychologist's diagnosis meets that requirement. Thus, you would want that psychologist's report to be made part of the PSR. That doesn't mean you should go and lie just to try and get the year off while in the BOP.

The final element of your lawyer's letter should be some color. I mean this literally. The cover page of the letter should have a color picture of you with your family or friends. When the probation officer gets the letter, the only other picture they will have of you is your booking photo. Giving them a family photo will show them that you are human and the stakes are high. It will show them there are more lives at stake here than just a criminal defendant's.

Sadly, most lawyers do not prepare these letters to probation officers. You should demand your lawyer put a letter together. You need to make sure that your lawyer is prepared to do this letter before you plead guilty. You need the letter to get to the probation officer as soon as the case is assigned to them. If you can beat the government to the punch, you will do yourself a lot of favors. If your lawyer is not doing this, then you may want to find a sentencing mitigation specialist to help with presenting your case to the probation officer.

Stage Two
The Interview

The probation officer is going to interview you. Before the interview takes place you will be expected to sign a bunch of consent forms for the probation officer to conduct an investigation into your background. Of course, these consent forms are by no means required. But rest assured that everything the probation officer wants to access with your consent has already been accessed by the prosecution without your consent. So there is really no reason not to allow the probation officer to investigate with your consent. However, if you and your lawyer decide that it would be best for your case to not consent, then you should seriously consider your lawyer's recommendation.

The interview is very important and you need to understand that when you are talking to the probation officer you are essentially talking to the judge. You are entitled to have your attorney present for the interview and you should demand that your lawyer attend. While there is very little for the lawyer to do, it can become quite helpful to have a credible witness present in the event there is a dispute as to what was said. If your lawyer did a proper letter, the interview should be a relatively painless experience. Even so, it is important to be fully prepared to answer all of the probation officer's questions. Be prepared to answer questions about your work history, finances, family life, educational background, military history, substance abuse history, full medical history and current medical issues (including your medications), and mental health treatment history.

If you are going into the interview without having sent an initial letter to the probation officer as discussed in Stage One, then everything mentioned up there will have to be brought up during the interview. The technical legal stuff like Guidelines calculations should be presented by your lawyer. But all of the factual stuff in Stage One will need to be discussed.

One thing that probation officers will look out for is to _hear_ your allocution. If a letter was sent, a written allocution was already sent to the probation officer. But it is more powerful if you can ALSO explain your criminal actions and contrition to the probation officer directly.

DO NOT JUST READ YOUR WRITTEN ALLOCUTION

You should prepare what you are going to say but do not be robotic. Make sure you aren't looking at some piece of paper when you say all this. And get used to explaining your criminal actions and contrition because everyone you encounter from here on out will look for that. In fact, the second you arrive at the Bureau of Prisons, a case manager is going to also ask you to explain your criminal actions.

Stage Three
Follow-up Letter

It is surprising how few lawyers actually take the time to draft a follow-up letter to the probation officer. You should make sure that your lawyer is going to do just that and take it seriously. The most basic level of professionalism dictates that a follow-up letter be sent to the probation officer. I mean, you just interviewed with the single most powerful person involved in determining your sentence. The judge is going to listen to this person. Giving them more information to work with or clarifying other information will only serve to help you.

The first thing the follow-up letter should address are any items that you and/or your lawyer said you would clarify. The probation officer is human and gets that you may not remember everything during the interview. This is your opportunity to complete the missing pieces to make the picture complete.

The second thing the follow-up letter needs to discuss is the defense's Guidelines calculation proposal. Yes, that was already done in the first letter. But who says you can't bring it up again? Nobody. Reminding the probation officer of your position as to the Guidelines calculation can't hurt.

You will want to make sure and provide the probation officer with specific statistics regarding the sentences imposed in cases similar to yours in your area. There are several ways to get sentencing statistics. The best way, in my opinion, is to use a sentencing statistics specialist to generate charts and reports for the probation officer and judge. I personally used Mark Allenbaugh who was with Sentencing Stats, LLC.[1] While his fee was expensive, it was well worth the cost. Allenbaugh reviewed all the facts of my case and compared them to all other "similarly situated" defendants in the federal system by using the United States Sentencing Commission's own data. If Mark is no longer around, it is possible to generate a wealth of statistical information by going to the United States Sentencing Commission's website and using their *Interactive Data Analyzer* (available to the public at https://ida.ussc.gov/analytics/saw.dll?Dashboard). Make sure your lawyer knows about both of these options. Even if you have an appointed lawyer, it is possible to hire someone like Allenbaugh. There is nothing that prohibits someone from gifting the service toward

---

[1] I haven't heard from Mark in some time. I don't know if sentencingstats is still around or not. If you are looking for an attorney who uses sentencing statistics routinely, contact Alan Ellis who used to work with Mark. His website is AlanEllis.com.

your defense. And, if the appointed lawyer is especially creative, they could even ask the court to approve the cost of the service as necessary for the defense under the Criminal Justice Act. But, no matter how you look at it, there is no excuse for not producing some statistics for the probation officer and judge. Giving them average and median sentences will help convince the probation officer to make a particular recommendation to the judge through their report. It may also convince them to suggest the judge give a downward variance.

The final thing you should give the probation officer, if you haven't already done so, are any character letters you intend on providing to the court. Most lawyers wait until sentencing to file character letters. **DON'T LET YOUR LAWYER WAIT THAT LONG.** If letters have been given to your lawyer from friends, family, colleagues, teachers, or any other important person in your life, now is the time to turn them over. If the probation officer is moved by them it could result in a great sentencing recommendation or the probation officer pointing out the letter to the judge personally.

Stage Four
Initial Disclosure

The rules require the probation officer to disclose a draft of the presentence report to your lawyer, you, and the prosecutor. At this stage, they are **not** allowed to disclose the report to the judge. This initial disclosure is the most important stage of this whole process. Technically, when the probation officer gives the report to your lawyer, they have given it to you. Notwithstanding that an argument can be made that the probation officer should mail you a copy personally, the fact remains that they will probably just give it to your lawyer. Bug your lawyer for this report. Do not let up. You should ask your lawyer for the first disclosure of the report every week following the follow-up letter. Be annoying with this. That absolute last thing you want is for anyone to claim that you never asked for it. Ask and ask and ask again.

Sometimes lawyers will tell you not to worry about it. "I'll take care of it." Hopefully, you aren't faced with that. But if you are, your response should be: "I don't care. I want a copy and I want it as fast as possible." If your lawyer is refusing to give you a copy for any reason, you should probably go to the judge and ask for a new a lawyer. The reason would be quite simple: "My lawyer and I have irreconcilable differences. He won't let me see the first disclosure of the presentence report and won't let me provide my input regarding any objections that are necessary." This is one of those times where you need to make sure the lawyer listens to you.

Here's why.

If you don't object to the first disclosure presentence report properly, **YOU COULD WAIVE ALL OBJECTIONS TO IT LATER**. All of them. That is a steep price to pay for the document that is literally going to run your life for decades to come. But that is the price of silence in court all the time. WAIVER. *Don't waive your right to object.* If you do, you will not be able to appeal it or convince anyone that anything in the PSR was wrong later.

Nobody is perfect. Probation officers are people who are also not perfect. There are parts of the PSR that can be fixed easily and will make your life significantly easier while you are in prison. Other parts may require some legal presentation arguing a position. And still other parts may state erroneous facts that you want to make sure are understood as not agreed.

The PSR is comprised of a number of sections. You will need to review each of these sections in much the same way as a plea agreement. Read it all. Line-for-line, paragraph-for-paragraph, page-for-page, section-for-section. And then read it again. On the third reading you will start to take notes about what you disagree with. There are some variations in the style of PSR's. Sections that we go over here may be in a different order in your case. But the information we are discussing will all be present in some form in your PSR.

You want to make sure and write some notes about each and every paragraph in the report. If there is nothing wrong with a paragraph in the report, then make sure and write a note saying there is nothing wrong. That way you don't have to keep going back. But, be picky. It doesn't matter how small of an error you may believe it is. All errors are important to get fixed. In this stage we are only concerned about taking notes about problems. We will discuss how to fix all the errors in Stage 5.

The very beginning of the PSR will have the case caption with your case number. It will also state who the judge is, the prosecutor's name, and your lawyers names. It will list the offenses with which you were convicted and the minimum/maximum penalties for each. Pay close attention to these because they are sometimes incorrect. If a charge is listed using verbiage you didn't agree to, then you may want to clarify the name of the charge for the PSR writer. The section titled "Release Status" is extremely important because it is what is used by the BOP to determine your jail credit. You get credit for every day you are held in jail (but not a halfway house or house arrest) that isn't applied to any other sentence. This can get complicated and it is something that I will be covering in another book, but suffice it to say you want every day that you were in jail (even if it was for one minute) to be mentioned.

There will also be a section with "Detainers" listed. A detainer is a notice filed by another law enforcement agency declaring an intention to prosecute you in some way. Some people say that you want to deal with your detainers before sentencing because they could prevent you from being designated to a minimum security camp. But, that isn't always the wisest move because if you "deal" with that detainer and it results in a separate state conviction, it *could* affect your criminal history score and raise your sentencing Guidelines range. If you can get a detainer dismissed and removed completely, then you should do that. Often times, detainers are simple citations for not paying your parking tickets or speeding tickets. Taking care of these loose ends will make your life simpler when you get to prison.

Finally, the opening pages will list if there are any "codefendants" or "related cases." The related cases can be important if your sentencing is going to be a global sentencing to deal with all of the cases you have outstanding. If your sentencing will include dealing with other cases, then those cases should be listed here. As for "codefendants," you want this to list all the ones you know because their sentences could become important when you are sentenced. Judges are supposed to avoid "unwarranted sentencing disparities" and this includes disparate sentences between codefendants. If your buddies all got time served, and you are facing 20 years, you will want to make sure the probation officer and judge see those case references.

Demographics (Also called "Identifying Data")

Out of everything here, there are two items that are absolutely essential to make sure are correct: your address and your education. Your address will dictate the prison you will be assigned to when you are designated. It will also be listed as your "release residence" within the Bureau of Prisons. If this is wrong it can be difficult to get it fixed later. It is common for defendants to be prosecuted in a district where they don't live in. This is especially true in drug trafficking and child pornography cases. If you don't ensure that your address specifies the correct district it will be difficult for you to convince anyone to change it later.

Your education level is key because it deeply affects your eligibility for programs in the BOP. It doesn't matter if you have a Ph.D. If you graduated from high school or received a GED you need this line to say: "High School Diploma VERIFIED" or "GED VERIFIED." If it doesn't say these words, the BOP will force you to enroll in the GED program and take the GED. I have seen the BOP force a medical doctor take the GED because his PSR didn't say these words. They don't care if you went to college. If the PSR doesn't say that your high school level was "verified" they will make you try and get proof sent into them and jump through a million hoops to convince them that it is real. If this needs to be fixed make sure that you write it in your notes. And make sure that your lawyer is provided with proof of your high school diploma or GED so he can ensure the probation officer gets it.

Next, you need to make sure that your citizenship is correct. If you are a U.S. citizen (naturalized or born) and it doesn't say that in the PSR, the BOP will treat you like an illegal immigrant. That will result in you not being able to access a multitude of programs including preventing you from going to a minimum security camp. If you are not a U.S. Citizen, then you also want it to correctly state your country of citizenship. If nothing else, you may qualify for an International Treaty Transfer. But if your citizenship is incorrectly stated, then the United States may not accept a request from your real country of residence.

You also want to make sure your military status, if any, is listed properly. Having your veterans status verified in the report can make it easier for you to work in Unicor while in the BOP (which is First Step Act time credit eligible). You will also be given access to VA representatives when they come around to answer questions.

Finally, you need to make sure your family members are all listed with their relationship to you. You want to make sure your grandparents, mother, father, brothers, sisters, wife/husband, and children are all listed because the Bureau of Prisons will immediately approve those visitors as "Immediate Family" for visiting purposes. If they aren't listed here, then the BOP will run a criminal background check on them and subject them to greater scrutiny to be able to visit you. Even if your family isn't supportive of you right now, still list them. You may eventually be able to patch things up and a failure to make sure this is correct will make it that much harder to do that.

There is one thing that you want to look at and write down and that's your "USM#." That stands for United States Marshal Number which is the same number that you will use for everything while you are in the BOP. And no, you don't need to go anywhere to "get your number." It was assigned to you the day you were processed by the Marshals in the courthouse and this is that number. A lot of know-it-alls will tell people that they have to go to Oklahoma "to get their number" or to some other random place out there. That isn't true at all. While centralized receiving may be common in the state systems, it is not in the federal system. Everything about you is processed in Grand Prairie, Texas without you present for it.

Part A: The Offense

Charges & Convictions

This section is going to detail all the charges and how you were convicted (plea or verdict). If some charges were dismissed (due to an agreement or a hung jury or something like that) they will also be listed with their disposition here. If there is a plea agreement, the probation officer is going to detail that out as well and discuss what the terms of the plea involve. Just make sure everything that is written is accurate. If anything is wrong, jot it down so it can be corrected. It is actually common for the probation officer to copy and paste the entire plea agreement into this section.

Pretrial Services Information

If you were given bail and placed in a halfway house or on house arrest pending your trial, the pretrial services information will be placed here. The probation officer could talk about literally anything from your time in pretrial services. If you caused problems, refused to follow rules, or go to therapy, that will be noted here. And, rest assured, it will be used against you by the prosecutor. If there is anything negative in this section, you need to discuss with your lawyer whether it is an accurate depiction of the events so the lawyer can try and convince the probation officer to remove it or at least put in your version of events.

The Offense Conduct

This will be a narrative of the offense from the prosecution's perspective. However, if your lawyer did his job and got the initial letter out as fast as possible, then the offense conduct could also have the defense's version in it. This section should be read for accuracy as well. You may not agree with some of the things in the section. The vast majority of it is supported by police reports. But, if there is something that isn't true, mark it because it is something you may need to object to later.

The probation officer will put anything they believe to be relevant to the court's consideration of your sentence. It is pretty dry, but when you read it the first hundred times, you will feel like it is a bash on you. To some degree, it is bashing on you, but not in the way that it feels like. The probation officer is just trying to give a rendition of the case for the judge to understand how you are standing there at that time. Some of them may be harsher than others, but most of them take pride in being neutral about this kind of stuff. So, again, make sure it is accurate and if something is totally outrageous or wrong, then notate it. But don't take it too personally.

Defendant's Version

This is where the probation officer is going to note what YOU have to say about the offense. This is the allocution we spoke of previously. Hopefully you already sent a written allocution to the probation officer through your lawyer. During the interview, if you gave a spoken allocution of some sort, it may also be reflected here. If you chose not to provide a statement, it will say so but that silence will not be used against you.

Victim Impact

This section is going to identify whether the government located any specific victims to your case. It will not discuss the impact your crime had on society or the community as a whole. But that doesn't mean the probation officer will view your crime as a victimless crime in any event. In fact, it is more likely than not that your crime will be viewed as having victims of some sort. If you have any identifiable victims, it is highly likely that you will be subject to some level of restitution order during sentencing. If any restitution requests have been made, they will be noted here too.

If any victims have submitted anything for the probation officer to look at and it is referenced in here, you have a right to see it. This includes their "Victim Impact Letters" whether written by them or someone else. Your lawyer should make sure and get copies of anything submitted by victims and scrutinize them. Names and address will likely be redacted or pseudonyms used for the victim's privacy.

If no victims have come forward specifically, this section will probably be blank.

Acceptance of Responsibility Adjustments

The probation officer will note here if they intend on awarding the acceptance of responsibility points during the Guidelines calculations. If you pleaded guilty, it is likely this section will agree to give you the acceptance points regardless. If you went to trial, you will not likely get acceptance points. But if somehow you wow the probation officer following a trial, then they could still award them.

Offense Level Computations

In this section, you will find all the detailed computations for the final Guidelines offense level. It is suggested that you get a copy of the Guideline sections used in this computation so you can follow along. Every enhancement will be discussed and the probation officer will discuss the facts in which they are using the justify the application of any points. **This is very important.** If points are awarded for a "fact" that you dispute, you need to mark it and be prepared to have a very detailed conversation with your attorney about it. **You have a right to object to every enhancement and the government then must prove the enhancement applies.** Sometimes it is a foregone conclusion and attacking the enhancement is a waste of time. But that isn't always the case. Sometimes the facts are wrong. Sometimes the enhancement doesn't apply to the facts. This is the most important section of the entire PSR because it is what will be used to determine your final Guidelines range.

You do **NOT** need to purchase the Sentencing Guidelines book. It is very expensive to purchase a bound version of it and it is unnecessary. Instead, it is available for free online by going to the United States Sentencing Commission's website (https://www.ussc.gov/guidelines). If you are in jail or prison, you can have your family print off and mail you the sections that you need to look at. Or, you can request your lawyer provide you a copy of each section that you require. If you are in a Federal Detention Center, the Guidelines are accessible on the Electronic Law Library through your Trulincs station. I am including the three most common Guidelines sections used in federal practice today for ease of reference in the Appendix of this book: 2D1.1 (common drug offenses), 2L1.2 (common immigration offenses), and 2G2.2 (common child pornography offenses).

There are three overall steps to calculating the offense level. The first step is selecting and computing the offense specific Guideline. Second, there is an analysis for role in the offense and obstruction of justice. Finally, there is a calculation for acceptance of responsibility points. If you are charged with multiple counts, they may be grouped together for the Guidelines calculation or calculated separately. That is determined through the instructions provided at Guidelines section 3D1.2. There is a list there for which calculations are never to be grouped together and also provides a list of calculations that are always grouped together. For instance, if you are convicted of a drug conspiracy, possession with intent to distribute and distribution, those will all be grouped into a single 2D1.1 analysis. But, if you are convicted of 21 U.S.C. § 843(a)(3), which is obtaining a controlled substance via fraud, then your Guideline section is 2D2.2 which is **not** grouped. Each individual count of that will be treated as a single "group."

To determine which Guideline section applies to you, you want to consult the "Statutory Index." The Statutory Index is located in the Appendix to the Guidelines manual. But, I am providing a copy of the entire index in the Appendix of Surviving Pretrial. Just find the statute code you are convicted of and look right next to it to find the Guideline section that applies. If you have multiple counts of conviction, look up EACH COUNT and be prepared to do a Guidelines calculation for each different Guidelines section that applies.

Guidelines Chapter 3A-3C controls the victim related, role in the offense, and obstruction of justice calculations. The most common calculations here are 3B1.1 (aggravated role), 3B1.2 (mitigating role) and 3C1.1 (obstruction). Defendants want a "mitigating role" adjustment if at all possible. With regard to aggravated role adjustments, if they can be avoided, they should be. Sometimes the Government will agree that there isn't any aggravated role adjustment that applies. The reason is if you are convicted of heroin or methamphetamine offenses under 21 U.S.C. § 841(a)(1) or 841(b)(1) AND you are found to have been a "leader, organizer, manager, or supervisor" of the conduct, then you will not be eligible to earn First Step Act time credits.

Obstruction of justice enhancements happen all the time. The most common reason for it is if you testify at any hearing or trial saying, under oath, that you are innocent of the charges, but are later convicted then you committed perjury under the eyes of the law that is obstruction. Most sane defense lawyers believe this is too harsh, but it is the current state of the law and it isn't going to get changed during your case. That means if you intend on testifying in your own defense and you plan on testifying that you are factually innocent of the crimes alleged, you could suffer this enhancement. It also happens that this enhancement is levied for your conversations with family and friends on jail phones. For instance, let's say you get on the phone and tell your family to turn off your Facebook account. The government could claim that your reason for doing so was to interfere with their investigation of your conduct. In fact, something very similar happened to me.

Because of the case, I had to close my business. When I did so, I had to transfer my clients' files to them. My brother informed me that the clients were in need of the files and asked for my passwords to access them. Not thinking that I would get in trouble for just making my clients whole, I gave my password to my brother. My brother then got the clients their files. Everyone was happy. Not Uncle Sam though. And it wasn't like they really cared. They just wanted to get the enhancement. They never even asked if we had copies of the files to be reviewed. But the enhancement still applied. And make no mistake, I fought it tooth and nail.

If you have been given an obstruction enhancement and it is not firmly supported by substantial evidence, you really should talk to your lawyer about challenging it.

If any of the calculations the probation officer came up with seem wrong to you in any way, you will want to notate those problems so you and your lawyer can discuss if there is any fight for a more favorable calculation. Sometimes probation officers get point-happy and the enhancements aren't proper. You will get an opportunity to fight any Guidelines calculations that eventually come out in the PSR through Stage Five.

Part B: The Defendant's Criminal History

Before we get into the particulars of criminal history in the PSR, we need to discuss one aspect of priors that is misunderstood. Federal defendants will routinely assert they are "first-time offenders" because the federal case is their first **FEDERAL** case. That doesn't make you a "first-time offender." A first time offender is someone who has **NEVER** been arrested, jailed, or convicted of any crime whatsoever. The jurisdiction doesn't matter. So, if you have a record, you don't want to get trapped in the weeds of asserting that you are a first-time offender. Now, that doesn't mean you will be assigned points for your priors. But, no judge or prosecutor would ever allow your lawyer to walk in to court and say you are a "first-time offender" if you have any priors regardless of the point structure.

Juvenile Adjudications
Most people believe that juvenile records are sealed and can't be used against you as an adult. The

feds have access to literally everything, and your juvie record is something that can be used in a federal criminal sentencing. And some of those juvenile issues may increase your criminal history score. You want to pay attention to two big factors. First, was the date of the federal crime five years or less following the juvenile conviction? If so, it may not count against you and your lawyer will have to object. Second, the facts of the juvenile adjudication may be incomplete and they may demonstrate you were not at as serious fault as the charge implies. For instance, if you have a juvenile conviction for domestic violence, that alone would make it appear that you were a violent kid. But if that crime was caused because your step-dad was beating your mom and you intervened, then it doesn't seem so bad. Make sure you communicate the facts of the juvenile case to your lawyer so they can make sure they are presented appropriately. Depending on your situation, lawyer may even be able to request the judge make a specific finding that the case wasn't as serious as the charge implies.

Adult Criminal Convictions

Next, the PSR will outline any criminal convictions that you sustained since turning 18. This will include MISDEMEANORS and FELONIES. What it won't include are civil infractions (like traffic tickets or child support issues). It is very important to pay attention to what the probation officer details as to the sentence that was imposed in the case because that will determine how many points you get. Also, if the sentence was served more than 15 years before the date of the alleged federal offense, it will not be assigned any points. If a conviction was vacated for any reason, but that isn't reflected in the PSR, then you need to make sure that gets fixed too.

Criminal History Computation

The probation officer will state the total points and the corresponding Criminal History Category for the Guideline. By way of reference, there are six criminal history categories:

- Category I: 0-1 points
- Category II: 2-3 points
- Category III: 4-6 points
- Category IV: 7-9 points
- Category V: 10-12 points
- Category VI: 13+ points

You can find the instructions for calculating your criminal history score by getting Guidelines sections 4B1.1 and 4B1.2. You can also find these Guidelines sections in the Appendix to this book.

Other Arrests

It is possible that the probation officer will list "other arrests" that you have suffered through the years. There is no hard and fast rule to this. The sentencing court can hear of pretty much anything that will help in determining an appropriate sentence. Often times, the probation officer will list as an "other arrest" a collateral state case that was dismissed so the feds could take over. In all of these cases, you want to make sure and provide your lawyer your version of each of these arrests so he can object or clarify the defense's version of those other "arrests."

Part C: Offender Characteristics

This is by far the most important section of the PSR. It is basically your life story and goes a long way to humanize you to the court. This part will likely be divided into a few sections: personal/family data, marital, physical/medical condition, mental/emotional health, substance abuse, educational/vocational, employment, military, and financial. Each of these sections is important for court, but they are even more important for the BOP. This is where the BOP will look to determine who your direct family members are (for visiting purposes). Your eligibility for RDAP (and the one-year off that comes with completion) is determined by what is written in the substance abuse section. Your medications, medical needs, and physical limitations will be determined this way as well. And your military status can move you up in the line to get into Unicor while you do your time.

With regard to how this section affects your upcoming sentencing, you need to see if it is lopsided. That means the narrative favors one viewing over another. If it is lopsided in your favor, then great. More likely than not, if it is lopsided at all, it will not be to your benefit. Nobody expects you to look like Jesus. But you don't want to appear like Jeffrey Dahmer either.

If it is negatively lopsided, then your lawyer will object and request that the defense's version of the section be provided. Your lawyer should develop an equally lopsided version of all the facts presented but toward your favor. Let me show you what I mean.

John got his initial draft PSR and sees that the probation officer spends a lot of time talking about his childhood. When discussing his childhood the probation officer says:

> *John was raised in a loving home with parents who cared for him and met all of his needs. Much to his*

> *parents' dismay, by 9th grade, John just wouldn't listen. He rebelled at home and school. According to his brother, John would always "run with the wrong crowd." It is apparent that John's history of drug dealing behavior took off during his freshman year of high school and progressed rapidly from there.*

John certainly doesn't sound like Jeffrey Dahmer, but the narrative suggests that John had a wonderful upbringing and his drug dealing behavior had no serious basis in his childhood experiences. In response, John's lawyer pulls out the psychology report he had developed before the interview and was provided to the probation officer. In that psychology report, the psychologist stated:

> *John's childhood was tumultuous. There is no reason to believe that his parents were abusive toward John in any physical or sexual way. But John reported a significant amount of arguing among his parents about lack of finances for necessities like medical care, food, and after-school care. This made John feel like a burden on his family. Moreover, his parents work schedules were rigorous leaving John to generally fend for himself. John recounts that his first experiences selling drugs were in the 9th grade at Main Street High School and his reasoning was to help his family with their struggling finances. He would routinely*

> place money into the cookie jar at the top of the fridge without anyone's knowledge. He also would keep some of the money for himself so he could acquire the items he wanted and needed as a young teen. When John graduated from high school, his family was excited that he got into college and planned on going. Affording college became a major stressor for John which pushed him further into the drug dealing behavior....

The psychologist's rendition of John's childhood shines a lot of light on what happened and how. His lawyer wants to make sure that the probation officer either fixes their lopsided narrative or, at the very least, put the defense's narrative into the PSR word-for-word. The lawyer's objections, that are prepared in Stage Five, provide the following:

The defense objects to the PSR's suggestion that John's childhood was perfect. While there is no dispute that John's family loves him, the fact remains that his youthful experiences shaped the man before the court today. According to Psychologist Dr. Jones, John's "childhood was tumultuous." He parents argued constantly about money and that made John "feel like a burden..." His first experiences selling drugs resulted in him helping his family without their knowledge. The court is not presented with the stereotypical drug dealer who is running through the streets, guns ablaze, and pushing drugs through violence and gangs. The defense requests the PSR more accurately reflect John's childhood to show that his drug dealing behavior was influenced greatly by negative family experiences regarding finances and his hope was to provide finances for his family. If that is not possible, then the defense requests that the Psychologist's narrative as presented above be placed into the PSR, in full, directly underneath the objected-to narrative.

There is nothing wrong with pushing to have the scales top in your favor as much as possible. One of the most famous images in law is the Scales of Justice. And you are allowed to add nuggets to your scale as much as the other side is. If you have characteristics that need to be put forward to the sentencing court, now is the time to do it.

Part D: Sentencing Options

This is where the rubber meets the road. This section will lay out every type of sentencing option available to the judge. It will cover everything from what the statute permits, to the Guidelines calculation, the impact of a plea agreement, probation or supervised release options or requirements, fines, and restitution. It is rare for a probation officer to get this part wrong. It is basically the sum of all the parts already discussed in the PSR. If you have objections to the Guidelines calculations, then that is probably not correct. The portions that you may want to pay particular attention to, and potentially object to, are the restitution, fine, and supervised release provisions.

Restitution

Restitution is imposed as a way to cover the victim's past and (possibly) future actual losses suffered as a result of your criminal actions. And it can be imposed to compensate any victim who makes a claim to the government. Furthermore, some offenses require the imposition of restitution. For instance, if you are convicted of any child pornography offense, then restitution is mandatory and will not be less than $3,000 per victim under 18 U.S.C. § 2259A. If you are convicted of certain other offenses, named in 18 U.S.C. § 3559A, you will also have mandatory restitution. There are a number of restitution statutes and if one is mentioned in your PSR, you will want to get a copy of that statute so you can see what the exact requirements are. Your inability to pay a fine is generally not a basis to not order restitution. Or, put another way, being poor doesn't release you from restitution. And if you have a restitution order, the BOP will effectively force you to make payments on it. So will the United States Attorney's Office.

You have a right to object to restitution calculations under 18 U.S.C. § 3664(e). The burden is on the government to prove the actual loss amount sustained by the victim by a preponderance of the evidence. They also have to prove that the loss sustained is tied to the crime with which you were convicted. That means the government must submit evidence supporting the claim for a specific amount of restitution. And, unless you stipulated to a specific restitution amount, you should object if the probation officer or government asserts that restitution must be paid. You have nothing to lose by making the government do its job.

When it comes to the reality of restitution, if you know that you damaged someone in some way (and yes, if you are a child porn offender, just downloading the pics hurts the victims), you may want to make an offer to settle any restitution claims. The government is very aware that the vast majority of restitution will never be fully paid and it is quite expensive for the government to actually collect it. (Don't dare think, for a second, that the government won't seek to collect though. They absolutely will.) The PSR will specify any victims who seek restitution and their bases for that restitution. If there is an amount you could pay immediately directly to the victim, it is definitely worth a shot to have your lawyer ask the prosecutor if the victim would accept it to just clear it up. But if you do this, you absolutely need to make sure you comply with the terms offered. If you offer to pay the amount in a lump sum immediately, then make sure that is going to happen. If you are agreeing to pay it off over the course of a year, make sure that happens. Your compliance with restitution obligations does help if you ever try and get back into court for any reason (like compassionate release).

Fines

Fines can get pretty crazy. Fines are an independent part of a sentence. The statute restricts when fines may be imposed such that it will probably only happen if you are financially stable at the time

Offense Level	A Minimum	B Maximum
3 and below	$200	$9,500
4-5	$500	$9,500
6-7	$1,000	$9,500
8-9	$2,000	$20,000
10-11	$4,000	$40,000
12-13	$5,500	$55,000
14-15	$7,500	$75,000
16-17	$10,000	$95,000
18-19	$10,000	$100,000
20-22	$15,000	$150,000
23-25	$20,000	$200,000
26-28	$25,000	$250,000
29-31	$30,000	$300,000
32-34	$35,000	$350,000
35-37	$40,000	$400,000
38 and above	$50,000	$500,000.

of sentencing. If paying a fine would impair your ability to support dependents, pay restitution, or interfere with your basic survival, then a fine would be inappropriate. If you required a public defender or have a significant amount of debt, then it is unlikely that you will be assessed a fine. But if the court finds you have the ability to pay a fine, then there are a couple of legal considerations that take place. First, how much does the statute of conviction authorize for a fine? Most felony statutes authorize a fine of up to $250,000 per count of conviction. But, if you are convicted of a drug offense, the fines can increase to mil-lions of dollars. Second, what does the Guideline say the fine should be? (Hint: Look at the table provided above).

Probation

It isn't common for probation to be "authorized" by the Guidelines. But if it is, this will be covered as an option for the judge to consider. If you do not have any mandatory minimum sentence that must be imposed and you weren't convicted of a Class A or B offense, you are legally eligible for probation. If your plea agreement doesn't prohibit it, you can argue for it so long as those requirements are met. But, the ultra-majority of federal defendants serve at least some time in jail or prison. If that happens and the judge orders you to have "time served" then you will technically be under the supervised release statute. The conditions of each are largely the same and there is very little practical difference between the two. The only real difference between the two are the terms authorized. If you are convicted of a felony offense, the minimum amount of probation that may be imposed is one year and the maximum is five years. If you violate probation, the proceedings will be the same as if you were on supervised release. However, the penalties for violating will be very different.

If you violate probation, the court can either extend the term of probation or can "revoke" it. If the court revokes it, it will sentence you fully to whatever terms were justified by the statute of conviction and recommended by the Guidelines. And make no mistake, most judges are not very forgiving if you violate probation by committing any new crime (no matter how minor it is). That means if you are lucky enough to get probation and never see the inside of a jail (extremely rare, but if you pulled it off, more power to you), then you need to keep your nose clean (literally and figuratively). The judge can literally put you away for the maximum term authorized by the statute(s) of conviction and include a term of supervised release to boot.

Supervised Release

Most defendants will be given a term of supervised release. A lot of defendants believe that supervised release cannot exceed the maximum terms set by the statute of conviction. That is incorrect. Supervised release is perfectly legal and has been upheld by the courts for some time. It will not likely go away any time soon. It is imposed as part of the sentence of imprisonment but it has it's own limits independent of the statute of conviction. 18 U.S.C. § 3583 establishes the general terms of supervised release permitted in any case. It is a little confusing how the statute is written so here are a couple of tables to help you:

Potential Statutory Penalty: Maximum of LIFE (it must use the word "life")
- Offense Classification: A
- Supervised Release Maximum: 5 years
- Maximum term in prison is you violate: 5 years

Potential Statutory Penalty: Maximum of 25 years or more (but does not have the word "life)
- Offense Classification: B
- Supervised Release Maximum: 5 years
- Maximum term in prison if you violate: 3 years

Surviving Pretrial · 435

Potential Statutory Penalty: Maximum of 10-25 years
- Offense Classification: C
- Supervised Release Maximum: 3 years
- Maximum term in prison if you violate: 2 years

Potential Statutory Penalty: Maximum of 5-10 years
- Offense Classification: D
- Supervised Release Maximum: 2 years
- Maximum Term in prison if you violate: 1 year

IF YOU ARE CONVICTED OF ANY DRUG OFFENSE

Convicted under 21 U.S.C. § 841(b)(1)(A)
- Potential Statutory Penalty: 10-Life
- Offense Classification: A
- Supervised Release Minimum: 5 years
- Supervised Release Maximum: LIFE
- Maximum term in prison if you violate: 5 years

Convicted under 21 U.S.C. § 841(b)(1)(B)
- Potential Statutory Penalty: 5-40 years
- Offense Classification: B
- Supervised Release Minimum: 4 years
- Supervised Release Maximum: Life

- Maximum term in prison if you violate: 3 years

Convicted under 21 U.S.C. § 841(b)(1)(C)
- Potential Statutory Penalty: 0-20 years
- Offense Classification: C
- Supervised Release Minimum: 3 years
- Supervised Release Maximum: Life
- Maximum term in prison if you violate: 2 years

Note: If you have a prior violent offense or drug offense conviction (as defined under the Controlled Substances Act) and an information was filed by the prosecutor under 21 U.S.C. § 851, the supervised release minimums double. Further, the imprisonment terms essentially double as well which could affect the maximum term in prison if you violate.

IF YOU ARE CONVICTED OF ANY FEDERAL SEX OFFENSE OR FAILURE TO REGISTER AS A SEX OFFENDER:

- Potential Statutory Penalty: ANY
- Offense Classification: ANY
- Supervised Release Minimum: 5 years
- Supervised Release Maximum: LIFE
- Maximum term in prison if you violate:

- If the maximum term authorized by statute of conviction is LIFE: 5 years
- If the maximum term authorized by statute of conviction is 25 or more years: 3 years
- If the maximum term authorized by statute of conviction is less than 25 years: 2 years

If anything in this section doesn't jive with the relevant statutes, then you will want to make sure and object. To be sure, if the judge imposes a sentence above that authorized by statute, it is illegal and can be vacated. But, you don't want to even have that as a problem. Let everyone know that you know what the maximum penalties are to protect yourself.

There is something else that you need to think about in this section. The Constitution demands that you be provided with all the information regarding the direct consequences of pleading guilty before pleading guilty. Direct consequences includes knowledge of potential immigration consequences, supervised release terms, the minimum sentence, and the potential maximum sentence. It does not include fines, restitution, forfeiture, or special penalty assessments. And it generally does not include the Guidelines calculation. If you were not provided some or any of this information and you would have insisted on going to trial had you known the real consequences, then you could move the court to vacate your plea. If you would not have insisted on trial had you understood the exact consequences of your plea, then you shouldn't move to vacate your plea.

Part E: Downward Departures

The probation officer is required to analyze whether any "downward departure" provisions of the Guidelines could apply to your case. It is uncommon for a probation officer to outright agree that a "downward departure" should apply. But if they do suggest one, then you and your lawyer will want to latch on it for sentencing because it is very powerful. More than anything, however, you want to see what the probation officer says about the application of downward departures and the facts they state in their analysis. If they got something wrong, then you need to say they are off base. It could help get the downward departure.

Mind you, downward departures are very hard to get because they are so specific in their application. That doesn't mean there aren't reasons for the judge to reduce your Guidelines offense level. But that's called a "downward variance." A downward variance is a reduction granted for any reason that is supported by the § 3553(a) factors but not necessarily the Guidelines. For instance, you probably will want to try and argue that your behavior was "aberrant." Aberrant behavior is a potential downward departure that the Guidelines establishes has specific circumstances associated with it:

§5K2.20 - ABERRANT BEHAVIOR (POLICY STATEMENT)

(a) In General.—Except where a defendant is convicted of an offense involving a minor victim under section 1201, an offense under section 1591, or an offense under chapter 71, 109A, 110, or 117, of title 18, United States Code, a downward departure may be warranted in an exceptional case if (1) the defendant's criminal conduct meets the requirements of subsection (b); and (2) the departure is not prohibited under subsection (c).

(b) Requirements.—The court may depart downward under this policy statement only if the defendant committed a single criminal occurrence or single criminal transaction that (1) was committed without significant planning; (2) was of limited duration; and (3) represents a marked deviation by the defendant from an otherwise law-abiding life.

(c) Prohibitions Based on the Presence of Certain Circumstances.—The court may not depart downward pursuant to this policy statement if any of the following circumstances are present:

(1) The offense involved serious bodily injury or death.

(2) The defendant discharged a firearm or otherwise used a firearm or a dangerous weapon.

(3) The instant offense of conviction is a serious drug trafficking offense.

(4) The defendant has either of the following: (A) more than one criminal history point, as determined under Chapter Four (Criminal History and Criminal Livelihood) before application of subsection (b) of §4A1.3

(Departures Based on Inadequacy of Criminal History Category); or (B) a prior federal or state felony conviction, or any other significant prior criminal behavior, regardless of whether the conviction or significant prior criminal behavior is countable under Chapter Four.

If you don't technically meet that standard in the Guidelines, your lawyer can request the judge reduce your Guidelines level anyways as a variance.

Let's say you were convicted of a crime involving a minor victim which precludes application of 5K2.20. If the other elements of the aberrant behavior Guideline applies, you may still be able to convince the judge that the Guidelines over-penalize your conduct because it was otherwise aberrant. In order to bring such an argument to the judge, you will have to make it known to the probation officer to consider when revising the report. A truly effective objection letter could actually convince the probation officer to agree with you that the conduct was otherwise aberrant based on their own review of the presented evidence. If the probation officer agrees they will say so in their revised report.

Stage Five
Corrections, Clarifications and Objections to the PSR

Rule 32(f) of the Federal Rules of Criminal Procedure specifically provides that either party (i.e. the government or the defendant) can object to any portion of the presentence report. But the objections absolutely need to be sent to the probation officer **NO LATER THAN 14-DAYS** after the report is disclosed to your lawyer. Those exact words are in the rule. Bug your lawyer after you are interviewed about whether it has been disclosed. That way he can`t feign ignorance that you didn`t want a copy of it. While the law says you are absolutely entitled to receive a copy of it, lawyers can be pretty bad about getting it to you with enough time to file objections. If the objections are going to be late for any reason (lawyer is sick, you guys are being prevented from conferring at the jail, zombie apocalypse starts, etc.) your lawyer needs to request an extension from the probation officer immediately. A simple email to the probation officer and the prosecutor requesting an extension is all it takes.

All the notes you took are going to be the basis for every correction, clarification, and objection you present. Corrections are easy. They usually involve misspellings of names, incorrect addresses, and the like. Clarifications seek to provide more information about a subject so the probation officer can include it in the report to be complete. Objections are disagreements with the probation officer's assessment of the facts or application of the law to your case.

> **Correction** The PSR reflects that the defendant's name is John Edward Smith. However, Mr. Smith's middle name is Edwin. Therefore, the PSR should be corrected to reflect that the defendant's name is John Edwin Smith.
>
> **Clarification** The PSR states that Mr. Smith lived in Quantico, Virginia while he was enlisted in the Marine Corps. However, that address is merely the headquarters location of the United States Marine Corps. Rather, Mr. Smith was stationed at Camp Lejeune in North Carolina and never resided in Virginia.
>
> **Objection** The PSR states that Mr. Smith intended to distribute 100 KG of heroin and applies a level 38 base offense level under 2D1.1(c). But,

Mr. Smith was convicted solely of conspiracy and his involvement did not include any distribution whatsoever. This is made clear through the ROI reports provided by the DEA during the course of the investigation. See ROI dated Jan. 5, 2020 at Bates 542. DEA Agent Mark Jones specifically stated that "it is obvious that target John Smith was unaware of the breadth of the conspiracy to which he became involved. The principals to the conspiracy routinely intimated to him that they were only going to sell 1 KG of heroin." Therefore, the defense objects to the incorrect base offense level and use of any language that alleges Mr. Smith of intending to distribute 1000 KG of heroin. Rather, he should only be held accountable for 1 KG of heroin which yields a base offense level of 30.

The above examples are completely made up. They are put here to demonstrate the purpose of each type of statement that is going to be made to the probation officer. The most important for sentencing purposes will be the "objections." But all of them are important because the PSR is your Bible for the rest of your life. That PSR will be relied on for literally everything from the BOP to probation when you are serving supervised release. You want to make sure that the small errors are corrected and that the full picture is provided to anyone who may read the document. That's why you have "corrections" and "clarifications." Objections not only preserve appeal issues but also can make a specific point to the judge and probation officer.

Most good lawyers prepare the Rule 32(f) Corrections, Clarifications, and Objections in letter format. They usually discuss everything in paragraph order. This makes the probation officer's life considerably easier. It is not advised to get cute with this letter and jump all over the place. Hopefully your lawyer already knows that! The letter should go paragraph-by-paragraph and note any corrections, clarifications, or objections you may have. And do not let your lawyer tell you that the correction, clarification, or objection is not necessary. That is for the probation officer or judge to decide. As it stands for your purposes, the PSR needs to be as perfect as possible. The probation officer may not agree with you and then the issue will be taken to the judge later. That procedure counsels that you should bring the issues up. Be a stickler here. The presentence report is that important.

Every PSR should have something to correct, clarify, **AND** object to. Note the "and." Probation officers who write the reports are human and make mistakes all the time. Just like anyone else. So do judges for that matter. That is why there are so many safety nets. If your lawyer tells you that there doesn't need to be a letter at all, I would suggest that you seek another lawyer. If you are stuck with a public defender or CJA counsel, then I would stress to them that you know how important the PSR is and that the chance of a human being not making a single error in its creation is ridiculous. If, after you make it known that you know of errors in the report, the lawyer still says there is nothing to file, then I would suggest that you file a motion with the court citing an "irreconcilable difference" with counsel and that new counsel is needed. This is a topic we covered in Part Four: Lawyers.

You will want to make sure the lawyer provides you with a copy of the letter to the probation officer showing all corrections, clarifications and objections to the report. You want to save this until you get the final PSR so you can compare.

Examples

There are number of common objections that are filed when draft PSR`s are disclosed. You should consider if the situation applies to your circumstances that you have a serious discussion with your lawyer to advance such an objection. This is hardly a complete list either. There are innumerable objections that can be advanced to a presentence report. Always remember, every point matters. And never forget that the BOP will use the PSR for your entire term of imprisonment and it will be considered gospel in all decisions regarding your imprisonment.

Supervised Release Conditions

The end of the PSR probably has supervised release conditions that the probation officer proposes should be included in the judgment. This is routinely ignored by lawyers but shouldn`t be. The proper procedure is to object to conditions before sentencing. If the probation officer disagrees (which they likely will), then you will have to bring the objection into court. Failure to object to supervised release conditions at this stage will waive any objection as to the legality of the conditions later. While that doesn`t mean you can`t request the court modify conditions later, when you waive the right to challenge the legality of the conditions, you make your life harder. Most lawyers don't look at this because their concern is trying to keep you from going to prison for the rest of your life. And we all agree they should be concerned about that. But, conditions can serve to put you back in prison if you violate them so challenging them to make them less onerous is also a priority.

Challenging conditions of supervised release can also have a psychological effect on the judge. That's because if you are pressing arguments that presume you will be released, then the judge's mind is going to see you as being released. If you are concerned with getting a literal life sentence and don't want your lawyer worrying about this, then you are probably right. But if you are expecting to survive prison and make it home, then you need to think about this.

You should read each condition and, if they seem ridiculous, then you should speak with your lawyer about the prospect of challenging those conditions. Your lawyer should research the law on the matter as there are a multitude of cases that have spoken of improper conditions and ways to fix them. If the conditions seem like they are livable and reasonable, then you probably don't need to challenge them.

Drug Weight

There is a really serious problem occurring in the court system and that's called "ghost dope." Ghost dope consists of any drug that the probation officer or government says was involved in the crime but has no actual evidence for it. For instance, if you plead guilty to conspiring to distribute 1 KG or more of heroin, then you are facing a 10 year mandatory minimum. That is a big range of possibilities. The Guidelines could be as low as base offense level 30, which starts at 87-121 months, or could be as high as 38, which starts at 235-293 months. The probation officer will read a lot of reports that say that their informant said you wanted to distribute 1 kilo of heroin 90 times over the course of the previous year. They don't have any other information than the informant, but they will hold you "accountable" for 90 kilograms of heroin. That is ghost dope and there is only one way to really challenge it. **<u>OBJECT</u>**.

You should demand the government prove the reliability of their informant's information because the informant is likely being paid with freedom to provide the information. The burden of proof at sentencing is lower than at trial, but it is still meaningful. All your lawyer has to do is request a hearing on the matter and he can further file a "Brady Motion" seeking information relating to the informant's deal in order to discredit the informant.

Ghost dope has reeked havoc on many people's cases and they are always upset when it is used to enhance their sentence. You may not win, but if you challenge the use of "ghost dope" as "unreliable" or "unproven by a preponderance of the evidence" you may have an appealable issue. The only way to get that is to object.

There is another aspect of drug weight that can seriously affect your case. That is the purity of the substance. It is unlikely that the offense involved a 100% pure substance. But when the presentence report comes back, it presumes that all the ghost dope and even drugs that were actually seized are 100% pure. It is important to demand your lawyer challenge this, especially with ghost dope. Taking the example above, the government's informant says you guys were talking about distributing a kilo of heroin 90 times. Well, was that going to be 100% pure heroin? What does the informant say about that? Unless you are Pablo Escobar's family, or you have access to poppy fields in Afghanistan, then you probably have little-to-no intention (or ability for that matter) of acquiring 100% pure heroin. An expert could easily testify that the ultra-majority of drug offenses involve drugs with a lower than 75% purity (or even less). That would allow you to argue that 90 kilograms is too much because if it was only going to be 75% pure, then the relevant conduct should "only" hold you accountable for 65.5 kilos, or a base offense level of 36 (188-235 months). If the government can invent ghost dope, then you can certainly invent intended purity! And there is no reason not to argue about it either. If enough people quibble with the government's use of ghost dope to increase drug weight amounts, then the courts will start rejecting its use as a waste of time.

Criminal History Calculations

In the Appendix of this book, you will find the Guidelines that concern calculating your criminal history. It's like doing taxes. But you need to become a pro at this. All too often, lawyers presume the probation officer got it right. But the probation officer is pulling your record from government computers and those can certainly be wrong. If you have prior offenses, then you need to be absolutely sure that your criminal history score is calculated correctly. If **_anything_** is wrong, then you need to object. Criminal history will affect the sentence you get and will also play a vital role in prison placement decisions. The Bureau of Prisons will look to your criminal history points to determine your base score for security purposes.

The idea here is to be clear and understandable for the probation officer. Many lawyers want to keep these documents short. But this is more like math than a book report. Take all the space you need to work it out. That doesn't mean to make an argument long for the sake of length. The probation officer should not be concerned with how many pages the objection letter comes to. Hopefully, the probation officer was correct and needed very little clarification on anything. It would be even better if the probation officer didn't say anything objectionable in the report. That isn't likely, but if that's the case, then cool. The point is, don't let your lawyer tell you that there isn't enough space to correct, clarify or object to part of the report.

Stage Six
Response to Government's Objections

It isn't very common for the government to object to the probation officer's assessment, but it does happen. And if it does happen, then you need to make sure your lawyer responds to the objection unless you are both satisfied that the government is absolutely correct about its objection (it is a rare day for a sane defendant to agree with anything the government says). The reason you need to make sure that your lawyer responds, and responds in a timely manner, is you will end up conceding the issue if you remain silent about it. Make sure your lawyer knows that you know a response is absolutely necessary if the government files any objections to the PSR. The response would go to the probation officer. While the response **could** be included in your own objections, if your lawyer waited that long to file your objection letter, then you should consider finding new counsel. Your objection letter needs to be detailed and well researched, but it should also be rapid fired. Your lawyer should **NOT** ask for more time or wait the entire 14 days to get this done.

Stage Seven
Final Disclosure

After the probation officer gets all the objections and responses, they will consider them. One way or another, you will be informed of the probation officer's decisions. They are required to note each and every objection, correction, and clarification and provide their own response for each. These will be at the beginning of the final PSR. You will need to go through and take note of any you lost and then determine if you will be pushing your issue further. Sometimes you will read what the probation officer says and agree with them. If that is the case, then you can move on. But if you disagree with there assessment, then it is time to declare a war.

Stage Eight
Formal Objections

The way to declare war is to file a set of formal objections with the judge. Your lawyer should put together a full motion and brief asking for everything you guys want. If the objection concerns a fact, especially a fact that goes to the Guidelines calculation, you want to make sure your lawyer demands an evidentiary hearing on the issue(s). This matters even if a fact doesn't go to the Guidelines but will likely effect the sentence. Don't be afraid to tell the government you want them to prove something that isn't provable. If it is clearly provable, you will want to leave it alone. Once the formal objections are filed, then the court will schedule any necessary hearings and will further set the case for sentencing.

Sentencing Mitigation Videos

There is a fantastic way to humanize you and tell your story to a judge and that's through the use of sentencing videos. Videography is something that has been used in trial work for years but is relatively new to the criminal sentencing world. The long of the short of it is that it works. There is nothing more effective at convincing anyone to do something than through video. The reason why Super Bowl commercials are so expensive is because they work.

There are number of people out there who provide video development services but none is more effective than Doug Passon from Arizona. Anyone else who produces sentencing videos probably called Doug for advice or training. His contact information is at the beginning of this book. Doug has spent his career as a criminal defense attorney. He worked in the Arizona state court as a public defender and went on to become a Federal Public Defender in the District of Arizona. All through his career, Doug has spent a significant amount of energy becoming an award winning video documentarian as well. He combined these two passions and has created the most effective sentencing advocacy available today. This is one of those services that I highly recommend you try and retain. If there is a toss up for funds to go to a private defense or getting a sentencing video, I would go with the appointed lawyer and seek to bring Doug on (using those donated funds or what's left of your own assets if you can access them).

What makes Doug an incredible sentencing video specialist is he is an attorney. Although, I joke with him constantly that he isn't really an attorney. That's because while he has a license and graduated from law school, he doesn't act like any typical attorney. He is easy to speak with and genuinely cares about your life. Make no mistake, he is vicious in a courtroom too. But these days, he concentrates mostly on sentencing mitigation consulting and video development. So, what does he do?

First thing Doug does is develops a "story board." He will try and pinpoint the most compelling story to tell the judge. And when I say "story" I don't mean to imply that it is a fictional representation of who you are. Doug's job is to bring the truth forward and show the judge that you are a normal person. Normal people have faults and have successes. It doesn't matter if they face a federal judge or not. Most people are not evil (like the prosecutor or news anchor will have everyone believe). In my case, I sent Doug a mini-autobiography detailing several aspects of my life that I thought could be relevant. After reading that and reviewing the case discovery, he put together the story board that would be used to develop my video.

With his story board, he puts together a list of people who need to be interviewed on camera to be used in the video. The video he puts together is a lot like what you would watch on the History Channel or Discovery. There should be several people who bring the story together because that is what gives any true story credibility. After videoing everyone who needs to be interviewed, Doug edits the whole thing and makes a video that is short enough for a judge's busy schedule (no more than 15 or 20 minutes). Doug also gathers any pictures and videos from your past that he believes could help tell the story to include in the video. The final product is really good. In fact, it will make you believe that you are being featured on prime time television.

Doug will be happy to show you videos that he produced. He only shows videos from clients who have given him prior authorization. As it happens, I am one of those clients. Just ask Doug to show you Bilal Khan's video and he will. Doug, using his many powers of persuasion, convinced the jail I was at to allow me to wear a button down shirt for the video. The fact that we were able to film in a jail was pretty impressive too. Doug has many ways to get things done.

Doug doesn't just do full-on sentencing movies either. He is a sentence mitigation specialist and is someone that you can contact early in your case. He can help guide your lawyer through plea negotiations and can even develop smaller videos to help those negotiations. One thing you will find about Doug is he is extremely fair on his pricing and he is well worth the cost.

Whether you use Doug or someone else, a sentencing video is something that can be extremely powerful to show the judge (and your family or friends, prosecutors, and probation officers) you are a person and that you accept responsibility for your mistakes while also telling the judge why the crime happened. During a sentencing hearing, you will only get a couple of minutes to give a statement. With a video, the judge is given a copy of it well before sentencing (with your sentencing memorandum) and can watch it "in chambers." The judge can digest it. And what is said in that video would take 50 pages (at least) in a brief to cover. The judge would prefer a 15 minute video than have to read a boring brief for an hour to get the same information. It also can save the judge a lot of time during a sentencing hearing because all your witnesses are presented in the video. They didn't have to come to court, be questioned, and be cross-examined. Sure, a prosecutor can cry that the witness wasn't cross-examined and could demand they be called as a witness, but rest assured, the judge isn't going to be too happy about it. Prosecutors creating more work for a judge is almost as bad as a defense lawyer doing it!

If you don't have the money for a sentencing video, it is possible to hire a "Sentencing Mitigation Specialist" for a lower price. In the State of Arizona, these people are common. I don't know how common they are in other state systems, but they are NOT common in federal court. Hopefully it becomes more common because they really do help. Think of a sentencing mitigation specialist as an investigator who concentrates only on sentencing. They are the ones who will develop everything for your lawyer to use to try and get you a lower sentence. There are a few federal specialists out there. One I know is Tess

Lopez who has worked with Alan Ellis substantially. She was involved in my case and helped generate our letters to the probation officer. As she was a federal probation officer in a previous life, she was very helpful in navigating those waters.

Because there is a high likelihood that you will face a federal sentencing court if you are reading this, my suggestion is to contact Doug as early in the process as possible. The help he provides can literally prevent you from rotting in prison for decades. Finally, if Doug doesn't think your money would be well spent using his services, he will tell you that. Put another way, he is not a money-grubbing shyster who wants to cheat you.

Sentencing Memorandum

Every federal lawyer should know that submitting a sentencing memorandum at least a week before the sentencing hearing is absolutely essential to advocate your case. Usually, this memorandum is written in tandem with your formal objections to the PSR, but the elements are very different. The objections are the objections. The sentencing memorandum advocates for a particular sentence. This is where your lawyer presents other cases that are similar to yours and other information to convince the judge the sentence you are asking for is appropriate. **Even if you have a locked in plea, your lawyer should still prepare a sentencing memorandum.** If you did a video, most of the information about you as a person will be presented there. There are still things the lawyer can do to advocate for you in writing though. And they should do this. The best way to make sure your lawyer gets this done is to always refer to the sentencing memorandum as a certainty in every conversation you have rather than asking "if" they will do a memorandum.

> *"You'll make sure to talk about that in the sentencing memorandum, I'm sure."*
>
> *"When you write the sentencing memorandum, please make sure to highlight the letter from my college professor."*

The sentencing memorandum should be prepared no later than the date all the objections are going to be filed. Whether they are in a single document or in separate documents is a stylistic issue that your lawyer can figure out. Make sure the lawyer gives you a copy to read. You'll know you are reading a sentencing memorandum if you see a section talking about the § 3553(a) factors. These are the factors a judge is **REQUIRED** to consider **BEFORE** imposing a sentence. Because most judges will decide what they are going to do **BEFORE** the hearing even kicks off, you want this to be presented with enough time for the judge to consider it all.

The § 3553(a) factors are:

(1) ▢ *the nature and circumstances of the offense and the history and characteristics of the defendant;*

(2) ▢ *the need for the sentence imposed--*

(A) ▢ *to reflect the seriousness of the offense, to promote respect for the law, and to provide just punishment for the offense;*

(B) ▢ *to afford adequate deterrence to criminal conduct;*

(C) ▢ *to protect the public from further crimes of the defendant; and*

(D) ▢ *to provide the defendant with needed educational or vocational training, medical care, or other correctional treatment in the most effective manner;*

(3) ▢ *the kinds of sentences available;*

(4) ▢ *the kinds of sentence and the sentencing range established for--*

(A) ▢ *the applicable category of offense committed by the applicable category of defendant as set forth in the guidelines--*

(i) ▢ *issued by the Sentencing Commission pursuant to section 994(a)(1) of title 28, United States Code , subject to any amendments made to such guidelines by act of*

Congress (regardless of whether such amendments have yet to be incorporated by the Sentencing Commission into amendments issued under section 994(p) of title 28); and

(ii) ☐that, except as provided in section 3742(g) , are in effect on the date the defendant is sentenced; or

(B) ☐in the case of a violation of probation or supervised release, the applicable guidelines or policy statements issued by the Sentencing Commission pursuant to section 994(a)(3) of title 28, United States Code , taking into account any amendments made to such guidelines or policy statements by act of Congress (regardless of whether such amendments have yet to be incorporated by the Sentencing Commission into amendments issued under section 994(p) of title 28);

(5) ☐any pertinent policy statement--

(A) ☐issued by the Sentencing Commission pursuant to section 994(a)(2) of title 28, United States Code , subject to any amendments made to such policy statement by act of Congress (regardless of whether such amendments have yet to be incorporated by the Sentencing Commission into amendments issued under section 994(p) of title 28); and

(B) ☐that, except as provided in section 3742(g) , is in effect on the date the defendant is sentenced. 1

> (6) ▢the need to avoid unwarranted sentence disparities among defendants with similar records who have been found guilty of similar conduct; and
>
> (7) ▢the need to provide restitution to any victims of the offense.

Your lawyer should talk about each of these factors in relation to your case. If you are trying to get the judge to accept a C-Plea, then the lawyer will spend more time showing the judge that the agreement is fair and doesn't offend other sentences imposed by creating an unwarranted disparity. If you are trying to get a judge to go with the government's recommendation, your lawyer will probably spend more time talking about your acceptance of responsibility and how the recommended sentence is fair. If you are facing a wide range and the Guidelines are being contested through objections, your lawyer needs to be detailed with each of these factors. The more discretion the judge has in fashioning your sentence, the more detailed the § 3553(a) section needs to be.

If your lawyer is balking at this and not preparing a sentencing memorandum, you may want to move the court for a new lawyer. Because you are so close to sentencing, you will want to explain to the judge that it is apparent that you aren't being provided with effective assistance of counsel at sentencing because your lawyer isn't preparing seriously for sentencing. An effective attorney would know that sentencing is very serious and requires as much diligence as a trial. While asking for a new lawyer will delay your sentencing hearing, if the lawyer isn't working hard for you, then you need someone else. This is where it all ends. Once you get to the sentencing hearing, the train has left the station and the roller coaster can't be called back. **DO NOT ASSUME YOU WILL BE ABLE TO WIN AN APPEAL IF YOU DON'T ASK FOR A NEW LAWYER.**

Sentencing Proceedings

We spoke generally about what the sentencing hearing entails before but there is so much more that needs to be done. Sentencing is usually the most stressful and most important aspect of the case for everyone facing a felony case. This is the hearing where the gavel falls and the sentence is imposed. There won't be any more guessing. Once the judge states what your sentence is, that is the sentence. The case is over. Regardless of whether you pleaded guilty or took the case to trial, you need to prepare hard for sentencing and make sure your lawyer is ready, willing and able to present your sentencing case.

If you submitted a sentencing video, it is imperative that your lawyer ensure that the judge was able to view it. Doug Passon makes it available via a secure web link **_and_** delivers a DVD to the judge's chambers for their convenience. It is also a great idea to make sure the DVD is filed on the record with the Clerk's office. This should have been done when you submitted the sentencing memorandum. But, it doesn't hurt for your lawyer to call chambers and ask the judge's secretary if there were any problems or if a replacement DVD is needed. If the judge needs a replacement, then by all means your lawyer needs to get them a replacement very quick. Who cares that there is a web link? The judge is old and probably just wants to insert a disc and watch. Make it easy for the judge. It goes a long way.

Hopefully the judge is moved by your video. If you didn't submit a sentencing video, then your lawyer hopefully submitted a kickass sentencing memorandum. There are a bunch of other things to take care of before you are actually sentenced. It all usually happens the same day, but it could take several days depending on how many objections you have to the PSR. Each objection to the PSR could take some time to resolve. These are the objections that you filed in Stage Eight. Aside from the objections, the judge will need to provide a final Guidelines calculation, hear from any victims, hear arguments from the prosecutor, hear arguments from the defense, and give you an opportunity to make a statement. After all that is done, then the judge will impose the sentence.

If the issue is factual, then the judge is going to give the lawyers an opportunity to bring in witnesses or evidence to prove their side of the case. The judge will have to decide who wins and, in most instances, the judge will make the decision right there. If it is a delicate or really difficult issue, the judge may want to postpone the sentencing until he can make a decision. Or, the judge can punt the decision if he wants to by stating that the judge will not rely on the fact at issue in determining your sentence. No matter what, one of these three things needs to happen. If you lose the objection, and you properly protected your appellate rights, then it is an issue that you could appeal. If the government loses, there are a number of rules they must abide by before they can appeal, but it is potentially appealable by them too.

If the issue is legal, then there doesn't need to be a taking of evidence. Each side will, however, be given an opportunity to present their arguments as to why a decision one way or the other is appropriate. The judge will have to decide who is right. Unlike factual issues, pretty much every legal issue will have to be resolved. Sometimes there are complicated legal issues that are presented and the judge will need time to stew on it before making a decision. Other times, the judge is well versed in the issue and has already decided the issue. The vast majority of issues will be decided right then for most cases because the issues would have been presented in the formal objections and sentencing memorandum. Presumably, the judge would have already researched the issue but will give the lawyers a chance to offer other argument. The more complicated issues that require more time usually involve steep statutory enhancements like the Armed Career Criminal Act or mandatory life sentences listed in 18 U.S.C. § 3559. As the stakes get higher, the judge will be more prudent and deliberate. That means it will take more time to decide. That`s good if you are facing these very complicated issues. You want the judge to think seriously before putting you away for life if there is a choice either way.

After the factual and legal issues are resolved, the judge will provide the final Guidelines calculation. Unless your lawyer is really terrible, there shouldn`t be any surprises here. Either you won your objections and you got the Guidelines calculation you wanted, you lost your objections and got the calculation provided in the PSR, or somewhere in between.

While it is rare for judges to impose sentences above the Guidelines, it does happen. If the court intends on going above the calculated Guidelines range (called an upward departure or upward variance), it absolutely must give you and your lawyer notice of its intention to do so **BEFORE THE SENTENCING HEARING.** The purpose of the notice is to warn you to really prepare to try and convince the judge to go lower. If you are served with one of these notices, your job is going to be a lot harder. If I were served with one of these notices, I would call in every favor I could and get enough money to call someone like Doug Passon or Alan Ellis because I don't know anyone else who could change a judge's mind after one of those notices comes out.

The most important part of the sentencing hearing will be when you get to speak. This is your last chance to convince the judge that he or she should give you the lowest possible sentence available. Up until this point, you should have submitted a statement to the probation officer and you also should have made a statement during the PSR interview. You need to presume the judge read or heard of everything you said previously. That means you need to prepare a little speech to give the judge. No judge wants to hear you read from a piece of paper. No judge wants to hear the same old song and dance that typical defendants spew to them every day. Federal judges have heard it all and they are phenomenal bullshit detectors. So don't try and overdo it.

I have helped a number of people prepare their allocutions. And the most successful are ones that truly come from the heart. Some defendants are religious and if you legitimately are, you may want to include things from your religion. One guy I helped, who was standing before a judge after molesting his boyfriend's son (and thought he would go away for 10 years), was able to convince the judge to give him probation by quoting a passage from the Bible. Everyone, including the defendant, was stunned. The passage was only part of the success though. He actually showed that he was legitimately sorry. Before that hearing, he was very good at blaming everyone else for what he did. He actually told me, point blank, that it wasn't his fault, and that his boyfriend started it all. I got pretty angry myself at the guy and told him that, as a grown man, he could have – and therefore should have – stopped the abuse. But instead of stopping it, he joined in. It was definitely his fault. Once I read him the riot act, he got his shit together and figured out that he actually was at fault and he exuded that fault in his allocution. That is what won him probation.

Someone else I tried to help didn't have such a good outcome and that's because he tried to bullshit the judge. Rather than actually believing he was at fault for dealing meth which killed a teenager, he had the audacity to get up and say, "I never intended anyone to get hurt. I would never hurt someone." The judge was fuming when he said that. Why? Because if a drug dealer never had any intention of hurting anyone, then why in the hell did he deal drugs to teens? Because of greed and that is what the judge knew. It would have been better if the guy listened to me and realized that the driving force for his criminal actions was greed. Had he told the judge, "I never wanted anyone to die. But, I didn't really care if anyone got hurt because all I saw were dollar signs. Dollar signs are what funded my own habits and I couldn't see past my own face to even care if anyone got hurt. For that I am sorry. I am fully aware that had I not been greedy, Timmy probably wouldn't have died." A judge would eat that up if it was said with sincerity.

What does sincerity mean though? It means that what you are saying matches up with what happened. If you were dealing drugs because you had to pay gambling debts and you had a gambling problem, then anything you say should talk about that. If you go in and say that you were greedy, but in reality your problem was you were trying to save your family from financial ruin, then greed shouldn't be your statement because it would be insincere. The financial ruin potential would be what mattered to you. Don't get caught up in trying to find sincerity though. If you are talking about what really drove you to commit the crime, then you will be sincere.

There are times a defendant *shouldn't* give a statement to the judge. If that is something that you and your lawyer have decided will happen, then it shouldn't be too difficult. The judge will ask you if you have anything to say. If you are *not* going to say anything simply say,

I do not wish to make a statement your Honor.

That's it. The judge will move on to the next phase of the proceedings.

If you have family or friends who want to attend the hearing and someone wants to speak to the judge on your behalf, you need to make sure and tell your lawyer *before* the hearing that this is going to happen. The lawyer will make sure and let the judge know that someone wants to speak on your behalf. It isn't really helpful to have your parents stand up and speak for you because it is expected what they will say will be positive. Even so, if someone wants to speak and you and your lawyer don't think it would hurt, then by all means have them speak. The judge will not have the time to listen to more than one person. Therefore, you and your lawyer want to choose the strongest possible person to speak on your behalf. When they will be allowed to speak will usually be right after your allocution, but the judge can do it any time. That is why your lawyer needs to know up front.

Sometimes lawyers tell their clients to not have their family or friends attend the hearing. While this is a personal choice for you and your family, I personally advocate the opposite. Having your family and friends there humanizes you to the judge. It shows you have support. It shows the judge that when you get out, there is some hope you will do well. **YOU** shouldn't advocate for anyone to come to the hearing either. Simply let your family and friends know the date of the hearing and the time. If they want to come, it is a public place and they can go. You can warn your family that if they go, they should expect the prosecution to make you sound like a monster and to not believe everything they hear. It does happen that friends go to these hearings, hear something, and then find they don't like the defendant any longer. That is one risk of people coming to your court hearings.

If your family or friends ask you "what should I say" if they are called to speak, your response should be "The truth." Do not offer anything. You shouldn't tell anyone what to say in court. Ever. **Just tell them to tell the truth.** That's it.

After everyone gets an opportunity to speak to the judge, the judge will take the time to speak to everyone. Often times, the judge will summarize what they just heard and make comments on the record to show they were paying attention. After they do this, they will go on to pronounce the sentence. No matter how important this part is, you aren't going to pay attention. It's way too stressful to pay attention. But, that is why there is a record. When the judge says, "It is the judgment of this Court that [your name] is guilty of [your crimes] and hereby sentences you to [time in prison, fines, supervised release, etc.]," everything that follows is your sentence. What is said will be written in a "Judgment" that will be sent to the Bureau of Prisons. You will be able to ask your lawyer for a copy of the judgment or ask your case manager in the prison.

After the sentence is pronounced, the hearing is over. The judge will ask if there is anything else. I believe you should lean over and tell your lawyer that you **want the lawyer to file a notice of appeal unless you got literally everything you wanted and all objections were in your favor.** In order to appeal anything, a "Notice of Appeal" must be filed. These are really simple documents and it takes a lawyer like 30 seconds to write. If you decide to withdraw the appeal and dismiss it later that's fine. It is way easier to dismiss an open appeal than it is to start an appeal too late. **You only have 14 days from the date the judgment is entered** (usually your sentencing date) **to file the notice of appeal.** If you miss that 14-days, you are hit. You will not be able to appeal.

IF YOU WANT TO APPEAL FOR ANY REASON, YOU SHOULD TELL YOUR LAWYER IMMEDIATELY. Don't wait for your lawyer to come and talk to you. Don't wait to meet with your lawyer another day. Say it before you leave the courtroom. Say, "I want to appeal and I want you to file a notice of appeal right now."

If you aren't able to speak to your lawyer and you want to appeal, then you can always send in your own notice of appeal. If you don't know if your lawyer did it, or you are having trouble contacting them, then mail off your own. It doesn't hurt if more than one notice shows up. But it hurts like hell if nobody sends a notice. Here is a notice of appeal you can use. Remember, you have to put in the caption with your case number like we talked about with writing motions.

> ### Notice of Appeal
>
> Defendant, [YOUR NAME], respectfully NOTIFIES the Court and the United States that he is appealing the Court's entry of judgment in the above captioned case to the [Your Court's Circuit] Circuit Court of Appeals.

Date it and sign it. Mail it to the United States District Court where you were sentenced. On the envelope, write "**Attn: CLERK OF THE COURT**" and in the front left corner write, "**URGENT: TIME SENSITIVE**." Make sure you make a copy. If you are in jail when you mail the notice of appeal, you will want to execute an Inmate Declaration of Mailing. To do that, just put the following at the bottom of your motion:

> I declare under the penalty of perjury that: I am an inmate confined at [NAME OF JAIL OR PRISON] and I deposited the foregoing Notice of

> *Appeal into the institution's internal mailing system and properly paid the required postage on [DATE YOU GAVE IT TO JAIL PERSONNEL TO MAIL IT] for delivery to the United States Postal Service.*

Date it and sign it. Make sure that you put a copy of this in the envelope too. **MAKE SURE THE JAIL OR PRISON LOGS THE MAIL IN THEIR OUTGOING LEGAL MAIL BOOK.** If you do all this and the mailing arrives late for whatever reason, you will be protected by the "Prison Mailbox Rule." But, try and get the notice to the court as fast as possible.

After the notice of appeal is filed, the case will be sent to the Court of Appeals. You will get more information about the appeal at a later time. For now, rest assured that your appeal is active. When you get to your designated prison, you can start that process.

Appendix A

Guidelines Sentencing Table

The Sentencing Table on the next page is the same table used in the Guidelines book. You need to make sure and calculate your criminal history score (for the x-axis calculation) and your offense level (the y-axis calculation) to determine which range your case falls in.

SENTENCING TABLE
(in months of imprisonment)

Zone	Offense Level	Criminal History Category (Criminal History Points)					
		I (0 or 1)	II (2 or 3)	III (4, 5, 6)	IV (7, 8, 9)	V (10, 11, 12)	VI (13 or more)
Zone A	1	0–6	0–6	0–6	0–6	0–6	0–6
	2	0–6	0–6	0–6	0–6	0–6	1–7
	3	0–6	0–6	0–6	0–6	2–8	3–9
	4	0–6	0–6	0–6	2–8	4–10	6–12
	5	0–6	0–6	1–7	4–10	6–12	9–15
	6	0–6	1–7	2–8	6–12	9–15	12–18
	7	0–6	2–8	4–10	8–14	12–18	15–21
	8	0–6	4–10	6–12	10–16	15–21	18–24
Zone B	9	4–10	6–12	8–14	12–18	18–24	21–27
	10	6–12	8–14	10–16	15–21	21–27	24–30
	11	8–14	10–16	12–18	18–24	24–30	27–33
Zone C	12	10–16	12–18	15–21	21–27	27–33	30–37
	13	12–18	15–21	18–24	24–30	30–37	33–41
Zone D	14	15–21	18–24	21–27	27–33	33–41	37–46
	15	18–24	21–27	24–30	30–37	37–46	41–51
	16	21–27	24–30	27–33	33–41	41–51	46–57
	17	24–30	27–33	30–37	37–46	46–57	51–63
	18	27–33	30–37	33–41	41–51	51–63	57–71
	19	30–37	33–41	37–46	46–57	57–71	63–78
	20	33–41	37–46	41–51	51–63	63–78	70–87
	21	37–46	41–51	46–57	57–71	70–87	77–96
	22	41–51	46–57	51–63	63–78	77–96	84–105
	23	46–57	51–63	57–71	70–87	84–105	92–115
	24	51–63	57–71	63–78	77–96	92–115	100–125
	25	57–71	63–78	70–87	84–105	100–125	110–137
	26	63–78	70–87	78–97	92–115	110–137	120–150
	27	70–87	78–97	87–108	100–125	120–150	130–162
	28	78–97	87–108	97–121	110–137	130–162	140–175
	29	87–108	97–121	108–135	121–151	140–175	151–188
	30	97–121	108–135	121–151	135–168	151–188	168–210
	31	108–135	121–151	135–168	151–188	168–210	188–235
	32	121–151	135–168	151–188	168–210	188–235	210–262
	33	135–168	151–188	168–210	188–235	210–262	235–293
	34	151–188	168–210	188–235	210–262	235–293	262–327
	35	168–210	188–235	210–262	235–293	262–327	292–365
	36	188–235	210–262	235–293	262–327	292–365	324–405
	37	210–262	235–293	262–327	292–365	324–405	360–life
	38	235–293	262–327	292–365	324–405	360–life	360–life
	39	262–327	292–365	324–405	360–life	360–life	360–life
	40	292–365	324–405	360–life	360–life	360–life	360–life
	41	324–405	360–life	360–life	360–life	360–life	360–life
	42	360–life	360–life	360–life	360–life	360–life	360–life
	43	life	life	life	life	life	life

November 1, 2016

Appendix B

Guideline 2D1.1

§2D1.1 - UNLAWFUL MANUFACTURING, IMPORTING, EXPORTING, OR TRAFFICKING (INCLUDING POSSESSION WITH INTENT TO COMMIT THESE OFFENSES); ATTEMPT OR CONSPIRACY

(a) <u>Base Offense Level (Apply the greatest):</u>

(1) 43, if the defendant is convicted under 21 U.S.C. § 841(b)(1)(A), (b)(1)(B), or (b)(1)(C), or 21 U.S.C. § 960(b)(1), (b)(2), or (b)(3), and the offense of conviction establishes that death or serious bodily injury resulted from the use of the substance and that the defendant committed the offense after one or more prior convictions for a similar offense; or

(2) 38, if the defendant is convicted under 21 U.S.C. § 841(b)(1)(A), (b)(1)(B), or (b)(1)(C), or 21 U.S.C. § 960(b)(1), (b)(2), or (b)(3), and the offense of conviction establishes that death or serious bodily injury resulted from the use of the substance; or

(3) 30, if the defendant is convicted under 21 U.S.C. § 841(b)(1)(E) or 21 U.S.C. § 960(b)(5), and the offense of conviction establishes that death or serious bodily injury resulted from the use of the substance and that the defendant committed the offense after one or more prior convictions for a similar offense; or

(4) 26, if the defendant is convicted under 21 U.S.C. § 841(b)(1)(E) or 21 U.S.C. § 960(b)(5), and the offense of conviction establishes that death or serious bodily injury resulted from the use of the substance; or

(5) the offense level specified in the Drug Quantity Table set forth in subsection (c), except that if (A) the defendant receives an adjustment under §3B1.2 (Mitigating Role); and (B) the base offense level under subsection (c) is (i) level 32, decrease by 2 levels; (ii) level 34 or level 36, decrease by 3 levels; or (iii) level 38, decrease by 4 levels. If the resulting offense level is greater than level 32 and the defendant receives the 4-level ("minimal participant") reduction in §3B1.2(a), decrease to level 32. [Note: THIS IS THE MOST COMMON WAY TO DETERMINE THE BASE OFFENSE LEVEL]

(b) Specific Offense Characteristics

(6) If a dangerous weapon (including a firearm) was possessed, increase by 2 levels.

(7) If the defendant used violence, made a credible threat to use violence, or directed the use of violence, increase by 2 levels.

(8) If the defendant unlawfully imported or exported a controlled substance under circumstances in which (A) an aircraft other than a regularly scheduled commercial air carrier was used to import or export the controlled substance, (B) a submersible vessel or semi-submersible vessel as described in 18 U.S.C. § 2285 was used, or (C) the defendant acted as a pilot, copilot, captain, navigator, flight officer, or any other operation officer aboard any craft or vessel carrying a controlled substance, increase by 2 levels. If the resulting offense level is less than level 26, increase to level 26.

(9) If the object of the offense was the distribution of a controlled substance in a prison, correctional facility, or detention facility, increase by 2 levels.

(10) If (A) the offense involved the importation of amphetamine or methamphetamine or the manufacture of amphetamine or methamphetamine from listed chemicals that the defendant knew were imported unlawfully, and (B) the defendant is not subject to an adjustment under §3B1.2 (Mitigating Role), increase by 2 levels.

(11) If the defendant is convicted under 21 U.S.C. § 865, increase by 2 levels.

(12) If the defendant, or a person for whose conduct the defendant is accountable under §1B1.3 (Relevant Conduct), distributed a controlled substance through mass-marketing by means of an interactive computer service, increase by 2 levels.

(13) If the offense involved the distribution of an anabolic steroid and a masking agent, increase by 2 levels.

(14) If the defendant distributed an anabolic steroid to an athlete, increase by 2 levels.

(15) If the defendant was convicted under 21 U.S.C. § 841(g)(1)(A), increase by 2 levels.

(16) If the defendant bribed, or attempted to bribe, a law enforcement officer to facilitate the commission of the offense, increase by 2 levels.

(17) If the defendant maintained a premises for the purpose of manufacturing or distributing a controlled substance, increase by 2 levels.

(18) If the defendant knowingly misrepresented or knowingly marketed as another substance a mixture or substance containing fentanyl (N-phenyl-N-[1-(2-phenylethyl)-4-

piperidinyl] propanamide) or a fentanyl analogue, increase by 4 levels.

(19) (Apply the greatest):

    (A) If the offense involved (i) an unlawful discharge, emission, or release into the environment of a hazardous or toxic substance; or (ii) the unlawful transportation, treatment, storage, or disposal of a hazardous waste, increase by 2 levels.

    (B) If the defendant was convicted under 21 U.S.C. § 860a of distributing, or possessing with intent to distribute, methamphetamine on premises where a minor is present or resides, increase by 2 levels. If the resulting offense level is less than level 14, increase to level 14.

    (C) If —

        i. the defendant was convicted under 21 U.S.C. § 860a of manufacturing, or possessing with intent to manufacture, methamphetamine on premises where a minor is present or resides; or

        ii. the offense involved the manufacture of amphetamine or methamphetamine and the offense created a substantial risk of harm to (I) human life other than a life described in subdivision (D); or (II) the environment,

increase by 3 levels. If the resulting offense level is less than level 27, increase to level 27.

    (D) If the offense (i) involved the manufacture of amphetamine or methamphetamine; and (ii) created a substantial risk of harm to the life of a minor or an incompetent, increase by 6 levels. If the resulting offense level is less than level 30, increase to level 30.

(20) If (A) the offense involved the cultivation of marihuana on state or federal land or while trespassing on tribal or private land; and (B) the defendant receives an adjustment under §3B1.1 (Aggravating Role), increase by 2 levels.

(21) If the defendant receives an adjustment under §3B1.1 (Aggravating Role) and the offense involved 1 or more of the following factors:

    (A) (i) the defendant used fear, impulse, friendship, affection, or some combination thereof to involve another individual in the illegal purchase, sale, transport, or storage of controlled substances, (ii) the individual received little or no compensation from the illegal purchase, sale, transport, or storage of controlled substances, and (iii) the individual had minimal knowledge of the scope and structure of the enterprise;

(B) the defendant, knowing that an individual was (i) less than 18 years of age, (ii) 65 or more years of age, (iii) pregnant, or (iv) unusually vulnerable due to physical or mental condition or otherwise particularly susceptible to the criminal conduct, distributed a controlled substance to that individual or involved that individual in the offense;

(C) the defendant was directly involved in the importation of a controlled substance;

(D) the defendant engaged in witness intimidation, tampered with or destroyed evidence, or otherwise obstructed justice in connection with the investigation or prosecution of the offense;

(E) the defendant committed the offense as part of a pattern of criminal conduct engaged in as a livelihood,

increase by 2 levels.

(22) If the defendant receives the 4-level ("minimal participant") reduction in §3B1.2(a) and the offense involved all of the following factors:

   (A) the defendant was motivated by an intimate or familial relationship or by threats or fear to commit the offense and was otherwise unlikely to commit such an offense;

   (B) the defendant received no monetary compensation from the illegal purchase, sale, transport, or storage of controlled substances; and

   (C) the defendant had minimal knowledge of the scope and structure of the enterprise,

   decrease by 2 levels.

(23) If the defendant meets the criteria set forth in subdivisions (1)–(5) of subsection (a) of §5C1.2 (Limitation on Applicability of Statutory Minimum Sentences in Certain Cases), decrease by 2 levels.

(c) Drug Quantity Table

Base Offense Level	Heroin	Cocaine	Crack (Cocaine Base)	Methamphetamine	Ice (Pure Meth)	Marijuana
38	≥90 KG	≥450 KG	≥25.2 KG	≥45 KG	≥4.5 KG	≥90,000 KG
36	30-90 KG	150-450 KG	8.4-25.2 KG	15-45 KG	1.5-4.5 KG	30,000 - 90,000 KG
34	10-30 KG	50-150 KG	2.8-8.4 KG	5-15 KG	500 g - 1.5 KG	10,000-30,000 KG
32	3-10 KG	15-50 KG	840 g-2.8 KG	1.5-5 KG	150-500 g	3,000-10,000 KG
30	1-3 KG	5-15 KG	280-840 g	500 g - 1.5 KG	50 -150 g	1,000-3,000 KG
28	700-1000 g	3.5-5 KG	196-280 g	350-500 g	35-50 g	700-1000 KG
26	400-700 g	2-3.5 KG	112-196 g	200-350 g	20-35 g	400-700 KG
24	100-400 g	500g-2 KG	28-112 g	50-200 g	5-20 g	100-400 KG
22	80-100 g	400-500 g	22.4-28 g	40-50 g	4-5 g	80-100 KG
20	60-80 g	300-400 g	16.8 - 22.4 g	30-40 g	3-4 g	60-80 KG
18	40-60 g	200-300 g	11.2-16.8 g	20-30 g	2-3 g	40-60 KG
16	20-40 g	100-200 g	5.6-11.2	10-20 g	1-2 g	20-40 KG
14	10-20 g	50-100g	2.8-5.6 g	5-10 g	500 mg - 1g	10-20 KG
12	<10 g	<50 g	<2.8 g	<5 g	<500 mg	5-10 KG
10						2.5-5 KG
8						1-2.5 KG
						<1 KG

(d) Cross References

(1) If a victim was killed under circumstances that would constitute murder under 18 U.S.C. § 1111 had such killing taken place within the territorial or maritime jurisdiction of the United States, apply §2A1.1 (First Degree Murder) or §2A1.2 (Second Degree Murder), as appropriate, if the resulting offense level is greater than that determined under this guideline.

(2) If the defendant was convicted under 21 U.S.C. § 841(b)(7) (of distributing a controlled substance with intent to commit a crime of violence), apply §2X1.1 (Attempt, Solicitation, or Conspiracy) in respect to the crime of violence that the defendant committed, or attempted or intended to commit, if the resulting offense level is greater than that determined above.

(e) Special Instruction

(1) If (A) subsection (d)(2) does not apply; and (B) the defendant committed, or attempted to commit, a sexual offense against another individual by distributing, with or without that individual's knowledge, a controlled substance to that individual, an adjustment under §3A1.1(b)(1) shall apply.

Appendix C

Guideline 2G2.2

§2G2.2 - TRAFFICKING IN MATERIAL INVOLVING THE SEXUAL EXPLOITATION OF A MINOR; RECEIVING, TRANSPORTING, SHIPPING, OR ADVERTISING MATERIAL INVOLVING THE SEXUAL EXPLOITATION OF A MINOR; POSSESSING MATERIAL INVOLVING THE SEXUAL EXPLOITATION OF A MINOR WITH INTENT TO TRAFFIC, POSSESSING MATERIAL INVOLVING THE SEXUAL EXPLOITATION OF A MINOR

(a) Base Offense Level

   (1) 18, if the defendant is convicted of 18 U.S.C. § 1466A(b), § 2252(a)(4), § 2252A(a)(5), or § 2252A(a)(7).

   (2) **22, otherwise.** [THIS IS THE MOST COMMON]

(b) Specific Offense Characteristics

   (1) If (A) subsection (a)(2) applies; (B) the defendant's conduct was limited to the receipt or solicitation of material involving the sexual exploitation of a minor; and (C) the defendant did not intend to traffic in, or distribute, such material, decrease by 2 levels.

(2) If the material involved a prepubescent minor or a minor who had not attained the age of 12 years, increase by 2 levels.

(3) (Apply the greatest):

(A) If the offense involved distribution for pecuniary gain, increase by the number of levels from the table in §2B1.1 (Theft, Property Destruction, and Fraud) corresponding to the retail value of the material, but by not less than 5 levels.

(B) If the defendant distributed in exchange for any valuable consideration, but not for pecuniary gain, increase by 5 levels.

(C) If the offense involved distribution to a minor, increase by 5 levels.

(D) If the offense involved distribution to a minor that was intended to persuade, induce, entice, or coerce the minor to engage in any illegal activity, other than illegal activity covered under subdivision (E), increase by 6 levels.

(E) If the offense involved distribution to a minor that was intended to persuade, induce, entice, coerce, or facilitate the travel of, the minor to engage in prohibited sexual conduct, increase by 7 levels.

(F) If the defendant knowingly engaged in distribution, other than distribution described in subdivisions (A) through (E), increase by 2 levels.

(4) If the offense involved material that portrays (A) sadistic or masochistic conduct or other depictions of violence; or (B) sexual abuse or exploitation of an infant or toddler, increase by 4 levels.

(5) If the defendant engaged in a pattern of activity involving the sexual abuse or exploitation of a minor, increase by 5 levels.

(6) If the offense involved the use of a computer or an interactive computer service for the possession, transmission, receipt, or distribution of the material, or for accessing with intent to view the material, increase by 2 levels.

(7) If the offense involved —

(A) at least 10 images, but fewer than 150, increase by 2 levels;

(B) at least 150 images, but fewer than 300, increase by 3 levels;

(C) at least 300 images, but fewer than 600, increase by 4 levels; and

(D) 600 or more images, increase by 5 levels.

(c) Cross Reference

(1) If the offense involved causing, transporting, permitting, or offering or seeking by notice or advertisement, a minor to engage in sexually explicit conduct for the purpose of producing a visual depiction of such conduct or for the purpose of transmitting a live visual depiction of such conduct,

apply §2G2.1 (Sexually Exploiting a Minor by Production of Sexually Explicit Visual or Printed Material; Custodian Permitting Minor to Engage in Sexually Explicit Conduct; Advertisement for Minors to Engage in Production), if the resulting offense level is greater than that determined above.

Commentary

Statutory Provisions: 18 U.S.C. §§ 1466A, 2252, 2252A(a)-(b), 2260(b). For additional statutory provision(s), see Appendix A (Statutory Index).

Application Notes:

1. Definitions.—For purposes of this guideline:

    - "Computer" has the meaning given that term in 18 U.S.C. § 1030(e)(1).
    - "Distribution" means any act, including possession with intent to distribute, production, transmission, advertisement, and transportation, related to the transfer of material involving the sexual exploitation of a minor. Accordingly, distribution includes posting material involving the sexual exploitation of a minor on a website for public viewing but does not include the mere solicitation of such material by a defendant.
    - "Distribution for pecuniary gain" means distribution for profit.
    - "The defendant distributed in exchange for any valuable consideration" means the defendant agreed to an exchange with another person under which the defendant

knowingly distributed to that other person for the specific purpose of obtaining something of valuable consideration from that other person, such as other child pornographic material, preferential access to child pornographic material, or access to a child.

- "Distribution to a minor" means the knowing distribution to an individual who is a minor at the time of the offense.
- "Interactive computer service" has the meaning given that term in section 230(e)(2) of the Communications Act of 1934 (47 U.S.C. § 230(f)(2)).
- "Material" includes a visual depiction, as defined in 18 U.S.C. § 2256.
- "Minor" means (A) an individual who had not attained the age of 18 years; (B) an individual, whether fictitious or not, who a law enforcement officer represented to a participant (i) had not attained the age of 18 years, and (ii) could be provided for the purposes of engaging in sexually explicit conduct; or (C) an undercover law enforcement officer who represented to a participant that the officer had not attained the age of 18 years.
- "Pattern of activity involving the sexual abuse or exploitation of a minor" means any combination of two or more separate instances of the sexual abuse or sexual exploitation of a minor by the defendant, whether or not the abuse or exploitation (A) occurred during the course of the offense; (B) involved the same minor; or (C) resulted in a conviction for such conduct.
- "Prohibited sexual conduct" has the meaning given that term in Application Note 1 of the Commentary to §2A3.1

(Criminal Sexual Abuse; Attempt to Commit Criminal Sexual Abuse).

- "Sexual abuse or exploitation" means any of the following: (A) conduct described in 18 U.S.C. § 2241, § 2242, § 2243, § 2251(a)-(c), § 2251(d)(1)(B), § 2251A, § 2260(b), § 2421, § 2422, or § 2423; (B) an offense under state law, that would have been an offense under any such section if the offense had occurred within the special maritime or territorial jurisdiction of the United States; or (C) an attempt or conspiracy to commit any of the offenses under subdivisions (A) or (B). "Sexual abuse or exploitation" does not include possession, accessing with intent to view, receipt, or trafficking in material relating to the sexual abuse or exploitation of a minor.

2. Application of Subsection (b)(3)(F).—For purposes of subsection (b)(3)(F), the defendant "knowingly engaged in distribution" if the defendant (A) knowingly committed the distribution, (B) aided, abetted, counseled, commanded, induced, procured, or willfully caused the distribution, or (C) conspired to distribute.

3. Application of Subsection (b)(4)(A).—Subsection (b)(4)(A) applies if the offense involved material that portrays sadistic or masochistic conduct or other depictions of violence, regardless of whether the defendant specifically intended to possess, access with intent to view, receive, or distribute such materials.

4. Interaction of Subsection (b)(4)(B) and Vulnerable Victim (§3A1.1(b)).—If subsection (b)(4)(B) applies, do not apply §3A1.1(b).

5. Application of Subsection (b)(5).—A conviction taken into account under subsection (b)(5) is not excluded from consideration of whether that conviction receives criminal history points pursuant to Chapter Four, Part A (Criminal History).

6. Application of Subsection (b)(7).—

   (A) Definition of "Images".—"Images" means any visual depiction, as defined in 18 U.S.C. § 2256(5), that constitutes child pornography, as defined in 18 U.S.C. § 2256(8).

   (B) Determining the Number of Images.—For purposes of determining the number of images under subsection (b)(7):

      i. Each photograph, picture, computer or computer-generated image, or any similar visual depiction shall be considered to be one image. If the number of images substantially underrepresents the number of minors depicted, an upward departure may be warranted.

      ii. Each video, video-clip, movie, or similar visual depiction shall be considered to have 75 images. If the length of the visual depiction is substantially more than 5 minutes, an upward departure may be warranted.

7. Application of Subsection (c)(1). —

   (A) In General. — The cross reference in subsection (c)(1) is to be construed broadly and includes all instances where the offense involved employing, using, persuading, inducing, enticing, coercing, transporting, permitting, or offering or seeking by notice or advertisement, a minor to engage in sexually explicit conduct for the purpose of producing any visual depiction of such conduct or for the purpose of transmitting live any visual depiction of such conduct.

   (B) Definition. — "Sexually explicit conduct" has the meaning given that term in 18 U.S.C. § 2256(2).

8. Cases Involving Adapted or Modified Depictions. — If the offense involved material that is an adapted or modified depiction of an identifiable minor (e.g., a case in which the defendant is convicted under 18 U.S.C. § 2252A(a)(7)), the term "material involving the sexual exploitation of a minor" includes such material.

9. Upward Departure Provision. — If the defendant engaged in the sexual abuse or exploitation of a minor at any time (whether or not such abuse or exploitation occurred during the course of the offense or resulted in a conviction for such conduct) and subsection (b)(5) does not apply, an upward departure may be warranted. In addition, an upward departure may be warranted if the defendant received an enhancement under subsection (b)(5) but that

enhancement does not adequately reflect the seriousness of the sexual abuse or exploitation involved.

Background: Section 401(i)(1)(C) of Public Law 108-21 directly amended subsection (b) to add subdivision (7), effective April 30, 2003.

Historical Note   Effective November 1, 1987. Amended effective June 15, 1988 (amendment 31); November 1, 1990 (amendment 325); November 1, 1991 (amendment 372); November 27, 1991 (amendment 435); November 1, 1996 (amendment 537); November 1, 1997 (amendment 575); November 1, 2000 (amendment 592); November 1, 2001 (amendment 617); April 30, 2003 (amendment 649); November 1, 2003 (amendment 661); November 1, 2004 (amendment 664); November 1, 2009 (amendments 733 and 736); November 1, 2016 (amendment 801).

Appendix D

Guideline 2L1.2

§2L1.2 - UNLAWFULLY ENTERING OR REMAINING IN THE UNITED STATES

(a) Base Offense Level: 8

(b) Specific Offense Characteristics

    (1) (Apply the Greater) If the defendant committed the instant offense after sustaining—

        (A) a conviction for a felony that is an illegal reentry offense, increase by 4 levels; or

        (B) two or more convictions for misdemeanors under 8 U.S.C. § 1325(a), increase by 2 levels.

    (2) (Apply the Greatest) If, before the defendant was ordered deported or ordered removed from the United States for the first time, the defendant engaged in criminal conduct that, at any time, resulted in—

        (A) a conviction for a felony offense (other than an illegal reentry offense) for which the sentence imposed was five years or more, increase by 10 levels;

(B) a conviction for a felony offense (other than an illegal reentry offense) for which the sentence imposed was two years or more, increase by 8 levels;

(C) a conviction for a felony offense (other than an illegal reentry offense) for which the sentence imposed exceeded one year and one month, increase by 6 levels;

(D) a conviction for any other felony offense (other than an illegal reentry offense), increase by 4 levels; or

(E) three or more convictions for misdemeanors that are crimes of violence or drug trafficking offenses, increase by 2 levels.

(3) (Apply the Greatest) If, after the defendant was ordered deported or ordered removed from the United States for the first time, the defendant engaged in criminal conduct that, at any time, resulted in—

(A) a conviction for a felony offense (other than an illegal reentry offense) for which the sentence imposed was five years or more, increase by 10 levels;

(B) a conviction for a felony offense (other than an illegal reentry offense) for which the sentence imposed was two years or more, increase by 8 levels;

(C) a conviction for a felony offense (other than an illegal reentry offense) for which the sentence imposed exceeded one year and one month, increase by 6 levels;

(D) a conviction for any other felony offense (other than an illegal reentry offense), increase by 4 levels; or

(E) three or more convictions for misdemeanors that are crimes of violence or drug trafficking offenses, increase by 2 levels.

Commentary

Statutory Provisions: 8 U.S.C. § 1253, § 1325(a) (second or subsequent offense only), § 1326. For additional statutory provision(s), see Appendix A (Statutory Index).

Application Notes:

1. In General.—

   (A) "Ordered Deported or Ordered Removed from the United States for the First Time".—For purposes of this guideline, a defendant shall be considered "ordered deported or ordered removed from the United States" if the defendant was ordered deported or ordered removed from the United States based on a final order of exclusion, deportation, or removal, regardless of whether the order was in response to a conviction. "For the first time" refers to the first time the defendant was ever the subject of such an order.

(B) Offenses Committed Prior to Age Eighteen.— Subsections (b)(1), (b)(2), and (b)(3) do not apply to a conviction for an offense committed before the defendant was eighteen years of age unless such conviction is classified as an adult conviction under the laws of the jurisdiction in which the defendant was convicted.

2. Definitions.—For purposes of this guideline:

- "Crime of violence" means any of the following offenses under federal, state, or local law: murder, voluntary manslaughter, kidnapping, aggravated assault, a forcible sex offense, robbery, arson, extortion, the use or unlawful possession of a firearm described in 26 U.S.C. § 5845(a) or explosive material as defined in 18 U.S.C. § 841(c), or any other offense under federal, state, or local law that has as an element the use, attempted use, or threatened use of physical force against the person of another. "Forcible sex offense" includes where consent to the conduct is not given or is not legally valid, such as where consent to the conduct is involuntary, incompetent, or coerced. The offenses of sexual abuse of a minor and statutory rape are included only if the sexual abuse of a minor or statutory rape was (A) an offense described in 18 U.S.C. § 2241(c) or (B) an offense under state law that would have been an offense under section 2241(c) if the offense had occurred within the special maritime and territorial jurisdiction of the United States. "Extortion" is obtaining something of value from another by the wrongful use of (A) force, (B) fear of physical injury, or (C) threat of physical injury.

- "Drug trafficking offense" means an offense under federal, state, or local law that prohibits the manufacture, import, export, distribution, or dispensing of, or offer to sell a controlled substance (or a counterfeit substance) or the possession of a controlled substance (or a counterfeit substance) with intent to manufacture, import, export, distribute, or dispense.

- "Felony" means any federal, state, or local offense punishable by imprisonment for a term exceeding one year.

- "Illegal reentry offense" means (A) an offense under 8 U.S.C. § 1253 or § 1326, or (B) a second or subsequent offense under 8 U.S.C. § 1325(a).

- "Misdemeanor" means any federal, state, or local offense punishable by a term of imprisonment of one year or less.

- "Sentence imposed" has the meaning given the term "sentence of imprisonment" in Application Note 2 and subsection (b) of §4A1.2 (Definitions and Instructions for Computing Criminal History). The length of the sentence imposed includes any term of imprisonment given upon revocation of probation, parole, or supervised release, regardless of when the revocation occurred.

3. Criminal History Points.—For purposes of applying subsections (b)(1), (b)(2), and (b)(3), use only those convictions

that receive criminal history points under §4A1.1(a), (b), or (c).

In addition, for purposes of subsections (b)(1)(B), (b)(2)(E), and (b)(3)(E), use only those convictions that are counted separately under §4A1.2(a)(2).

A conviction taken into account under subsection (b)(1), (b)(2), or (b)(3) is not excluded from consideration of whether that conviction receives criminal history points pursuant to Chapter Four, Part A (Criminal History).

4. Cases in Which Sentences for An Illegal Reentry Offense and Another Felony Offense were Imposed at the Same Time.—There may be cases in which the sentences for an illegal reentry offense and another felony offense were imposed at the same time and treated as a single sentence for purposes of calculating the criminal history score under §4A1.1(a), (b), and (c). In such a case, use the illegal reentry offense in determining the appropriate enhancement under subsection (b)(1), if it independently would have received criminal history points. In addition, use the prior sentence for the other felony offense in determining the appropriate enhancement under subsection (b)(2) or (b)(3), as appropriate, if it independently would have received criminal history points.

5. Cases in Which the Criminal Conduct Underlying a Prior Conviction Occurred Both Before and After the Defendant Was First Ordered Deported or Ordered Removed.—There may be cases in which the criminal conduct underlying a prior conviction occurred both before and after the defendant was ordered deported or ordered removed from the United States

for the first time. For purposes of subsections (b)(2) and (b)(3), count such a conviction only under subsection (b)(2).

6. Departure Based on Seriousness of a Prior Offense.—There may be cases in which the offense level provided by an enhancement in subsection (b)(2) or (b)(3) substantially understates or overstates the seriousness of the conduct underlying the prior offense, because (A) the length of the sentence imposed does not reflect the seriousness of the prior offense; (B) the prior conviction is too remote to receive criminal history points (see §4A1.2(e)); or (C) the time actually served was substantially less than the length of the sentence imposed for the prior offense. In such a case, a departure may be warranted.

7. Departure Based on Time Served in State Custody.—In a case in which the defendant is located by immigration authorities while the defendant is serving time in state custody, whether pre- or post-conviction, for a state offense, the time served is not covered by an adjustment under §5G1.3(b) and, accordingly, is not covered by a departure under §5K2.23 (Discharged Terms of Imprisonment). See §5G1.3(a). In such a case, the court may consider whether a departure is appropriate to reflect all or part of the time served in state custody, from the time immigration authorities locate the defendant until the service of the federal sentence commences, that the court determines will not be credited to the federal sentence by the Bureau of Prisons. Any such departure should be fashioned to achieve a reasonable punishment for the instant offense.

Such a departure should be considered only in cases where the departure is not likely to increase the risk to the public from further crimes of the defendant. In determining whether such a departure is appropriate, the court should consider, among other things, (A) whether the defendant engaged in additional criminal activity after illegally reentering the United States; (B) the seriousness of any such additional criminal activity, including (1) whether the defendant used violence or credible threats of violence or possessed a firearm or other dangerous weapon (or induced another person to do so) in connection with the criminal activity, (2) whether the criminal activity resulted in death or serious bodily injury to any person, and (3) whether the defendant was an organizer, leader, manager, or supervisor of others in the criminal activity; and (C) the seriousness of the defendant's other criminal history.

8. *Departure Based on Cultural Assimilation.*—There may be cases in which a downward departure may be appropriate on the basis of cultural assimilation. Such a departure should be considered only in cases where (A) the defendant formed cultural ties primarily with the United States from having resided continuously in the United States from childhood, (B) those cultural ties provided the primary motivation for the defendant's illegal reentry or continued presence in the United States, and (C) such a departure is not likely to increase the risk to the public from further crimes of the defendant.

In determining whether such a departure is appropriate, the court should consider, among other things, (1) the age in childhood at which the defendant began residing continuously in the United States, (2) whether and for how long the defendant attended school in the United States, (3) the duration of the defendant's continued residence in the

United States, (4) the duration of the defendant's presence outside the United States, (5) the nature and extent of the defendant's familial and cultural ties inside the United States, and the nature and extent of such ties outside the United States, (6) the seriousness of the defendant's criminal history, and (7) whether the defendant engaged in additional criminal activity after illegally reentering the United States.

Historical Note   Effective November 1, 1987. Amended effective January 15, 1988 (amendment 38); November 1, 1989 (amendment 193); November 1, 1991 (amendment 375); November 1, 1995 (amendment 523); November 1, 1997 (amendment 562); November 1, 2001 (amendment 632); November 1, 2002 (amendment 637); November 1, 2003 (amendment 658); November 1, 2007 (amendment 709); November 1, 2008 (amendment 722); November 1, 2010 (amendment 740); November 1, 2011 (amendment 754); November 1, 2012 (amendment 764); November 1, 2014 (amendment 787); November 1, 2015 (amendment 795); November 1, 2016 (amendment 802); November 1, 2018 (amendment 809).

Appendix E

Guidelines Used for Calculating Criminal History

§4A1.1 - CRIMINAL HISTORY CATEGORY

The total points from subsections (a) through (e) determine the criminal history category in the Sentencing Table in Chapter Five, Part A.

(a) Add 3 points for each prior sentence of imprisonment exceeding one year and one month.

(b) Add 2 points for each prior sentence of imprisonment of at least sixty days not counted in (a).

(c) Add 1 point for each prior sentence not counted in (a) or (b), up to a total of 4 points for this subsection.

(d) Add 2 points if the defendant committed the instant offense while under any criminal justice sentence, including probation, parole, supervised release, imprisonment, work release, or escape status.

(e) Add 1 point for each prior sentence resulting from a conviction of a crime of violence that did not receive any points under (a), (b), or (c) above because such sentence was treated as a single sentence, up to a total of 3 points for this subsection.

Commentary

The total criminal history points from §4A1.1 determine the criminal history category (I–VI) in the Sentencing Table in Chapter Five, Part A. The definitions and instructions in §4A1.2 govern the computation of the criminal history points. Therefore, §4A1.1 and §4A1.2 must be read together. The following notes highlight the interaction of §4A1.1 and §4A1.2.

Application Notes:

1. §4A1.1(a). Three points are added for each prior sentence of imprisonment exceeding one year and one month. There is no limit to the number of points that may be counted under this subsection. The term "prior sentence" is defined at §4A1.2(a). The term "sentence of imprisonment" is defined at §4A1.2(b). Where a prior sentence of imprisonment resulted from a revocation of probation, parole, or a similar form of release, see §4A1.2(k).

   - Certain prior sentences are not counted or are counted only under certain conditions:
   - A sentence imposed more than fifteen years prior to the defendant's commencement of the instant offense is not counted unless the defendant's incarceration extended into this fifteen-year period. See §§4A1.2(e).
   - A sentence imposed for an offense committed prior to the defendant's eighteenth birthday is counted under this subsection only if it resulted from an adult conviction. See §§4A1.2(d).
   - A sentence for a foreign conviction, a conviction that has been expunged, or an invalid conviction is not counted. See §4A1.2(h) and (j) and the Commentary to §4A1.2.

2. §4A1.1(b). Two points are added for each prior sentence of imprisonment of at least sixty days not counted in §4A1.1(a). There is no limit to the number of points that may be counted under this subsection. The term "prior sentence" is defined at §4A1.2(a). The term "sentence of imprisonment" is defined at §4A1.2(b). Where a prior sentence of imprisonment resulted from a revocation of probation, parole, or a similar form of release, see §4A1.2(k).

- Certain prior sentences are not counted or are counted only under certain conditions:
- A sentence imposed more than ten years prior to the defendant's commencement of the instant offense is not counted. See §4A1.2(e).
- An adult or juvenile sentence imposed for an offense committed prior to the defendant's eighteenth birthday is counted only if confinement resulting from such sentence extended into the five-year period preceding the defendant's commencement of the instant offense. See §4A1.2(d).

- Sentences for certain specified non-felony offenses are never counted. See §4A1.2(c)(2).
- A sentence for a foreign conviction or a tribal court conviction, an expunged conviction, or an invalid conviction is not counted. See §4A1.2(h), (i), (j), and the Commentary to §4A1.2.
- A military sentence is counted only if imposed by a general or special court-martial. See §4A1.2(g).

3. §4A1.1(c). One point is added for each prior sentence not counted under §4A1.1(a) or (b). A maximum of four points may be counted under this subsection. The term "prior sentence" is defined at §4A1.2(a).
   - Certain prior sentences are not counted or are counted only under certain conditions:
     - A sentence imposed more than ten years prior to the defendant's commencement of the instant offense is not counted. See §4A1.2(e).
     - An adult or juvenile sentence imposed for an offense committed prior to the defendant's eighteenth birthday is counted only if imposed within five years of the defendant's commencement of the current offense. See §4A1.2(d).
     - Sentences for certain specified non-felony offenses are counted only if they meet certain requirements. See §4A1.2(c)(1).
     - Sentences for certain specified non-felony offenses are never counted. See §4A1.2(c)(2).
     - A diversionary disposition is counted only where there is a finding or admission of guilt in a judicial proceeding. See §4A1.2(f).
     - A sentence for a foreign conviction, a tribal court conviction, an expunged conviction, or an invalid conviction, is not counted. See §4A1.2(h), (i), (j), and the Commentary to §4A1.2.
     - A military sentence is counted only if imposed by a general or special court-martial. See §4A1.2(g).

4. §4A1.1(d). Two points are added if the defendant committed any part of the instant offense (i.e., any relevant conduct) while under any criminal justice sentence, including probation, parole, supervised release, imprisonment, work release, or escape status. Failure to report for service of a sentence of imprisonment is to be treated as an escape from such sentence. See §4A1.2(n). For the purposes of this subsection, a "criminal justice sentence" means a sentence countable under §4A1.2 (Definitions and Instructions for Computing Criminal History) having a custodial or supervisory component, although active supervision is not required for this subsection to apply. For example, a term of unsupervised probation would be included; but a sentence to pay a fine, by itself, would not be included. A defendant who commits the instant offense while a violation warrant from a prior sentence is outstanding (e.g., a probation, parole, or supervised release violation warrant) shall be deemed to be under a criminal justice sentence for the purposes of this provision if that sentence is otherwise countable, even if that sentence would have expired absent such warrant. See §4A1.2(m).

5. §4A1.1(e). In a case in which the defendant received two or more prior sentences as a result of convictions for crimes of violence that are treated as a single sentence (see §4A1.2(a)(2)), one point is added under §4A1.1(e) for each such sentence that did not result in any additional points under §4A1.1(a), (b), or (c). A total of up to 3 points may be added under §4A1.1(e). For purposes of this guideline, "crime of violence" has the meaning given that term in §4B1.2(a). See §4A1.2(p).

- For example, a defendant's criminal history includes two robbery convictions for offenses committed on different occasions. The sentences for these offenses were imposed on the same day and are treated as a single prior sentence. See §4A1.2(a)(2). If the defendant received a five-year sentence of imprisonment for one robbery and a four-year sentence of imprisonment for the other robbery (consecutively or concurrently), a total of 3 points is added under §4A1.1(a). An additional point is added under §4A1.1(e) because the second sentence did not result in any additional point(s) (under §4A1.1(a), (b), or (c)). In contrast, if the defendant received a one-year sentence of imprisonment for one robbery and a nine-month consecutive sentence of imprisonment for the other robbery, a total of 3 points also is added under §4A1.1(a) (a one-year sentence of imprisonment and a consecutive nine-month sentence of imprisonment are treated as a combined one-year-nine-month sentence of imprisonment). But no additional point is added under §4A1.1(e) because the sentence for the second robbery already resulted in an additional point under §4A1.1(a). Without the second sentence, the defendant would only have received two points under §4A1.1(b) for the one-year sentence of imprisonment.

Background: Prior convictions may represent convictions in the federal system, fifty state systems, the District of Columbia, territories, and foreign, tribal, and military courts. There are jurisdictional variations in offense definitions, sentencing structures, and manner of sentence pronouncement. To minimize problems with imperfect measures of past crime seriousness, criminal history categories are based on the maximum term imposed in previous sentences rather than on other measures, such as whether the conviction was designated a felony or misdemeanor. In recognition of the imperfection of this measure however, §4A1.3 authorizes the court to depart from the otherwise applicable criminal history category in certain circumstances.

Subsections (a), (b), and (c) of §4A1.1 distinguish confinement sentences longer than one year and one month, shorter confinement sentences of at least sixty days, and all other sentences, such as confinement sentences of less than sixty days, probation, fines, and residency in a halfway house.

Section 4A1.1(d) adds two points if the defendant was under a criminal justice sentence during any part of the instant offense.

Historical Note   Effective November 1, 1987. Amended effective November 1, 1989 (amendments 259-261); November 1, 1991 (amendments 381 and 382); October 27, 2003 (amendment 651); November 1, 2007 (amendment 709); November 1, 2010 (amendment 742); November 1, 2013 (amendment 777); November 1, 2015 (amendment 795).

§4A1.2 - DEFINITIONS AND INSTRUCTIONS FOR COMPUTING CRIMINAL HISTORY

(a) Prior Sentence

(1) The term "prior sentence" means any sentence previously imposed upon adjudication of guilt, whether by guilty plea, trial, or plea of nolo contendere, for conduct not part of the instant offense.

(2) If the defendant has multiple prior sentences, determine whether those sentences are counted separately or treated as a single sentence. Prior sentences always are counted separately if the sentences were imposed for offenses that were separated by an intervening arrest (i.e., the

defendant is arrested for the first offense prior to committing the second offense). If there is no intervening arrest, prior sentences are counted separately unless (A) the sentences resulted from offenses contained in the same charging instrument; or (B) the sentences were imposed on the same day. Treat any prior sentence covered by (A) or (B) as a single sentence. See also §4A1.1(e).

For purposes of applying §4A1.1(a), (b), and (c), if prior sentences are treated as a single sentence, use the longest sentence of imprisonment if concurrent sentences were imposed. If consecutive sentences were imposed, use the aggregate sentence of imprisonment.

(3) A conviction for which the imposition or execution of sentence was totally suspended or stayed shall be counted as a prior sentence under §4A1.1(c).

(4) Where a defendant has been convicted of an offense, but not yet sentenced, such conviction shall be counted as if it constituted a prior sentence under §4A1.1(c) if a sentence resulting from that conviction otherwise would be countable. In the case of a conviction for an offense set forth in §4A1.2(c)(1), apply this provision only where the sentence for such offense would be countable regardless of type or length.

"Convicted of an offense," for the purposes of this provision, means that the guilt of the defendant has been established, whether by guilty plea, trial, or plea of nolo contendere.

(b) Sentence of Imprisonment Defined

(1) The term "sentence of imprisonment" means a sentence of incarceration and refers to the maximum sentence imposed.

(2) If part of a sentence of imprisonment was suspended, "sentence of imprisonment" refers only to the portion that was not suspended.

(c) Sentences Counted and Excluded

Sentences for all felony offenses are counted. Sentences for misdemeanor and petty offenses are counted, except as follows:

(1) Sentences for the following prior offenses and offenses similar to them, by whatever name they are known, are counted only if (A) the sentence was a term of probation of more than one year or a term of imprisonment of at least thirty days, or (B) the prior offense was similar to an instant offense:

- Careless or reckless driving
- Contempt of court
- Disorderly conduct or disturbing the peace
- Driving without a license or with a revoked or suspended license
- False information to a police officer
- Gambling
- Hindering or failure to obey a police officer
- Insufficient funds check
- Leaving the scene of an accident
- Non-support
- Prostitution
- Resisting arrest
- Trespassing.

(2) Sentences for the following prior offenses and offenses similar to them, by whatever name they are known, are never counted:

- Fish and game violations
- Hitchhiking
- Juvenile status offenses and truancy
- Local ordinance violations (except those violations that are also violations under state criminal law)
- Loitering
- Minor traffic infractions (e.g., speeding)
- Public intoxication
- Vagrancy.

(d) Offenses Committed Prior to Age Eighteen

(1) If the defendant was convicted as an adult and received a sentence of imprisonment exceeding one year and one month, add 3 points under §4A1.1(a) for each such sentence.

(2) In any other case,

(A) add 2 points under §4A1.1(b) for each adult or juvenile sentence to confinement of at least sixty days if the defendant was released from such confinement within five years of his commencement of the instant offense;

(B) add 1 point under §4A1.1(c) for each adult or juvenile sentence imposed within five years of the defendant's commencement of the instant offense not covered in (A).

(e) Applicable Time Period

(1) Any prior sentence of imprisonment exceeding one year and one month that was imposed within fifteen years of the defendant's commencement of the instant offense is counted. Also count any prior sentence of imprisonment exceeding one year and one month, whenever imposed, that resulted in the defendant being incarcerated during any part of such fifteen-year period.

(2) Any other prior sentence that was imposed within ten years of the defendant's commencement of the instant offense is counted.

(3) Any prior sentence not within the time periods specified above is not counted.

(4) The applicable time period for certain sentences resulting from offenses committed prior to age eighteen is governed by §4A1.2(d)(2).

(f) Diversionary Dispositions

Diversion from the judicial process without a finding of guilt (e.g., deferred prosecution) is not counted. A diversionary disposition resulting from a finding or admission of guilt, or a plea of nolo contendere, in a judicial proceeding is counted as a sentence under §4A1.1(c) even if a conviction is not formally entered, except that diversion from juvenile court is not counted.

(g) Military Sentences

Sentences resulting from military offenses are counted if imposed by a general or special court-martial. Sentences imposed by a summary court-martial or Article 15 proceeding are not counted.

(h) Foreign Sentences

Sentences resulting from foreign convictions are not counted, but may be considered under §4A1.3 (Departures Based on Inadequacy of Criminal History Category (Policy Statement)).

(i) Tribal Court Sentences

Sentences resulting from tribal court convictions are not counted, but may be considered under §4A1.3 (Departures Based on Inadequacy of Criminal History Category (Policy Statement)).

(j) Expunged Convictions

Sentences for expunged convictions are not counted, but may be considered under §4A1.3 (Departures Based on Inadequacy of Criminal History Category (Policy Statement)).

(k) Revocations of Probation, Parole, Mandatory Release, or Supervised Release

(1) In the case of a prior revocation of probation, parole, supervised release, special parole, or mandatory release, add the original term of imprisonment to any term of imprisonment imposed upon revocation. The resulting total is used to compute the criminal history points for §4A1.1(a), (b), or (c), as applicable.

(2) Revocation of probation, parole, supervised release, special parole, or mandatory release may affect the time period under which certain sentences are counted as provided in §4A1.2(d)(2) and (e). For the purposes of determining the

applicable time period, use the following: (A) in the case of an adult term of imprisonment totaling more than one year and one month, the date of last release from incarceration on such sentence (see §4A1.2(e)(1)); (B) in the case of any other confinement sentence for an offense committed prior to the defendant's eighteenth birthday, the date of the defendant's last release from confinement on such sentence (see §4A1.2(d)(2)(A)); and (C) in any other case, the date of the original sentence (see §4A1.2(d)(2)(B) and (e)(2)).

(l) Sentences on Appeal

Prior sentences under appeal are counted except as expressly provided below. In the case of a prior sentence, the execution of which has been stayed pending appeal, §4A1.1(a), (b), (c), (d), and (e)) shall apply as if the execution of such sentence had not been stayed.

(m) Effect of a Violation Warrant

For the purposes of §4A1.1(d), a defendant who commits the instant offense while a violation warrant from a prior sentence is outstanding (e.g., a probation, parole, or supervised release violation warrant) shall be deemed to be under a criminal justice sentence if that sentence is otherwise countable, even if that sentence would have expired absent such warrant.

(n) Failure to Report for Service of Sentence of Imprisonment

For the purposes of §4A1.1(d), failure to report for service of a sentence of imprisonment shall be treated as an escape from such sentence.

(o) Felony Offense

For the purposes of §4A1.2(c), a "felony offense" means any federal, state, or local offense punishable by death or a term of imprisonment exceeding one year, regardless of the actual sentence imposed.

(p) Crime of Violence Defined

For the purposes of §4A1.1(e), the definition of "crime of violence" is that set forth in §4B1.2(a).

Commentary

Application Notes:

1. Prior Sentence.—"Prior sentence" means a sentence imposed prior to sentencing on the instant offense, other than a sentence for conduct that is part of the instant offense. See §4A1.2(a). A sentence imposed after the defendant's commencement of the instant offense, but prior to sentencing on the instant offense, is a prior sentence if it was for conduct other than conduct that was part of the instant offense. Conduct that is part of the instant offense means conduct that is relevant conduct to the instant offense under the provisions of §1B1.3 (Relevant Conduct).

2. Under §4A1.2(a)(4), a conviction for which the defendant has not yet been sentenced is treated as if it were a prior sentence under §4A1.1(c) if a sentence resulting from such conviction otherwise would have been counted. In the case of an offense set forth in §4A1.2(c)(1) (which lists certain misdemeanor and petty offenses), a conviction for which the defendant has not yet been sentenced is treated as if it were a prior sentence under §4A1.2(a)(4) only where the offense is similar to the instant offense (because sentences for other offenses set forth in §4A1.2(c)(1) are counted only if they are of a specified type and length).

3. Sentence of Imprisonment.—To qualify as a sentence of imprisonment, the defendant must have actually served a period of imprisonment on such sentence (or, if the defendant escaped, would have served time). See §4A1.2(a)(3) and (b)(2). For the purposes of applying §4A1.1(a), (b), or (c), the length of a sentence of imprisonment is the stated maximum (e.g., in the case of a determinate sentence of five years, the stated maximum is five years; in the case of an indeterminate sentence of one to five years, the stated maximum is five years; in the case of an indeterminate sentence for a term not to exceed five years, the stated maximum is five years; in the case of an indeterminate sentence for a term not to exceed the defendant's twenty-first birthday, the stated maximum is the amount of time in pre-trial detention plus the amount of time between the date of sentence and the defendant's twenty-first birthday). That is, criminal history points are based on the sentence pronounced, not the length of time actually served. See §4A1.2(b)(1) and (2). A sentence of probation is to be treated as a sentence under §4A1.1(c) unless a condition of probation requiring imprisonment of at least sixty days was imposed.

4. Application of "Single Sentence" Rule (Subsection (a)(2)).—

(A) Predicate Offenses.—In some cases, multiple prior sentences are treated as a single sentence for purposes of calculating the criminal history score under §4A1.1(a), (b), and (c). However, for purposes of determining predicate offenses, a prior sentence included in the single sentence should be treated as if it received criminal history points, if it independently would have received criminal history points. Therefore, an individual prior sentence may serve as a predicate under the career offender guideline (see §4B1.2(c)) or other guidelines with predicate offenses, if it independently would have received criminal history points. However, because predicate offenses may be used only if they are counted "separately" from each other (see §4B1.2(c)), no more than one prior sentence in a given single sentence may be used as a predicate offense.

5. For example, a defendant's criminal history includes one robbery conviction and one theft conviction. The sentences for these offenses were imposed on the same day, eight years ago, and are treated as a single sentence under §4A1.2(a)(2). If the defendant received a one-year sentence of imprisonment for the robbery and a two-year sentence of imprisonment for the theft, to be served concurrently, a total of 3 points is added under §4A1.1(a). Because this particular robbery met the definition of a felony crime of violence and independently would have received 2 criminal history points under §4A1.1(b), it may serve as a predicate under the career offender guideline.

6. Note, however, that if the sentences in the example above were imposed thirteen years ago, the robbery independently would have received no criminal history points under §4A1.1(b), because it was not imposed within ten years of the defendant's commencement of the instant offense. See

§4A1.2(e)(2). Accordingly, it may not serve as a predicate under the career offender guideline.

(C) Upward Departure Provision.—Treating multiple prior sentences as a single sentence may result in a criminal history score that underrepresents the seriousness of the defendant's criminal history and the danger that the defendant presents to the public. In such a case, an upward departure may be warranted. For example, if a defendant was convicted of a number of serious non-violent offenses committed on different occasions, and the resulting sentences were treated as a single sentence because either the sentences resulted from offenses contained in the same charging instrument or the defendant was sentenced for these offenses on the same day, the assignment of a single set of points may not adequately reflect the seriousness of the defendant's criminal history or the frequency with which the defendant has committed crimes.

7. 4. Sentences Imposed in the Alternative.—A sentence which specifies a fine or other non-incarcerative disposition as an alternative to a term of imprisonment (e.g., $1,000 fine or ninety days' imprisonment) is treated as a non-imprisonment sentence.

6. Sentences for Driving While Intoxicated or Under the Influence.—Convictions for driving while intoxicated or under the influence (and similar offenses by whatever name they are known) are

always counted, without regard to how the offense is classified. Paragraphs (1) and (2) of §4A1.2(c) do not apply.

7. Reversed, Vacated, or Invalidated Convictions.—Sentences resulting from convictions that (A) have been reversed or vacated because of errors of law or because of subsequently discovered evidence exonerating the defendant, or (B) have been ruled constitutionally invalid in a prior case are not to be counted. With respect to the current sentencing proceeding, this guideline and commentary do not confer upon the defendant any right to attack collaterally a prior conviction or sentence beyond any such rights otherwise recognized in law (e.g., 21 U.S.C. § 851 expressly provides that a defendant may collaterally attack certain prior convictions).

8. Nonetheless, the criminal conduct underlying any conviction that is not counted in the criminal history score may be considered pursuant to §4A1.3 (Departures Based on Inadequacy of Criminal History Category (Policy Statement)).

9. Offenses Committed Prior to Age Eighteen.—Section 4A1.2(d) covers offenses committed prior to age eighteen. Attempting to count every juvenile adjudication would have the potential for creating large disparities due to the differential availability

of records. Therefore, for offenses committed prior to age eighteen, only those that resulted in adult sentences of imprisonment exceeding one year and one month, or resulted in imposition of an adult or juvenile sentence or release from confinement on that sentence within five years of the defendant's commencement of the instant offense are counted. To avoid disparities from jurisdiction to jurisdiction in the age at which a defendant is considered a "juvenile," this provision applies to all offenses committed prior to age eighteen.

10. Applicable Time Period.—Section 4A1.2(d)(2) and (e) establishes the time period within which prior sentences are counted. As used in §4A1.2(d)(2) and (e), the term "commencement of the instant offense" includes any relevant conduct. See §1B1.3 (Relevant Conduct). If the court finds that a sentence imposed outside this time period is evidence of similar, or serious dissimilar, criminal conduct, the court may consider this information in determining whether an upward departure is warranted under §4A1.3 (Departures Based on Inadequacy of Criminal History Category (Policy Statement)).

11. Diversionary Dispositions.—Section 4A1.2(f) requires counting prior adult diversionary dispositions if they involved a judicial determination of guilt or an admission of guilt in open court. This reflects a policy that defendants who receive the benefit of a rehabilitative sentence and continue to commit crimes should not be treated with further leniency.

12. Convictions Set Aside or Defendant Pardoned.—A number of jurisdictions have various procedures pursuant to which previous convictions may be set aside or the defendant may be pardoned for reasons unrelated to innocence or errors of

law, e.g., in order to restore civil rights or to remove the stigma associated with a criminal conviction. Sentences resulting from such convictions are to be counted. However, expunged convictions are not counted. §4A1.2(j).

13. Revocations to be Considered.—Section 4A1.2(k) covers revocations of probation and other conditional sentences where the original term of imprisonment imposed, if any, did not exceed one year and one month. Rather than count the original sentence and the resentence after revocation as separate sentences, the sentence given upon revocation should be added to the original sentence of imprisonment, if any, and the total should be counted as if it were one sentence. By this approach, no more than three points will be assessed for a single conviction, even if probation or conditional release was subsequently revoked. If the sentence originally imposed, the sentence imposed upon revocation, or the total of both sentences exceeded one year and one month, the maximum three points would be assigned. If, however, at the time of revocation another sentence was imposed for a new criminal conviction, that conviction would be computed separately from the sentence imposed for the revocation.

14. Where a revocation applies to multiple sentences, and such sentences are counted separately under §4A1.2(a)(2), add the term of imprisonment imposed upon revocation to the sentence that will result in the greatest increase in criminal history points. Example: A defendant was serving two probationary sentences, each counted separately under §4A1.2(a)(2); probation was revoked on both sentences as a result of the same violation conduct; and the defendant was

sentenced to a total of 45 days of imprisonment. If one sentence had been a "straight" probationary sentence and the other had been a probationary sentence that had required service of 15 days of imprisonment, the revocation term of imprisonment (45 days) would be added to the probationary sentence that had the 15-day term of imprisonment. This would result in a total of 2 criminal history points under §4A1.1(b) (for the combined 60-day term of imprisonment) and 1 criminal history point under §4A1.1(c) (for the other probationary sentence).

15. Application of Subsection (c). —

(A) In General. — In determining whether an unlisted offense is similar to an offense listed in subsection (c)(1) or (c)(2), the court should use a common sense approach that includes consideration of relevant factors such as (i) a comparison of punishments imposed for the listed and unlisted offenses; (ii) the perceived seriousness of the offense as indicated by the level of punishment; (iii) the elements of the offense; (iv) the level of culpability involved; and (v) the degree to which the commission of the offense indicates a likelihood of recurring criminal conduct.

(B) Local Ordinance Violations. — A number of local jurisdictions have enacted ordinances covering certain offenses (e.g., larceny and assault misdemeanors) that are also violations of state criminal law. This enables a local court (e.g., a municipal court) to exercise jurisdiction over such offenses. Such offenses are excluded from the definition of local ordinance violations in §4A1.2(c)(2) and, therefore, sentences for such offenses are to be treated as if the defendant had been convicted under state law.

(C) Insufficient Funds Check.—"Insufficient funds check," as used in §4A1.2(c)(1), does not include any conviction establishing that the defendant used a false name or non-existent account.

Background: Prior sentences, not otherwise excluded, are to be counted in the criminal history score, including uncounseled misdemeanor sentences where imprisonment was not imposed.

Historical Note   Effective November 1, 1987. Amended effective November 1, 1989 (amendments 262-265); November 1, 1990 (amendments 352 and 353); November 1, 1991 (amendments 381 and 382); November 1, 1992 (amendment 472); November 1, 1993 (amendment 493); November 1, 2007 (amendment 709); November 1, 2010 (amendment 742); November 1, 2011 (amendment 758); November 1, 2012 (amendment 766); November 1, 2013 (amendment 777); November 1, 2015 (amendment 795); November 1, 2018 (amendment 813).

Acknowledgements

This book has been a work in progress for many years. As is the case with any book, it couldn't have been completed without the support and encouragement of friends and family. This is especially true for an independent author who is in prison. First, I need to thank Hunter Grey whose tireless efforts in making this book go from a manuscript to a formatted and bound book will never be forgotten. He has been incredible in taking all the time necessary to make sure this book became a reality for the thousands of federal defendants who need it. Next, I want to thank Jeff, Ryan, Matt, and Jim, the first friends I have ever made in my life because they all know the real me, who pushed me to finish and showed me every day that anything is possible - even from behind the prison walls. Their experiences are part of this book and I hope they are always part of my life. Doug Passon, the incredible documentarian, videographer, and attorney who has been my friend, mentor, and lawyer through some of the toughest times I have ever faced, was instrumental is making sure I didn't spend the rest of my life behind bars which gave me the boost of self-esteem needed to even start this book. He also taught me the importance of humanization in advocacy. To Vince Ward, the best trial lawyer in the country who literally saved my life while also teaching me that the art of advocacy is not a right of popularity.

Finally, my family is always there and always supportive. But, I would be remiss to not specifically mention my Mother, Marie, my Father, Khalid, and my Sister, Sarah. Out of everyone, they have been the three to continually remind me that I am part of a family and that I have a life worth living. They stuck by me through everything, even those frantic phone calls where I was scared to death and pushed them to their emotional limits. I hope I make them proud.

Made in the USA
Middletown, DE
12 April 2023